A LITERARY GUIDE TO

IRELAND

Susan and Thomas Cahill

WOLFHOUND PRESS

Printed in the United States of America

Published 1979
Wolfhound Press
98 Ardilaun   Portmarnock
County Dublin (452162)

ISBN 0 905473 35 3 (Cloth)
ISBN 0 905473 36 1

ACKNOWLEDGMENTS

The Bodley Head for extracts from ULYSSES by James Joyce. Reprinted by permission of The Bodley Head, Ltd.

Constable & Company, Ltd. for the extract from IN THE MIDDLE OF THE FIELDS by Mary Lavin. Reprinted by permission of Constable & Company.

Coward-McCann, Inc. for "The Balls of the Goat" from THE ORGY by Muriel Rukeyser. Copyright 1965 by Muriel Rukeyser. Reprinted by permission of Coward-McCann, Inc.

The Devin-Adair Company for "She Moved Through The Fair" from COLLECTED POEMS OF PADRAIC COLUM by Padraic Colum, copyright 1953 by Padraic Colum; extracts from THE TAILOR AND ANSTY by Eric Cross, copyright 1942 by Eric Cross; extracts from "If Ever You Go To Dublin Town," "Canal Bank Walk," "Tale of Two Cities," from COLLECTED POEMS by Patrick Kavanagh, copyright 1964 by Patrick Kavanagh; and the extract from

ume II, PROSE (ed. Allan Price); Volumes III and IV, PLAYS (ed. Ann Saddlemyer). Reprinted by permission of Oxford University Press.

For "She Moved Through The Fair" from THE POET'S CIRCUITS by Padraic Colum. Reprinted by permission of Oxford University Press.

Kathleen Raine, for the extract from "Words for the Boatman on Lough Key" by Kathleen Raine. Used by permission of the author.

Random House, Inc. for the extracts from ULYSSES by James Joyce, copyright 1914, 1918, by Margaret Caroline Anderson, 1934 by The Modern Library, Inc., 1942, 1946 by Nora Joseph Joyce; from THE COMPLETE WORKS OF JOHN M. SYNGE, copyright 1935 by The Modern Library, Inc., renewed 1960 by the executors of the estate of Edward Synge and Lillian Mary Stephens; and from THE ARAN ISLANDS AND OTHER WRITINGS OF SYNGE, copyright 1962 by Random House. Reprinted by permission of Random House, Inc.

St. Martin's Press, Inc. for the extracts from I KNOCK AT THE DOOR by Sean O'Casey, copyright 1939 by The Macmillan Company, renewed 1966 by Eileen O'Casey, Breon O'Casey and Shivaun Kenig, and from RED ROSES FOR ME by Sean O'Casey. Reprinted by permission of St. Martin's Press, Inc. and the Macmillan Co. of Canada.

The Viking Press, Inc. for the extracts from A PORTRAIT OF THE ARTIST AS A YOUNG MAN by James Joyce, copyright 1916 by B. W. Huebsch Inc., 1944 by Nora Joyce, 1964 by The Estate of James Joyce; from "The Dead" from DUBLINERS by James Joyce, originally published in 1916 by B. W. Huebsch, Inc., copyright 1967 by The Estate of James Joyce; from THE LETTERS OF JAMES JOYCE, Vol. II, ed. by Richard Ellmann, copyright 1966 by F. Lionel Monro as administrator of The Estate of James Joyce, all rights reserved; and "She Weeps Over Rahoon" from "Pomes Pennyeach" from COLLECTED POEMS by James Joyce, copyright 1927 by James Joyce. Reprinted by permission of The Viking Press, Inc.

Walker and Company for the extract from "The Workman's Friend" in AT SWIM-TWO-BIRDS by Flann O'Brien. Copyright 1951, 1966 by Brian Nolan. Reprinted by permission of Walker and Company, Ltd.

Extracts from COLLECTED POEMS by W. B. Yeats by permission of M. B. Yeats and the Macmillan Co. of London & Basingstoke.

For

Florence and Frank Neunzig

and

Margaret and Patrick T. Cahill

ACKNOWLEDGMENTS

WE WOULD LIKE TO THANK the following people for their help and hospitality: Mr. J. P. McGarry, Mrs. Sheelah Kirby, Mrs. Kathleen Moran, and the officers and faculty of the Yeats International Summer School, Sligo; Professor Kevin B. Nowlan of University College, Dublin; Mr. Tom McGreevy; Mrs. Lily Stephens; Mr. Bryan MacMahon; Mr. William Maxwell and Aer Lingus; Mr. Aidan O'Hanlon, Mr. John Kennedy, Miss Helen D'Arcy, Miss May Boyd, Mr. Robert Grier, and Bord Failte Eireann; Mr. Vincent Tobin and the Shannon Free Airport Development Corporation; Miss Frances MacNally; Mr. and Mrs. McNeil O'Lochlainn; Professor Sean Lucy of University College, Cork, and Mrs. Lucy; and especially Mr. and Mrs. Michael Marlborough and family.

CONTENTS

THE
WRITERS'
IRELAND

GIANT'S
CAUSEWAY

SLIGO
W.B. Yeats

MAYO
Anthony Raftery

ROSCOMMON
John McGahern

INISHKEEN
Patrick Kavanagh

COOLEY
Cuchulainn

LOUGH CARRA
George Moore

BOYNE VALLEY
Newgrange
Mary Lavin

CONNEMARA
Oliver St. John Gogarty
Patrick Pearse

EDGEWORTHTOWN
Maria Edgeworth

"SWEET AUBURN"
Oliver Goldsmith

GALWAY
James Joyce

DUBLIN

ARAN ISLANDS
J.M. Synge
Liam O'Flaherty

CLONMACNOIS

CELEBRIDGE
Jonathan Swift

Jonathan S
G.B. Shaw
James Joyc
Sean O'Cas
Brendan Be
Flann O'Bri
Samuel Bec

THOOR BALLYLEE
W.B. Yeats

COOLE PARK
Lady Gregory

WICKLOW
J.M. Synge
Tom Moore

CLARE Brian Merriman
Biddy Early

SHANNON

KILKENNY

CASHEL

DINGLE

CORK
Edmund Spenser
Elizabeth Bowen
Eileen O'Leary

KILLORGLIN
Puck Fair

KILLARNEY
Tennyson
Egan O'Rahilly

RING OF
KERRY

CORK CITY
Frank O'Connor
Sean O'Faolain

BEARE

GOUGANE BARRA
"The Tailor"

CARBERY COAST
Somerville and Ross

A LITERARY GUIDE TO
IRELAND

Glenmalure, Co. Wicklow. Thomas Cahill

INVITATION

◇◇◇◇◇◇◇◇◇◇◇◇◇◇◇◇◇◇◇◇◇◇◇◇◇◇◇◇◇◇◇◇◇◇◇◇◇◇

Come and Dance with Me in Ireland

I am of Ireland,
And of the holy land
  Of Ireland.
Good Sir, pray I thee,
For of *saint charité*—
Come and dance with me
  In Ireland.

ANONYMOUS, 14TH CENTURY·

IRELAND IS such a little place that on a map of the world it looks like an elbow of England, a geographical afterthought of Europe. But what it lacks in extent it has more than made up for in time, for the sources of its spirit go deep into the past. Sometimes, as with the country's subterranean waterways, the Irish spirit will rush to the surface and course into full view in all its alien vigor, taking the tourist's breath away. More often, the spirit of the land—the mysterious voice in the poem above—beckons us softly to the hidden and the unsuspected.

Travelling in Ireland is like discovering that your own backyard is a multilevel site of ancient human habitation.

/ 3

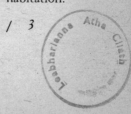

You thought you knew what was there—a smaller, under-populated and unspoiled version of Britain, with a synthetic leprechaun or two propped up by the Tourist Board, but what you find in this outpost of Europe is a richly layered, archaic civilization that went its own way, sprouted and flowered, languished and blossomed again, but never became merely a little Britain or a little Europe. The loveliness of the landscape and the friendliness of the people may lull you at first into thinking that you know this terrain, that you speak the same language. But the sense of familiarity, of having come this way before, can grow imperceptibly into a feeling—equally real—of touching lost land, of having discovered Atlantis, an island that the ocean of history should long ago have washed away.

At the height of their expansion in the centuries before Christ, the Celtic peoples inhabited vast tracts of Europe and Asia Minor. Though their myths and mores have fascinated commentators from Julius Caesar to Matthew Arnold, their culture has all but disappeared from the face of the earth, and the Irish are the only Celtic people to survive as a modern nation-state. As citizens of the twentieth century the Irish of course share much in common with the rest of us. All the same, they have kept alive traditions and attitudes that died out elsewhere centuries ago.

With sea and ocean for its territorial borders, Ireland was left unstirred by many of the major currents of European history. It was never annexed to the Roman empire, never knew the discipline of Roman law and government. Only the weakest, outermost wave of the Renaissance reached its

4 /

shores, so that Ireland was barely touched by the gentle softening of humanism. The industrial revolution has yet to darken Irish skies and waters. Successive invaders did indeed make their contributions—as well as cause terrifying suffering—but they often became in their turn "more Irish than the Irish themselves." Insular remoteness allowed the Irish to wed themselves completely to their island home.

Though the hilltop fires of Maytime no longer light the pagan night, they may flicker in the eyes of your drinking companion as he "stands you a few jars" and tells you of the evening he met a man without a head on a road outside the village. If you warm to his tale, he will warm to the telling: image will pile upon image and the voice will rise to incantation, till language becomes a being between you, a great whip that wields its own strength. Here, words are wondrous things, and whether they tell a story or make up a passing jibe, they can take over the speaker and fill a room with their presence.

For the Irish the world is still magical. Mountains and rivers are named for the banished gods. In many a field stands a faery mound, which the plowman painstakingly avoids, for he would not risk disturbing it. For unnumbered centuries barefoot penitents have climbed jagged hills to inaccessible sanctuaries of pilgrimage. There are paths no man will cross because of the unbearable hunger that will seize him, for here the peasants lay down and died in the Great Famine. Kerry celebrates a yearly fair where a he-goat is exalted on a platform high above the town in promise of fertility, and people dance for three nights in the square. The countryside is dotted with prehistoric stone configurations, ancient churches, and spectacular, haunted Georgian houses. Each place has its strange story.

To visit Ireland is to come in touch with the Irish imagination. For this reason, the best guide to Ireland is the words of its writers, the men and women who have interpreted this landscape to the world. From the beginning, literature, above all other arts, has flourished here. The panoramic inventiveness of Irish myth and saga often rivals the Greek. Ireland had the first vernacular literature of Europe, and in the Dark Ages the intricately illuminated manuscripts of Irish monks kept alive the traditional sacredness of words and fed the dying flame of learning on the continent. In the eighteenth century Swift, Goldsmith, Sheridan, and Farquhar invigorated English literature, while outlaw "hedge schoolmasters" continued to instruct peasant children in Irish, Latin, and Greek. Wilde and Shaw came next, and then the great outpouring of the Irish Literary Renaissance. In Yeats, Lady Gregory, Synge, Joyce, O'Casey, Beckett, O'Faolain, O'Connor, Behan, Flann O'Brien, Mary Lavin (the list is much longer), twentieth-century Ireland has given to the English language gifts wholly out of proportion to her meagre island population.

Because the writers have taken so much of their inspiration from local settings, Ireland offers the great joy of recognition: here are the gardens of Swift's secret rendezvous with Vanessa, Yeats's mythical landscapes, Joyce's streets and strands, Synge's glens, and Behan's pubs. For those who treasure Yeats or puzzle over Joyce, seeing *the place* is an unforgettable revelation. It is easy to grasp why the writers are so alive to the spirit of place, why their imaginations are so wedded to localities. The landscape is dramatic and involving: within short spaces mountains give way to seascapes, rocky cliffs to incredibly green plains, brooding mists to bright sun and rainbows. In such a world one understands Yeats's preoccupation with magic and the gods or Synge's respect for the legends and tales of ordinary people.

WE BEGIN in Wicklow, just south of Dublin, make a circuit of Ireland, and save the complexities of the capital for the final chapters. We have pretty much passed up the locales of authors whose works are out of print, and have scrupulously omitted whatever we thought was dull. A few writers—Sheridan, Wilde, Shaw, most notably—appear less frequently than we might like, because their geographical connections are minimal. We do, however, include places, whenever they fall across our path, that have no direct literary associations but shed light on the shaping of Irish imagination. The book may be used for a week's holiday, a month's stay, or longer. But however you use it, discard the impulse to move on quickly. Stay a while and savor. Forget the whole and—as the writers have done—let one place sink in. Above all, listen to the Irish, to whom all things are magical and the heart above all. "Well," says Pegeen Mike in *The Playboy of the Western World*, "the heart's a wonder." That's the way you dance in Ireland.

Cliffs of Moher, Co. Clare. Irish Tourist Board

INCIDENTAL
PLEASURES
AND PERILS

◇◇◇◇◇◇◇◇◇◇◇◇◇◇◇◇◇◇◇◇◇◇◇◇◇◇◇◇◇◇◇◇◇◇

I RELAND IS a relatively inexpensive country to get to
and travel through. Airfare from North America is
cheaper than to any other European country. For most travellers Aer Lingus, Irish International Airlines, offers the
most economical plans, especially the three-week "package"
which includes flight, a car, and lodging at a guesthouse.
(The guesthouse-gift is somewhat useless after a few days if
you want to travel around.) Typical Irish pleasures—a pint
of Guinness, a goodly measure of Paddy whiskey, Abbey
Theatre tickets—cost little. Prehistoric monuments and
medieval buildings are abundant and almost always ad-
mission-free. The benignly negligent Irish have returned
these to the care of Nature, whose idea of upkeep can be a
bit peculiar since she thinks in terms of centuries. (Your
problem with the monuments will be an occasional difficulty

in locating the key-keeper. The advantage to this, however, is that you may get to meet everyone in the village before getting the key.) Traditional Irish products—Waterford and Galway glass, Belleek china, Donegal tweeds—are to be had, not for a song but for a sizable saving in towns throughout the country. Standun's in Spiddal, just north of Galway City, is especially good for tweedy things; the shops around Clanbrassil Street, Dublin, often have bargain antiques; and Shannon Airport's Duty-Free Shop is the place to buy your whiskey for the return flight.

The Road

A car and petrol are the most expensive—and necessary—items. It is wise to book the car in advance through the Irish Tourist Board. Irish roads, though narrow and curved, are excellently maintained and signposted, and often quite empty of traffic. Should you, however, be driving around pub closing-time (11:30 P.M. in summer), caution is recommended. The Tourist Board publishes a good scenic map, and in the bookstores of the cities you will find the very detailed Ordinance Survey Maps. Especially useful are the series of five ($\frac{1}{4}$ inch to 1 mile) covering the whole island, Sheet 7 ($\frac{1}{2}$ inch to 1 mile) for Sligo, and the large Dublin City map. The Irish give enjoyable, if sometimes uninformative directions; and, if you are unsure of the route, you should not go too far without getting an alternate opinion. An eternal conundrum is the division of Irish topography into "townlands," unmapped and unmarked boundaries that only a native knows. Irish spelling of proper and place names is another imponderable and ranges freely from pristine Gaelic (Medhbh, Cuailnge) to English approximation (Maeve, Cooley). "Strands" are beaches suitable for bathing.

Every town has a Tourist Information Office. With the single exception of the office in O'Connell Street, Dublin (use, instead, the office in Dawson Street), these are staffed with agreeable, knowledgeable people, who are capable at a moment's notice of finding whatever kind of accommodation you require. The offices abound in leaflets, some highly informative, others merely eccentric, and in notices of local plays, games, and sports. Provincial theatrical performances can be worth your attention. The players are local amateurs, but the enthusiastic audiences contribute much to the drama.

Northern Ireland

Northern Ireland—the six counties of Ireland that are part of the United Kingdom—occupies little space in our book. The troubles you have read about are confined exclusively to this area, and are in fact almost entirely limited to the cities of Derry and Belfast. The twenty-six counties of the Irish Republic have long been peaceful.

Accommodations

Most Irish hotels are indifferent, or worse. The situation is saved, however, by the many private homes that accommodate visitors for bed and breakfast and sometimes for additional meals. These are inexpensive (about £1 or $3 for bed and breakfast) and have limited services, but are always clean, hospitable places. They are listed, with their locations and the rates charged, in two Tourist Board booklets, "Supplementary Guide to Town and Country Homes and Farmhouses" and "Farmhouse Holidays." Almost never risk an accommodation not approved by the Tourist Board and, where convenient, choose a farmhouse. There is no necessity to book in advance; just stop when you're tired. As for the really good hotels, they are usually expensive, often converted castles, and are rated A or A ★ in the Tourist Board booklet, "Official Guide to Hotels, Guesthouses, Holiday Camps, and Hostels." The hotels rated B ★, B, and C seem to have been given their ratings arbitrarily. Some, like the Imperial Hotel in Sligo Town or the Odeon in Galway City, are comfortable and friendly; others are horrors. Hotels and houses are seldom centrally heated and can be a trifle damp even in summer. Rain, usually a light mist, falls at least a small part of most days. Summer weather is temperate but often quite cool. Pack accordingly.

Food

The Tourist Board publishes a booklet, "Guide to Good Eating," that you will find an indispensable aid in ferreting out some excellent restaurants, which may be housed in such unlikely places as an eighteenth-century farmhouse or an old Wesleyan church. These offer appetizing continental fare and bountiful wine cellars. Standard Irish cuisine, however, which you will sooner or later find yourself up against, is another matter.

The best Irish meal is breakfast—bacon, eggs, sausage, tomato, home-baked breads, and strong tea. (If you must have coffee, it is wise to bring along your own instant and ask for boiling water.) Irish cooking is unadorned and overdone. Because of the abundance of rich grazing lands, steaks and chops can be inexpensive and superb. Instead of ordering your steak rare, however, ask the waitress merely to introduce it to the flame. Cold chicken is also a safe choice. Hotel dining rooms are often the only places for meals (consult the "Hotels" booklet for prices), though some towns have cafés where you will be served the same unremarkable fare that the hotels provide, but at cheaper prices and in more dreary surroundings. Cooking in private homes is often surprisingly better than what the hotels serve. As for snacks on the road, every village has shops where you can buy passable cheese and the most delicious fruit, tomatoes, and brown bread. The fresh seafood is always a pleasure.

In Dublin the cuisine prospects brighten a bit. The good restaurants are: The Lord Edward, opposite Christchurch, for fine seafood; the Unicorn in Merrion Row; the Quo Vadis in St. Andrew Street for Italian food (if you order pasta, specify *al dente*); the Tain Grill in the Gresham Hotel in O'Connell Street; Daly's Grill in Eden Quay; the Old Stand in Wicklow Street for a typical pub meal; the Old Hob and Snaffles, both basement restaurants in Lower Leeson Street; the Old Dublin in Francis Street; and

Bewley's Oriental Cafés in Westmoreland, Grafton, and George's streets for wonderful cakes and scones.

Entertainment

Dublin has a variety of theatres, museums, galleries, and concert halls (see Chapter 12 for some of these and also consult the Dublin newspapers) and pubs (see the end of Chapter 13). Throughout Ireland folk music is a prime pleasure and often a spontaneous outburst. In the Dublin area, the Abbey Tavern in Howth and the Old Sheeling in Raheny have particularly merry evenings of song. The Dubliners and the Wolfe Tones are singing groups not to be missed, if you should be in the vicinity of one of their performances. The same holds true for the Chieftains and Ceoltoiri Cualann, ensembles devoted to classical Gaelic music. Warning: the sign "Ballads Tonight" may only mean rehashed Frank Sinatra.

The hearth is still the hub of village life, and church and pub are the other centers of social activity. The church hall sometimes pulses with vigorous folk dancing. Most pubs have two sections, the lounge for both sexes and the bar, which sometimes discourages female company ("You'll feel more comfortable in the lounge, Missus"). But in the pub—and especially at the cramped, smoke-filled bar—wit is at its most distilled. Perhaps because the Irish have so much of fresh air and open spaces, they are unbothered by airless rooms and physical proximity; they rub against you unconsciously, and seem to want to look through your eyes to get at your soul. (They are bothered by sunglasses.) The trick of Irish conversation is that it is not conversation at all. It is a

performance. The speaker sets his scene, builds his characters and plot with only seeming carelessness (this is part of
his art), then finally explodes the structure with his final
line. For your part, you are expected to encourage him with
small noises and phrases like "You don't say," but never to
interrupt with your own train of thought. When he is
finished, you are welcome, of course, to try a performance
of your own, while he plays audience. Or you may sing a
song. Occasionally your contribution is required, but usually you are allowed to remain a listener, observing in fascinated silence the age-old origins of Irish literature.

St. Kevin's Church, Glendalough, Co. Wicklow. Irish Tourist Board.

1.
HOLY CITIES AND HOMELESS PEOPLE

◇◇◇◇◇◇◇◇◇◇◇◇◇◇◇◇◇◇◇◇◇◇◇◇◇◇◇◇◇◇◇

Counties Wicklow, Kilkenny, and Tipperary

Still south I went and west and south again,
Through Wicklow from the morning till the night,
And far from cities, and the sights of men,
Lived with the sunshine, and the moon's delight.

I knew the stars, the flowers, and the birds,
The grey and wintry sides of many glens,
And did but half remember human words,
In converse with the mountains, moors, and fens.

J. M. SYNGE, "PRELUDE"

JOHN MILLINGTON SYNGE was born in suburban Rathfarnham, four miles southwest of Dublin, at No. 2 Newtown Villas, a stucco Victorian house up the hill from Lower Dodder Road and left off Braemor Road. But aside from a commemorative plaque and a woodcut of his handsome head, the place holds nothing of Synge. Look for him rather in the Dublin and Wicklow Mountains, where his solitary wanderings gave him, as he later wrote, "a passionate and receptive mood like that of early man."

On the outskirts of Rathfarnham you can pick up the Military Road (L. 94) and take it south, as Synge in flight from the drawing room did, through the mountainy heather deserts of Wicklow, six times as old as the Alps and Himalayas but fresh as Synge's language and the earthy wisdom of his characters. For in Wicklow he heard the idioms of the earth speaking in his own body, and his art records their sensual, liberating harmonies and their deep vibrations of mortality. In the wooded valley of Glencree, to the right of the Military Road beyond the statue of the Good Shepherd, he roamed with his beloved Molly Allgood:

> My arms are around you, and I lean
> Against you, while the lark
> Sings over us, and golden lights, and green
> Shadows are on your bark.
>
> There'll come a season when you'll stretch
> Black boards to cover me:
> Then in Mount Jerome I will lie, poor wretch,
> With worms eternally.

Not long after he had written these words, "To the Oaks of Glencree," he was dead, aged thirty-seven. But Glencree rustles still with lights and shadows, and the Military Road, also known as the Wilderness Highway, wends through the magnificent Liffey Head Bog where Joyce's Anna Livia rises and begins her "goolden wending" down into Kildare, northwards to enter County Dublin near Leixlip, and eighty miles later, having "lapped so long" passes out "sad and weary" through Dublin Bay into the arms of her "cold mad feary father," the Irish Sea.

What the city on the Liffey is to Joyce's stories and novels, the open road is to Synge's plays: the dominant image of liberation, of the limitless possibilities of life when it is experienced as a journey. By following his routes and those of his picaresque heroines and heroes, you may be converted to the mystique of the road, gaining as soul-mates Moses, Paul, Chaucer, Huck Finn, Synge, and Jack Kerouac. A risky pilgrimage, true. Defining life as a journey to freedom means, among other things, that like the passionate young Nora of *In the Shadow of the Glen*, the wise old couple of *The Well of the Saints*, and the travelling people in *The Tinker's Wedding*, you can never go back or settle down in quite the same way again.

A few miles south of Glencree, where Sally Gap cuts through the Military Road to form Ireland's highest crossroads, there was posted in Synge's day a warning, "These Lands Are Poisonous." Synge's nephew, Edward Stephens, remembers his uncle laughing at the sign's absurdity and going his merry, independent way. He often turned left at Sally Gap and walked east (L. 161) and stopped above Lough Tay, an utterly peaceful and miragelike radiance, part of the road's sorcery, compelling you to stare for hours and then scramble down to where it glistens on the glen floor, buttressed by the black walls of Fancy Mountain. A few miles beyond Lough Tay (also called Luggala), the Old Calary Road leading north from Sraghmore beckons you away from the main Dublin road (T. 61). Synge knew the bedevilling paths up Djouce Mountain, to the left of the road, and, too, the grand views from the summit: to the west Liffey Head Bog, to the east the coast of Leinster from Wexford Town to the Mountains of Mourne, and, on a clear day, Wales. Understanding that mobility liberates, he gladly exchanged creature comforts for the rugged joys and visions of the road. Jack B. Yeats, W. B.'s brother, remembered Synge as "an old dog for a hard road and not a young pup for a tow-path":

Synge was by nature well equipped for the roads. Though his health was often bad he had beating under his ribs a brave heart that carried him over rough tracks. He gathered about him very little gear, and cared nothing for comfort except perhaps that of a good turf fire.

Nowadays, in northeastern Wicklow—on the roads near the pretty village of Enniskerry, the Dargle Glen, and the Great Sugar Loaf—you don't see many signs of the tramp life that flourished in Synge's day and inspired his essay "The Vagrants of Wicklow." Very anglicized and conventionally scenic, this section attracts tourism, a respectable trade, and disdains the wandering tinkers one still meets in the outposts of western Ireland. For Synge, however, these were the poets of the road, the liberators of the culture's imagination, representing the connection between mobility as a life-style and a living art:

In all the circumstances of this tramp life there is a certain wildness that gives it romance and a peculiar value for those who look at life in Ireland with an eye that is aware of the arts also. In all the healthy movements of art, variations from the ordinary types of manhood are made interesting for the ordinary man, and in this way only the higher arts are universal. . . . Art . . . [is] founded on the variations which are a condition and effect of all vigorous life.

As superhighways are images of efficient mobility, secondary roads suggest the slow-motion journey of surprises, revealing the world unpredictably, like the flow of experience itself. Leaving the beaten track, wind south from the Great Sugar Loaf towards Ashford on the less-travelled roads that twist to the west of T. 7; stop to explore the weird Devil's Glen one mile northwest of Ashford, first asking the owner's permission. On the village green in Roundwood, Synge photographed the markets and fairs and remembered the talk. There's plenty of that—and tasty cold chicken along with your pint—in the bar of the Wicklow Hills Hotel. From Roundwood, a signposted back road leads to Lough Dan, a long black tongue of mountain water connected to Lough Tay by the Cloghoge River and a hidden footpath. It's easy to lose, or want to lose, all sense of direction back here on the twisty roads and paths around Lough Dan, but suddenly you're in the village of Annamoe, where north of the bridge to the left you can still find the millrace that almost ended Laurence Sterne's life when he was a child growing up in Ireland. He fell through it while the mill was turning, but was taken out miraculously unharmed. Today the decayed wheel leans against the old mill wall, and a powerless stream trickles by.

Splendidly remote and culturally revealing is Castle

Kevin, the Georgian house in which Synge summered from 1892 to 1907. It stands dramatically atop a hill at the end of a long driveway, just outside Annamoe. (From the bridge bear right for a very short distance and then right again till you come to the high stone gates. Owners' permission should be sought to explore the demesne.)

Behind the house, the walled garden has been landscaped and planted since the days when Synge walked here among the weeds and ruins and pondered the old regime's crumbling, the subject of his essay "A Landlord's Garden in County Wicklow":

A stone's throw from an old house where I spent several summers in County Wicklow, there was a garden that had been left to itself for fifteen or twenty years. . . . Everyone is used in Ireland to the tragedy that is bound up with the lives of farmers and fishing people; but in this garden one seemed to feel the tragedy of the landlord class also, and of the innumerable old families that are quickly dwindling away. These owners of the land are not much pitied at the present day, or much deserving of pity; and yet one cannot quite forget that they are the descendants of what was at one time, in the eighteenth century, a high-spirited and highly cultivated aristocracy. The broken green-houses and mouse-eaten libraries that were designed and collected by men who voted with Grattan, are perhaps as mournful in the end as the four mud walls that are so often left in Wicklow as the only remnants of a farmhouse.

Today the stone bench where he often sat musing and writing stands beside the door to the garden. The orchards, the avenue of limes, the graceful and generous proportions of the house, all suggest the quality of the Anglo-Irish contribution to Ireland's social evolution.

Castle Kevin is a reminder that Anglo-Protestant culture gave to Ireland most of what she knows about Renaissance and modern values: the sense of proportion and individuality, and thence social consciousness; burgher efficiency; and parliamentary democracy. By uniting the country under one crown, the Anglo-Irish also succeeded in suppressing tribal identity and factionalism and gave the Irish—as one of the many ironies of Irish history—their identity as a nation.

But the contribution of the Anglo-Irish must be weighed against their awful destructiveness. The settlers from England attempted at first to eradicate a whole culture—the same culture that the Anglo-Irish Synge, Yeats, and Lady Gregory would in the twentieth century try so painstakingly to resurrect. They outlawed the precious religion of the natives and hounded their priests. They outlawed the Irish language and ancient customs. They made it virtually impossible for the indigenous inhabitants to own land or to have a voice in the government of their country. In short, they created a nation of slaves; and the conditions of that slavery, according to observers of the time, were worse than anything that prevailed in the American colonies. Finally, the already impoverished tenant farmers were reduced to starvation in the nineteenth century by the failures of the potato crop. England's response was insufficient, for to provide the radically necessary relief would be to commit the cardinal sin: interference with free enterprise. By the end of the century the population had been reduced by starvation and consequent emigration to four million—just half of its strength in 1840. Thus crushed, the fierce pride of the

Gael was transmuted into new forms. Usually, it was reduced to the obsequiousness of all conquered people who know they must fawn to survive. Sometimes it would burst forth in inept rebellion, often encouraged and led by disaffected Anglo-Irishmen who wanted a free Ireland. Always it seethed in the memory, fostering the undying enmities that still erupt in Northern Ireland.

From one point of view, however, the record of England's cultural imperialism can be read as an ironic story of creative destruction. For, dispossessed of their native language, the Irish came to outtalk the English in their own tongue, giving it the sound of poetry "as fully flavoured as a nut or apple" in the words of Synge's Preface to *The Playboy of the Western World*. It was not in the parlor of Castle Kevin that he heard the "rich and living" language of his plays. His dialogue came from native places like Tomrilands Farm, still a simple country house and garden at the end of a tree-lined laneway, a half mile north along the tarred road from Castle Kevin, the last house on the left before Tomrilands Crossroads:

When I was writing *In the Shadow of the Glen*, some years ago, I got more aid than any learning could have given me from a chink in the floor of the old Wicklow house where I was staying, that let me hear what was being said by the servant girls in the kitchen. . . . In Ireland, for a few years more, we have a popular imagination that is fiery and magnificent, and tender; so that those of us who wish to write start with a chance that is not given to writers in places where the springtime of the local life has been forgotten, and the harvest is a memory only, and the straw has been turned into bricks.

Brick has yet to blight the fresh world of this runaway from the Big House, though parts of Ireland are dangerously ripe for the developers' harvest. Mining companies have, in fact, been gouging about in Wicklow for some time. But you may be blissfully unaware of the ugly scars of modern industry as you pass through the gentle Vale of Clara, south of Annamoe and Laragh, then through Rathdrum, farther south, which looks much as it did when Synge went to its fairs. (Rathdrum's Avonbrae is a comfortable, sylvan guest-house.) Avondale, yet farther south, was once the home of Charles Stewart Parnell, great nineteenth-century champion of home rule; Synge visited here. But at the meeting of the Avonmore and Avonbeg rivers, a small stretch of blight sets in. "There is not in this wide world a valley so sweet/As that vale in whose bosom the bright waters meet," wrote Tom Moore in "The Meeting of the Waters," but today he might sing a different tune. The government has transformed the scene of his sentimental reverie into a sort of suburban patio, all concrete and rectangular, with the tree under which he sat given pride of place, though it is now quite dead from generations of souvenir-strippers. His beloved Vale of Avoca, where the Avonmore and Avonbeg flow south together, is studded with billboards and gashed with mines. To erase such images, head southwest (L. 32) through the valley of Aghavanagh and then northeast across the southern portion of the Military Road to Drumgoff Cross, and turn left. Catching sight of the majestic sweep of Lugnaquilla's heights (3,039 feet), you know you're back on the trail of an artist. Destination: Glenmalure, the setting

/ 25

of *In the Shadow of the Glen*, Synge's play about marriage Wicklow-style.

Nora Burke, the young wife of a wheezy old farmer, lives in "the last cottage at the head of a long glen in County Wicklow," a restless prisoner in a marriage as bleak as the valley in winter. But like the ewes and tups that play on the mountainsides, she and various shepherds who "do be reared in the Glen Malure" take their pleasures whenever the glen is clear. Having been found out one night when her crafty mate lay wrapped in a shroud pretending to be dead, she runs away with an eloquent Tramp who woos her with words of the open road:

Come along with me now, lady of the house, and it's not my blather you'll be hearing only, but you'll be hearing the herons crying out over the black lakes, and you'll be hearing the grouse and the owls with them, and the larks and the big thrushes when the days are warm, and it's not from the like of them you'll be hearing a talk of getting old like Peggy Cavanagh, and losing the hair off you, and the light of your eyes, but it's fine songs you'll be hearing when the sun goes up, and there'll be no old fellow wheezing, the like of a sick sheep, close to your ear.

Ironically, his description of the itinerant's paradise fits perfectly the beauty of the glen they leave behind. Glenmalure is the grandest and most historic of all the Wicklow glens. In 1580 Fiach MacHugh O'Byrne, the great Wicklow chief, routed the troops of Elizabeth's Deputy, Lord Grey, while Grey's secretary, Edmund Spenser, looked on, recording the defeat in his notebook. From Drumgoff Cross, the road twists three miles along the glen floor, a narrow slash between two massive slants of rock that rule all space between the snaky road and drifting sky. Through the trees on the left appears Carrowaystick Fall, a magic water-dance with cliff and wind. The path beside it, a tough, zigzaggy climb, leads to Kelly's Lough, at 2,000 feet the highest lake in Wicklow, and finally to Lugnaquilla, the highest point in Ireland outside Kerry. The road ends in a car-park at Baravore Ford. From here, you can pick your steps across the Avonbeg and follow the path that leads upstream past the ruin of Baravore, or Harney's Cottage, on the left. Accustomed to stopping in here on his walks, Synge had this lonesome place in mind as tyrannous Dan Burke's house. Nora and the Tramp fled from here up the glen, past where the campers' hostel is now situated, and over Table Mountain to Brittas. For Synge every road was a path to freedom.

To Nora, Glenmalure may have seemed a prison with its fortresslike walls, but the visitor is more overwhelmed by the sights and sounds of exploding energy, especially in April when the Avonbeg rushes blue and clear, the new lambs gambol frantically, yellow gorse shines everywhere, and always the mountaintops aim at the sky and tumbling clouds, and sudden shots of sunlight sweep the whole valley. "The worst vice is slight," wrote Synge in his first Wicklow play, *When the Moon Has Set*,

compared with the guiltiness of a man or woman who defies the central order of the world. . . . The only truth a wave knows is that it is going to break. The only truth a bud knows is that it is going to expand and flower. The only truth we know is that we are a flood of magnificent life, the fruit of some frenzy of the earth.

GLENDALOUGH, the Glen of the Two Lakes over the mountain from Glenmalure, belongs to the geography of human liberation. Continuing northeast on the Military Road from Drumgoff Cross past "Ladies Rock," the traveller turns to the west at Laragh and suddenly sees a round tower thrusting its ancient stone head through the trees. Over one thousand years old, its bold contour embodies the original spirit of Glendalough, scene of an eruption of spiritual, intellectual, and moral energy.

It all started in the sixth century when Saint Kevin fled here from a rotting pagan civilization. He desired not companionship, but the solitude in which to be alone with God and to transform himself into a new man. Thus, he settled, not in the area of the round tower, but in the valley's most inaccessible reaches—the cliff that borders the southern shore of the dazzling Upper Lake. If you take the path along the northern shore, you can look across the lake to St. Kevin's Bed, a hole in the rock wall—four feet wide, seven feet deep, three feet high—where Kevin lived, mortifying his flesh in order to free his soul. Soon, however, he was joined by others, groping, like the saint himself, towards some personal psychic revolution. The arrival of the neophytes necessitated a move to less precarious circumstances. The little community, with Kevin as its spiritual guide, settled down near the eastern shore of the Upper Lake, where the traces of their habitation are still visible: on a hill the foundations of a monkish cell and little Reefert Church; stone crosses and a fort on flatter ground. But even in these more gentle surroundings, silence and solitude were of supreme importance. If you climb the steep bank behind St. Kevin's bee-

hive cell and follow the forest road to the northern brow of
Derrybawn Mountain, the Upper Lake stretches out below
in all the ecstatic wonder it must once have had for the mystical ascetics of Glendalough.

St. Kevin's foundation grew at last into the university of
Glendalough, clustered about the round tower east of the
Lower Lake, which drew thousands of students from all
over Europe, drop-outs from a civilization in decline, men in
search of a counter-culture. They passed under the arched
Gateway, now opposite the Royal Hotel, and traced with
their fingers, as you can do today, the cross carved into the
right-hand wall, a sign that this is a sanctuary for pilgrims.
Within the walls lay the great monastic city. Its larger and
later stone buildings (eleventh to twelfth century) still
stand, though the wattle huts of the monks and scholars have
long since turned to dust. The Venerable Bede weaves a
tableau of Glendalough in full swing:

Many of the nobles of the English nation and lesser men also had
set out thither, forsaking their native island either for the grace of
sacred learning or a more austere life. And some of them indeed
soon dedicated themselves faithfully to the monastic life, others re-
joiced rather to give themselves to learning, going about from one
master's cell to another. All these the Irish willingly received, and
saw to it to supply them with food day by day without cost, and
books for their studies, and teaching, free of charge.

Here, then, was a human eco-system, a self-sufficient living
organism in the midst of a dying world. The Celtic interla-
cing of plants and animals carved on the churches and
crosses reveal the medieval harmony between the kingdom

/ 29

of nature and the kingdom of the spirit. Everything has its rightful role, and the world abounds in symmetries, parallels, and unexpected twists and resonances, as in Robin Flower's translation of an old monastic poem, "The Scholar and His Cat":

I and Pangur Ban my cat,
'Tis a like task we are at:
Hunting mice is his delight,
Hunting words I sit all night.

'Tis a merry thing to see
At our tasks how glad are we,
When at home we sit and find
Entertainment to our mind.

'Gainst the wall he sets his eye,
Full and fierce and sharp and sly;
'Gainst the wall of knowledge I
All my little wisdom try.

So in peace our task we ply,
Pangur Ban, my cat and I;
In our arts we find our bliss,
I have mine and he has his.

Part of the bliss of living in Glendalough must have been the freedom to chase ideas while strolling the valley. But then the sinister Viking ships appeared on the horizon, and the rich monasteries had to use their great round bell towers—those singular Irish contributions to ecclesiastical architecture—for hiding from barbarian hands the vessels of gold and precious gems. The round towers were customarily built without ground-level doorways. The monks entered at one of the upper-storey openings by means of a rope ladder, which could then be pulled up after them, thus denying access to an enemy. Terror and uncertainty could only have injured peace and scholarship.

The monks themselves crossed the seas, which was the most heroic thing they could think to do—to leave the land they loved so and become exiles for Christ. Without the diaspora of Irish scholars on the continent, without the gorgeously illuminated manuscripts they brought with them from monastic Ireland, the Dark Ages of Europe could never have given birth to medieval learning. Throughout Europe, in fact, "Scotus," the Latin word for Irishman, became a synonym for "scholar": Clemens Scotus headed Charlemagne's palace school; Johannes Scotus Eriugena instructed the court of Charles the Bald; Sedulius Scotus, possibly the author of "The Scholar and His Cat," taught at Liège, Metz, and Cologne, where his drinking songs were famous.

On the far side of the stream from St. Kevin's Kitchen and half a mile east is St. Saviour's Priory, hidden in a grove of fir trees. If you linger here in late afternoon, you may feel the quickening of the spirit Yeats describes in "Stream and Sun at Glendalough":

> What motion of the sun or stream,
> Or eyelid shot the gleam
> That pierced my body through?
> What made me live like these that seem
> Self-born, born anew?

On the priory's chancel arch and east window the rich Romanesque decorations still stand out clearly, inventive and joyful celebrations of new men in a new world.

By Synge's time the Irish Church had hitched its interests to the British Crown and made its worldly business the extinction of liberators. In *The Well of the Saints* Synge has the tyrannical Saint sleep at Glendalough, or the "Seven Churches" as it is called in Wicklow, while the free-spirited Martin and Mary Doul reject the priest's scheme of things and take to the roads. Glenmacnass waterfall, a few miles north of Glendalough and best seen when approached from Laragh on the Military Road, is an apt metaphor of these renegade souls. Its constant energy and stark setting inspired Synge's love poem, "Queens":

> Seven dog-days we let pass,
> Naming Queens in Glenmacnass,
> All the rare and royal names
> Wormy sheepskin yet retains.
> . . . .
> Yet these are rotten—I ask their pardon—
> And we've the sun on rock and garden;
> These are rotten, so you're the Queen
> Of all are living, or have been.

From Glenmacnass, the journey through his beloved Wicklow mountains comes to a dramatic scenic conclusion as you climb north to Sally Gap, turn left through the "Coronation Plantation," a memorial grove to honor Victoria's accession, and at Blessington head south through Donard for the Glen of Imaal.

KILKENNY CITY on the River Nore is an enchanting assemblage of medieval fragments and an important page in Ireland's bloody history. The first Kilkennians were the saints and scholars of St. Cannice's sixth-century monastery. But the only relic of their settlement is a restored round tower outside St. Cannice's Cathedral on the western end of town. In the twelfth century the monastic city was transformed into a secular town by a handful of the Norman adventurers who in the face of Irish disunity had little trouble establishing their castles, abbeys, and towns throughout the south and east. That these invaders, unlike the Vikings, contributed a soft, humanizing strain to the fierce Celtic temper is obvious from the special beauty of St. Cannice's Cathedral, built in the thirteenth century, used as a stable by Cromwell, and restored in 1863–64. From the outside, its lines are deliberately austere, suggesting the emotional control that marks the Norman temperament. Inside, the Gothic structure and quatrefoil windows of the clerestory have all the exultant sensuality of the Provençal love poetry that the Normans brought to Ireland. Irish versions of the troubadour's lyrics became so popular among the clerics and monks of Kilkenny that the fourteenth-century Bishop de Ledrede forbade all profane singing on holy days. The tombs within the cathedral, among them the bishop's, constitute one of the finest collections of medieval monuments to be seen anywhere. Historians say that the Normans became "more Irish than the Irish themselves." The little carvings of the "weepers"—the Norman warriors and saints that line the chests below the black marble effigies—give the evidence: their faces are so engagingly Irish-looking, and from the wild frizziness of their hair they obviously went their way through the Irish mist.

Far from being crushed, the Irish cast the spell of their culture over the so-called conquerors. In 1366 the Norman authors of the Statutes of Kilkenny tried to break the spell by making it illegal for Anglo-Normans to speak the Irish language, entertain Irish poets, play hurling, or marry Irish women; the natives, forbidden to live within a walled town, were banished to "Irishtown," the rows of one-storey cottages still seen on the outskirts of most towns and cities. If you walk along Dean and Abbey streets from St. Cannice's, you can see the architecture of apartheid in the medieval walls and gates, and beyond the walls the huts of the old native ghettos. Although the political and economic control of Kilkenny was monopolized eventually by ten Norman families—one of whose houses still stands, Rothe House in Parliament Street, a captivating building with a cobblestone court—the notorious Statutes of Kilkenny were in the end unenforceable: the Irish never lost their power over the hearts of their invaders.

Kilkenny also boasts a famous witch, one Dame Alice Kyteler. Her fourteenth-century house, the oldest in Kilkenny, has been restored as Kyteler's Inn, an excellent restaurant in Kieran Street just down the slip from High Street. In the candlelit cellar-dining room you can examine the strange identations in the original stone walls, presumably the markings left by her satanic rituals. She and her disciples were accused of sacrificing black cocks to the Devil and of brewing foul mixtures of their entrails with herbs, insects, and the hair and nails of unbaptized children and dead

men whose corpses she allegedly provided by killing three
of her four husbands. To satisfy her unnatural lusts Alice
was also said to have summoned an incubus, Robert son of
Art, under the forms of a cat, a black dog, and a Negro. But
these weird doings may only have been the imaginings of
Alice's accuser, Bishop de Ledrede (also known as Leather-
head), who had obviously been driven mad by all that
courtly love poetry. Though Alice escaped and was never
heard of again, her maid, Petronilla, was burned at the stake.
Yeats, who took these matters of the occult quite seriously,
used them in his poem, "1919," as an image of the mindless,
violent politics he abhorred:

> There lurches past, his great eyes without thought
> Under the shadow of stupid straw-pale locks,
> That insolent fiend Robert Artisson
> To whom the love-lorn Lady Kyteler brought
> Bronzed peacock feathers, red combs of her cocks.

Today, Alice's restaurant has helped to give the witch a
new image as a popular folk heroine. On Halloween, Kilkennians gather in her backyard for a rollicking dance presided over by a merry mistress of ceremonies on a broom-
stick. But even in the friendliest Irish crowd, strangers
would do well to leave unexplored the Yeatsian connections
between Alice's rituals and the bloody birth of the Irish Republic.

At the eastern end of town, Kilkenny Castle, impressively immense, crowns a hill commanding a splendid view
of the River Nore. From the secluded riverside path, perpendicular to John's Bridge, you can look across to the

grounds of Kilkenny College, where William Congreve, George Farquhar, Jonathan Swift and George Berkeley studied, and then climb to the castle's demesne up a stairway concealed in the hillside. Strongbow, Ireland's original Norman conqueror, picked this spot for his fortress, which was replaced in 1204 by a stone castle, of which three towers and the north wall have survived. In 1391 James Butler, third Earl of Ormonde, bought it, thus making Kilkenny the capital of Butler country. When the Confederation of Kilkenny, the Catholic Confederacy of 1645, met here to try to unify Ireland's many factions before Oliver Cromwell's onslaught, the Butlers extended their Irish hospitality as a way of controlling the balance of power and protecting their special interests. Old Gaelic kings, Old Norman magnates, and New English landlords also played the politics of greed and guile. The Confederation fell apart in factitious feuding, and Cromwell's butchers advanced unopposed by any united Irish front. The consequent devastation of the land, the ruin of the abbeys and churches, and the slaughter of many thousands must be blamed, not only on Cromwell and his minions, but on the self-seeking blindness of the Irish nobility. Kilkenny Castle is a reminder of tribal Ireland before it was a nation.

COUNTY TIPPERARY HAS its sad pleasures and grim stone celebrations of Ireland's shuddery past. The graveyard at Ahenny (south of Kilkenny and four and a half miles north of Carrick-on-Suir on L. 26) is dominated by two eighth-century monoliths, perhaps the earliest extant examples of the Celtic high cross. The intricate geometry of their carved designs shows them to be near cousins of the Book of Kells, that airy tour de force of Irish art now in Trinity Library, Dublin, but they have none of the lightsome grace that would later be achieved in the great tapered crosses of Clonmacnois and Monasterboice. Rather, their stark symmetry emphasizes overwhelming weight and mass, and their phallic caps make them seem more the work of powerful druids than of peace-loving contemplatives.

Continue southwest from Ahenny through the luminous valley of Slievenamon, and follow the signs for Ballypatrick from the Clonmel-Kilkenny-Dublin road (T. 6). One mile north of the Ballypatrick crossroads, a turn to the right leads straight down an avenue to the laurel-covered ruins of Kilcash castle on the southeast slope of Slievenamon. Once the seat of a branch of the Butlers, it has stood through the centuries as a symbol of the proud Kingdom of Ireland, beaten but never broken. The top of the tower affords a panoramic view of the lush countryside, once thick with forests. The haunting presence of this ruin inspired an anonymous Gaelic bard of the early eighteenth century to sing a song that Yeats would later use as a quarry for metaphors:

What shall we do for timber?
  The last of the woods is down.
Kilcash and the house of its glory
  And the bell of the house are gone,
The spot where that lady waited
  Who shamed all women for grace
When earls came sailing to greet her
  And Mass was said in the place.

My grief and my affliction
  Your gates are taken away,
Your avenue needs attention,
  Goats in the garden stray.
The courtyard's filled with water
  And the great earls where are they?
The earls, the lady, the people
  Beaten into the clay. . . .*

FIFTEEN MILES the other side of the mountain (Ballypatrick-
Templeetney-L. 154-L. 111), the Rock of Cashel juts
against the clouds, an outcropping of limestone cliff on
which is set the most impressive collection of medieval architecture in Ireland. Rising like the spires of Chartres from
the surrounding plain, the abbeys and churches of the Rock
ascend to two hundred feet. But, unlike Chartres, which ex-
tends its gentle invitation for miles, the ominous Rock seems
to threaten. From here the lords of Munster ruled and in the
Christian era took to themselves the double role of king and
bishop. On the spot where the high cross now stands, Saint
Patrick baptized King Aengus, the Rock's first Christian occupant. In the course of the ceremony, so the story goes, the
saint accidentally stuck his crozier through the king's foot.
The proud, unflinching warrior said nothing, thinking the
pain a part of his new religion.

The pain of the new religion, wedded to the old life style,

---

* Translation from the Irish by Frank O'Connor, *Kings, Lords, and Commons*. Except where otherwise noted all quoted translations from the Irish are from this
work.

finds a more serious expression in Cormac's chapel, the country's finest Romanesque remain. The delicacy of the chapel's lines is betrayed by the carvings within: severed human heads hang from the altar arch; in the tympanum of the main door a centaur slays a lion; and on a tomb in the west end serpents slither in a lattice of Viking design. In Austin Clarke's historical novel *The Singing Men of Cashel*, Gormlai, the innocent virgin bride of King Cormac, enters the chapel one night in confusion and terror to pray. "In the mingled light and shadow" she discerns her husband "abased on the flags. His robe was stripped from his back and there were long, dark weals on his flesh." Unbeknownst to her, Cormac has resolved to submit himself to the ancient tradition of Cashel—to be consecrated as king-bishop and live a celibate life—and put Gormlai away in a nunnery. He has been flagellating his body beneath "that arch of mocking heads" in order to mortify his evil desire to visit his own marriage bed.

The arrangement of the buildings on Cashel Rock is not harmonious like the abbeys of the high Middle Ages, but almost brutal. At a distance, when the sky is brooding, the great complex of stone can seem an apparition of unyielding cruelty, demanding obeisance. One could imagine that the men who made it belonged to a different, distant species.

Cathedral and River Lee, Cork. Irish Tourist Board

2.

GREAT EPICS
AND SMALL TALES

◇◇◇◇◇◇◇◇◇◇◇◇◇◇◇◇◇◇◇◇◇◇◇◇◇◇◇◇◇◇◇◇◇◇

County Cork

Eᴌɪᴢᴀʙᴇᴛʜᴀɴ Eɴɢʟᴀɴᴅ rattled into Ireland, not in
all its dazzle, but in all its myopic cruelty.
Though this first British experiment in colonialism had no
laureate-defender quite so pious as Kipling, among the
minor functionaries who profited from the occupation was
Edmund Spenser, who came to Ireland as secretary to the
savage Lord Deputy Grey de Wilton and stayed on as
Clerk to the Council of Munster and Sheriff of Cork. Spenser lived here for twenty-six years, and Irish places—under
invented names—are threaded through his sonorous lines.
The territory best known to him lies southwest of Cashel:

> All those faire forrests about Arlo hid,
> And all that Mountaine, which doth over-looke
> The richest champain that may else be rid;

And the faire Shure in which are thousand
                              Salmons bred.

The Glen of Aherlow—Spenser's "Arlo"—is sheltered on the north by the long ridge of Slievenamuck and on the south by the Galtee Mountains, rising abruptly from the plain of Tipperary to form the country's most imposing interior range. The Galtees and their southwest extension, the Ballyhoura Hills, comprise Spenser's "Old Mole" and bear ancient associations with Irish gods and warriors. In the *Cantos of Mutabilitie,* classical, rather than Celtic, deities assemble on Galtymore ("Arlo Hill"), the tallest peak in the chain, to treat of the philosophical problem of change.

The Ireland of Spenser's day could not have been more mutable and unstable; and when the immortals abandoned Arlo Hill, the rapparees—the rebel Irish—took over. The Galtee area was then, as was much of Ireland, thickly wooded; and from the mountain forests the dispossessed natives, who eked out there their scrappy existence, would sometimes emerge to raid and terrorize the colonists:

                . . . best and fairest hill
That was in all this holy Islands hights
Was made the most unpleasant and most ill
. . . .
Since when those Woods, and all that goodly Chase
Doth to this day with Wolves and thieves abound;
Which too-too true that land's in-dwellers
                            since have found.

Spenser himself was to find out too-too well the violence that dispossessed people are capable of. His estate of Kilcolman once spread for three thousand acres under the shadow of the Ballyhoura Hills. On the way there from Aherlow you pass Kildorrery, where Elizabeth Bowen grew up. Like Spenser, her family came to Ireland in the sixteenth century and were granted confiscated lands. Though the Italianate house of Bowen's Court has been pulled down and the estate is now a very ordinary farm, readers of *The Last September* may still detect the faint sadness of that last soft autumn of the Anglo-Irish aristocracy before the dispossessed at last wrested the land from British domination. *Bowen's Court*, the history she wrote of her family, is a sympathetic evocation of her class and of this countryside. It begins:

Up in the north-east corner of County Cork is a stretch of limestone country—open, airy, not quite flat; it is just perceptibly tilted from north to south, and the fields undulate in a smooth flowing way. Dark knolls and screens of trees, the network of hedges, abrupt stony ridges, slate glints from roofs give the landscape a featured look—but the prevailing impression is emptiness. This is a part of Ireland with no lakes, but the sky's movement of clouds reflects itself everywhere as it might on water, rounding the trees with bloom and giving the grass a sheen. In the airy silence, any sound travels a long way. The streams and rivers, sunk in their valleys, are not seen until you come down to them.

Little enough is left of Kilcolman Castle, which stands by a marshy, fishless lake three miles north of Doneraile on the road to Charleville. The fortress-house where Spenser lived has disappeared, and of the castle only a tower remains, covered in laurel, with turret stairs and vaulted chamber. Little tributaries of the Awbeg River, itself a tributary of the

Blackwater, intersect the fields. In Spenser, this "pleasant playne" is called "Armulla Dale," and the shiny Awbeg is Old Mole's daughter, "Mulla."

Spenser bedded his bride at Kilcolman to the trumpets of *Epithalamion*:

> Ye Nymphes of Mulla, which with carefull heed
> The silver scaly trouts doe tend full well,
> And greedy pikes which use therein to feed;
> (Those trouts and pikes all others doo excell;
> And ye likewise, which keepe the rushy lake,
> Where none doo fishes take;)
> Bynd up the locks the which hang scattered light,
> And in his waters, which your mirror make,
> Behold your faces as the christall bright,
> That when you come whereas my love doth lie,
> No blemish she may spie.
> And eke, ye lightfoot mayds, which keepe the deere,
> That on the hoary mountayne used to towre;
> And the wylde wolves, which seeke them to devoure,
> With your steele darts doo chace from comming neer;
> Be also present heere,
> To helpe to decke her, and to help to sing,
> That all the woods may answer, and your eccho ring.

In addition to its excellent fishing directions, *Epithalamion*, like the rest of Spenser's work, rings out with all the proud confidence of Renaissance man, certain of his centrality in the universal scheme. But these exuberant notes sounded with alien hostility over the Irish landscape. The natives resisted the conquerors and the spread of the new culture; the Elizabethans marshalled their Renaissance skill and technical superiority toward breaking the outrageous obstinacy of "the wylde Irishe." When the lands of the old chieftains were confiscated and they hid in the forests, the Elizabethans chopped down the trees—sacred to the Irish, with each species representing a letter of the Irish alphabet —and left the bare slopes and plains one sees everywhere today. (Defoliation as an antiguerrilla technique is no more novel than cultural imperialism.) Spenser, that eminent Elizabethan, advocated starvation and genocide, as well as clearing the forests, to bring the Irish under the gentle sway of England's Faerie Queen. All too many Englishmen had no need of his encouragement.

At Kilcolman Spenser wrote much of his poetry and waited, like Swift after him, for London preferments that never came:

> Tho, backe returning to my sheepe again,
> I from thenceforth have learn'd to love more deare
> This lowly quiet life which I inherit here.

The quiet was shattered forever one day in 1598 when the dispossessed descended, burned Kilcolman, scattered the livestock, and laid waste to the lands. A child and some books of *The Faerie Queene* are thought to have perished in the flames. Spenser himself died miserably, ironically in London a year later "for want of bread."

In the demesne of Doneraile Court, at the edge of Doner-aile village, a great house associated with Spenser still stands. "A lyrical place," Elizabeth Bowen describes it. "Carriage drives loop about; there are bamboo groves, a soporific lime walk, a clotted lily pond." Spenser recalled reclining here

/ 45

"among the cooly shade of the green alders," in conversation with Raleigh and Sydney. Outside the village's Catholic church a memorial to Canon Sheehan, obscure turn-of-the-century novelist and parish priest of Doneraile, eulogizes this kindly man as "an author of worldwide fame."

ALMOST AS UNKNOWN to the world as Canon Sheehan and yet so worthy of fame is *The Lament for Art O'Leary*, written in Irish and surely one of the most poignantly beautiful poems in any language. Art O'Leary, like most of the Gaelic noblemen whose families survived into the eighteenth century with their genealogies intact, was a commissioned officer in a continental army. He was among the very few who had managed to maintain a portion of his ancestral Irish land and to preserve, despite all harassment, some vestige of the ancient ways. But on a May evening in 1773 O'Leary was murdered in cold blood at the age of twenty-six for refusing to sell his splendid mare to a man named Morris for the meagre sum of five pounds. (Catholics were prohibited by law from owning a horse worth more than this.) O'Leary's wife, Dark Eileen, an O'Connell of Derrynane and an aunt of Daniel O'Connell, is the author of *The Lament*. In part, it is an answer to her husband's sister, who had apparently ridiculed her for not being present at his wake. (She went to soothe her weeping children, she replies.) More importantly, it is a love poem, a panegyric to the Gaelic ideal of manhood, and one long wail of anguish and outrage, perfectly sustained and controlled and worthy of Greek tragedy at its best:

Till Art O'Leary rise
This grief will never yield
That's bruising all my heart
Yet shut up fast in it,
As 'twere in a locked trunk
With the key gone astray,
And rust grown on the wards.

The route to the places of the O'Learys takes you west from Mallow along the Blackwater, then south through Millstreet to the village of Carriganimma between the mountains. A terra-cotta house in the village, one of the very few multiple-storey thatched dwellings left in Ireland, was the inn from which O'Leary set out for his home the night of his death. Directly across the street from Walsh's pub is an opening to a narrow path, which passes a deserted stone house and leads to a footbridge. On the far side of the bridge, turn left into a wide grassy path that parallels the river. In the eighteenth century this was the coach road. The third bush along the bank is a white thorn with furze at its base:

I never lingered
Till I found you lying
By a little furze-bush
Without pope or bishop
Or priest or cleric
One prayer to whisper
But an old, old woman,
And her cloak about you,
And your blood in torrents—
Art O'Leary—

/ 47

> I did not wipe it off,
> I drank it from my palms.

The river flows by clear and full from the modest slopes of the Derrynasaggart range in the northwest. To the east cattle graze. Neither man nor nature has taken notice of the murder of a passionate woman's passionate husband:

> But noble Art O'Leary,
> Art of hair so golden,
> Art of wit and courage,
> Art the brown mare's master,
> Swept last night to nothing
> Here in Carriganimma—
> Perish it, name and people!

Dark Eileen's first magnetic meeting with her future husband beside the markethouse in Macroom (the present markethouse is nineteenth century) is thoroughly in the Celtic love tradition:

> My love and my delight,
> The day I saw you first
> Beside the markethouse
> I had eyes for nothing else
> And love for none but you.

Just outside Macroom on the road to Killarney along the Sullane River, the first left brings you to a small green gatehouse, the entrance to Raleigh House, where the O'Learys lived. When we were there, the place seemed abandoned and a pack of starved, mad dogs roamed the grounds. The building itself is a pleasant but modest eighteenth-century house with a charming triple-arch window above the main door and, at a tangent, an odd ornamental rampart. Despite the relative simplicity of these surroundings, the O'Learys displayed the old flair and preserved their high sense of themselves:

You gave me everything.
There were parlours whitened for me,
Bedrooms painted for me,
Ovens reddened for me,
Loaves baked for me,
Joints spitted for me,
Beds made for me
To take my ease on flock
Until the milking time
And later if I pleased.
. . . .

My love and my fortune
'Tis an evil portion
To lay for a giant—
A shroud and a coffin—
For a big-hearted hero
Who fished in the hill-streams
And drank in bright halls
With white-breasted women.
. . . .

My rider of the bright eyes,
What happened you yesterday?
I thought you in my heart,
When I bought you your fine clothes,
A man the world could not slay.

The Lament, read aloud in its entirety, gives one, as few other things can, a concrete feeling for the ways of the aristocratic Gael—the fierce pride and dignity, the thrilling lustiness, the love of display, the depth of affection, the undying enmities, the profound understanding of tragedy. Appropriately, this poem is the last word of the old aristocracy, before its final submergence.

Three and one half miles west-southwest of the bridge that spans the River Bride at Ovens the body of Art O'Leary is laid to rest in the southeast corner of the nave of Kilcrea Abbey. His epitaph, probably composed by Eileen, sums up in three adjectives the ideals of the Gaelic order:

LO ARTHUR LEARY
GENROUS HANDSOME BRAVE
SLAIN IN HIS BLOOM
LIES IN THIS HUMBLE GRAVE

CORK CITY-DWELLERS, with a sly charm all their own, present the visitor with a baffling play of contradictions. On the one hand, they know that, like Kilkennians, Limerickmen, Galwegians, and Dubliners, they live in one of the places prominent on the map of Ireland's shame: most Irish cities were originally just monastic settlements or good port sites until the usurpers—Danish, Norman, and English—turned them into towns after bringing the natives to their knees. Saint Finbarr's monastic Cork became a secular city with a little help from the Danes. Corkmen, a bit waspish and defensive, have a chip on their shoulder about something and maybe it's their history. At the same time they can almost make you believe, as *they* do, that Cork is the most beautiful city in—not just Ireland—the world. (Some visitors do compare it with Florence.) To get in the mood for such delirious civic pride, drive west from Kilcrea Abbey through the lush Bride valley to Farran, crossing the Lee into Coachford within sight of a gracious Georgian mansion. Follow the Lee valley eastward along the river's northern shore: few cities offer a more harmonious overture than the River Lee, rolling greenly towards its home, passing on the way the city, flat on its back on the bed of the valley, stretched by fine arched bridges north and south:

> the spreading Lee, that like an island fayre
> Encloseth Corke with his divided flood . . .

Spenser saw that Cork's beauty was largely of the river.

That view becomes climactically apparent from the steep side of the city, north of Patrick's Bridge: from Shandon steeple on Shandon Hill, especially, from the summit of Patrick's Hill, and from the slopes of Montenotte (a swanky suburb farther east, called Montesnottie by inner-city loyalists). But wary of heights and visions, most Corkmen get their spirit of place from the bells of Shandon, still resounding through the warrens off Shandon Hill as they once rock-a-byed "Father Prout" (Francis Sylvester Mahony, 1804–66,) into growing up and making them famous in his song:

> With deep affection,
> And recollection,
> I often think of

> Those Shandon bells,
> Whose sounds so wild would,
> In the days of childhood,
> Fling around my cradle
> Their magic spells.
> On this I ponder
> Where'er I wander,
> And thus grow fonder,
> Sweet Cork, of thee;
> With thy bells of Shandon,
> That sound so grand on
> The pleasant waters of the River Lee.

Cork's liberal physical beauty, only from a distance like Florence's, masks her provincial soul. The world admires Frank O'Connor and Sean O'Faolain as Cork writers; but Cork boasts of Father Prout. Two good restaurants, one Chinese, one Italian, both in Washington Street, are filled nightly with diners ordering Irish beef and mounds of chips. The Arbutus Lodge in Montenotte offers continental cuisine and whispery elegance in the dining room, but locks up the bar at 11 P.M. and snarls "house rules" at any resident so bold as to ask for a midnight drink.

Frank O'Connor (born Michael O'Donovan), who grew up on a northside hill with a view of the river-bed city, looked into her provincial heart and wrote a dozen of the finest short stories in our language. For a sense of the territory of his childhood, real and fictional, hike west—down Shandon Hill and up Blarney Street—passing the old "shawlies," the children, sticky and streetsure, the mean cottages and tough faces, not much changed since he made them the background of "The Drunkard," the story of the little Blarney Lane boy who is sent by his mother to keep his Da from getting fluthered after a funeral and, sneaking his Da's stout, winds up drunk and sick himself and having to be steered home to an outraged mother by a coldly sober, terrified Da.

A hundred yards north of the top of Blarney Street (and the rubble heap at No. 5 that was O'Connor's birthplace) is Strawberry Lane, dropping down past his first school and the Good Shepherd orphanange (where his mother grew up) into Sunday's Well, the middle-class enclave where James Joyce's father lived. Any home could be the setting of O'Connor's "The Mad Lomasneys" who "lived on Sunday's Well in a small house with a long sloping garden and a fine view of the river and the city." Take the right fork as far as the quays, and then swing up again, this time on Summerhill, past St. Luke's Cross and Gardiner's Hill to No. 9 Harrington Square, "an uneven unlighted piece of ground between the Old Youghal Road and the Ballyhooley Road that seemed to have been abandoned by God." Neighborhood children, who will show you the O'Donovan bungalow, now read O'Connor's stories in school, and some residents of the Square enjoy reminiscing about the little boy who went off to join the I.R.A. and "was very good to his mother, I'll give him the bush for that."

Probably no one knew the sensitive, lonely child of "The Genius," "My Oedipus Complex," "The Study of History," "First Confession," and "The Duke's Children" whose secret garden was a rubbish-filled quarry, a short walk from the Square and commanding the same view he remembers in the first volume of his autobiography, *An Only Child*:

Then there was the quarry that fell sheer from the neighbourhood of the barrack to the Ballyhooley Road. It was a noisome place where people dumped their rubbish and gangs of wild kids had stoning matches after school and poor people from the lanes poked among the rubbish for spoil, but I ignored them and picked my way through the discarded bully-beef tins and climbed to some ledge of rock or hollow in the quarry face, and sat there happily, surveying the whole neighborhood from Mayfield Chapel, which crowned the hillside on the edge of the open country, to the spire of Saint Luke's Church below me, and below that again, in the distance was the River Lee with its funnels and masts, and the blue hills over it.

O'Connor quarried his native Cork and, like the poor people who still live in the lanes, found among the rubbish precious spoil—the stuff of over one hundred stories and "all I should ever know of God."

He found plenty of material, too, down in the "flaat o' deh city," where the Cork accent continues as entertainly ripe as it is reproduced in his stories and those of Sean O'Faolain (born at No. 1 Half Moon Street, a block south of the new Opera House). "Every Corkman has the gift of words," O'Faolain wrote. The fun is hearing them flaunt it.

Any native will be glad to give you an entertaining rundown on the Patrick Street statue of Father Theobold Mathew, Apostle of Temperance. At the Carnegie Public Library on Grand Parade where O'Connor as an adolescent and later as librarian made himself an authority on world lit-

erature and the Irish language (the Christian Brothers having decided he was too slow to learn from them), today's li-
brarians will stage-whisper an explanation of the National
Libraries' mysteries and check out your books in exchange
for their price, refunded upon return. Cork voices fill the
tiny Group Theatre in South Main Street, where Irish
dramas are played; and the excellent Everyman Theatre in
Castle Street (telephone: 224331), which has a refreshingly
international tone, has produced in recent seasons Anouilh,
Lorca, Pinter, Tennessee Williams, and Beckett. More the-
atrics spark the pubs in the neighborhood of the South quays
where even the most tight-lipped Corkmen—and they exist,
too—would be moved to poetry by the view from the South
Main Street Bridge, a collage of river, quays, old grey buildings, trees, sea gulls, and the triumphal spire of St. Finbarr's
mock-Gothic cathedral, which hides behind it the Georgian
façades of Deane Street.

The play of contradictions winds up in and around University College in College Road where Stephen Dedalus in
A Portrait of the Artist sees the word "foetus" cut on a desk
in the anatomy theatre. The campus's Honan Chapel,
surely the most beautifully appointed church in the country,
is named for a Cork merchant family that got rich scalping
the poor during the Great Famine. Across Western Road,
the Mardyke, a once-lovely river-walk, where Stephen
Dedalus sees "the leaves of the trees along the Mardyke
. . . astir and whispering in the sunlight," had its trees
tarred man-high by Cork vice squads to stop lovers from
leaning against them at night.

A healthy trek east of the city center is the Marina, a

tree-shaded river-walk unmolested by vigilantes and relatively unchanged since the Sunday mornings Frank O'Connor and his cronies swapped stories here while the rest of Cork went faithfully to Mass. It's a good place to sit and look across at the evening lights twinkling on the hills of Montenotte or to enjoy some more O'Connor stories in the place where many of them began. He helps you notice what you may have missed in seeing and hearing the city. Underneath her spitfire charm, Cork is a town—a small one at that.

ALONG THE COAST of County Cork are the inletted towns of Youghal and Kinsale. Sir Walter Raleigh was Warden (Governor) of Youghal. His house, Myrtle Grove, is one of the few Elizabethan manors remaining in Ireland. He seems to have spent very little time at Myrtle Grove, though according to local tradition, he often sat at the bay window to write to Queen Elizabeth, smoked Virginia tobacco under the yew in the yard, and planted here the first potatoes from the New World.

Kinsale has all the decayed charm of a seaport that technology has passed by. The town is terraced into the slope of Compass Hill, its narrow, winding lanes bordered by a fine collection of crumbling Georgian houses. In 1601 the armies of the north under Hugh O'Neill, Earl of Tyrone, suffered decisive defeat here at the hands of the English Lord Deputy Mountjoy. Ever since, Kinsale has been a synonym for the final fighting failure of Gaelic society.

The Carbery Coast—the stretch from Clonakilty to Ballydehob—has, in addition to its pretty scenery, the most concentrated collection of batty inhabitants you are likely to stumble on anywhere. This is the country of those writing cousins, Somerville and Ross, and the setting for their *Irish R.M.* stories. Though the office of R.M. (Resident Magistrate) has been abolished, the people have not changed. The country cottages and leaking, ramshackle Big Houses still shelter roguish horse dealers, carpenters who have never used a hammer, titled and dotty Anglo-Irish relicts, and their wily, zany servants. We could name names, but Somerville and Ross, who carefully invented every proper noun in their books, would thoroughly disapprove of such tastelessness. The traveller, however, will need little help in coming across present-day replicas of Somerville and Ross's characters, for lunacy is usual here. You cannot be more than an hour or so in these parts without running smack into the gleeful, hopeless inefficiency of Carbery people. Skibbereen, the capital and whackiest part of the area, is the backdrop for most Dublin anecdotes about the farcical improbabilities of provincial life.

For our first meal in "Skibb," we chose an inviting dining room off the main street, filled with animated conversationalists and very white tablecloths. After the amiable waitress had seated us and gone off on an interminable search for a menu, we were hit by a disturbing olfactory sensation: beneath the happy customers, the floors were strewn with cow dung. Surely the beast, whoever she'd been, was a worthy descendant of Somerville and Ross's other self-assured bovine trail blazer: "A path with the angles of a flash of lightning indicated the views of the local cow as to the best method of dealing with the situation." As we considered our situation, Somerville and Ross's technique of ending their alluringly quiet sentences with an unexpected punch came back to us: "My most immediate concern, as any one who has spent nine weeks at Mrs. Raverty's hotel will readily believe, was to leave it at the earliest opportunity." For all we know, the waitress may still be searching for the menu.

The revelation that the authors were women came as a blow to Victorian bookmen. It was really quite upsetting that women's prose should be so savory and their minds so piquant. "Martin Ross" (Violet Florence Martin) was born at Ross in Galway, but much of the duo's writing was done southeast of Skibbereen in Castletownshend, a pretty village with a steep main street that runs down to the Atlantic. Drishane House, Edith Œnone Somerville's family home, is on the right at the top of the hill, shaded by yews and scrupulously maintained. At the bottom of the hill in St. Barrahane's graveyard, the cousins are buried behind the church, a cross for Violet and a slab for Edith.

The villagers are unimpressed by the fame of Dr. Somerville, Castletownshend's most famous daughter. "She made her money by making fun of the poor Irish," said the postmistress. So she did, but the cousins dealt evenhandedly with gentry and peasantry, and demonstrated in passing how much influence the indigenous Celt and the Anglo-Irish settler had exercised on one another to produce a nation of improbable eccentrics. For the stony-faced postmistress a landowning Protestant is not an Irishman. The long history of religious bitterness and class struggle have made it impossible for planter and Gael to realize how much they share in common. Somerville and Ross knew better.

NORTH OF SKIBBEREEN and northeast of Bantry between Kealkill and Ballingeary, just after the Pass of Keimaneigh, on T. 64 the road to the left slides down into Gougane Barra—St. Finbarr's Basin, "Gougane of the Saints" in Eileen O'Leary's *Lament*, and one of Ireland's hidden treasures. Set deep in the scooped-out hollow is a small jewel of a lake, the source of the River Lee. On a tiny island, reachable by causeway from the lake's rim, the obscure Saint Finbarr lived in his hermitage before sailing downriver to found the monastery that became Cork City. At the head of the glen a modern fir forest darkens the hills; but, aside from two unobtrusive hotels, the sharp slopes of St. Finbarr's Basin look uninhabited.

In J. J. Callinan's lush Victorian poem, "Gougane Barra," he imagines the Irish bards of a century earlier gathering together on these hills to sing their last songs. Indeed, through the 1700's penniless poets would meet in the forgotten hamlets of West Cork and East Kerry to hear one another's new work and give mutual encouragement. These Courts of Poetry, as they were called, were a desperate holding action against the gradual death of the Irish language, and the last of them is still held each Twelfth Night in the nearby Irish-speaking village of Coolea. But the wandering bards were not so impractical as to gather "in the cleft of thy rocks, and the depth of thy heather," as Calli-

/ 59

nan's poem describes them. They met over drinks by a warm fire.

The atmosphere of the Courts is preserved in some measure whenever Irish people who love stories and songs sit together around a fireside at night, the licking flames creating a random, mystical rhythm. One of the merriest firesides that ever was was in the cottage of "The Tailor" of Gougane Barra; nor has there ever been a better storyteller than Timothy Buckley, the Tailor himself. He and his wife Ansty lived in the green cottage surrounded by high hedges, the second-to-last house on the left before the lake. In the thirties and early forties O'Connor, O'Faolain, and many others visited this cottage often, for the Tailor was a genuine shanachie, an Irish wiseman steeped in the folk tradition. "Living is like a man fishing with a seine," said he.

He throws his net into the sea, and then hauls it home with his catch. But the catch isn't much use to him unless he gets rid of it and sells it. If he keeps it, he gets no profit. It goes bad on him. That is what happens to a deal of people. Whatever they catch in their net goes bad on them.

It was not so in the old days. A man exchanged his catch with his neighbour, and there was plenty, and plenty of variety for all. There was more poetry in the old days, and there were more poets and better poets. I remember long before I ever saw the first pair of bellows for blowing up the fire, hearing it described this way:

> My back it is deal,
> My belly's the same,
>   And my sides are well bound with good leather.
> My nose it is brass,
> There's a hole in my ass,

And I'm very much used in cold weather.

There is no one nowadays could give you such a witty riddle about a bellows. . . . Those were the airy times and those were the airy people.

It is all there in Eric Cross's book, *The Tailor and Ansty* —the delight in difference and in words and people, the Shakespearian art of changing the pace from serious to silly, or from rambling to crisp, the Rabelaisian bawdy, the bottomless store of wit, wisdom, and memory, as various as the flickering fire. In Cross's retelling of the Tailor's perfectly fashioned tales one touches the wellsprings of the tradition that made possible the stories of O'Connor, O'Faolain, and a host of others. O'Connor called the Tailor "a rural Dr. Johnson," but some of his epigrams are far more ancient, and others far more modern, than the comparison might suggest. "It may be," he mused one evening, "that the people we think to be mad are the really sane ones, and it is we ourselves who are mad."

In 1943 the madmen in the de Valera government banned the book, soon after its publication, as "indecent." (The Tailor and Ansty, O'Connor explains, "both regarded sexual relations as the most entertaining subject for general conversation; a feature of life in Irish-speaking Ireland even in my youth, but which began to die out the moment English became the accepted language.") One night three priests—also mad—forced the old man, on his knees, to burn his copy of the book in his own hearthfire. The Tailor died soon after, and is buried with Ansty in the shore cemetery of Gougane Barra beneath the tombstone carved by Seamus Murphy, with an epitaph chosen by Frank O'Connor:

A STAR DANCED AND
UNDER THAT WAS I BORN

When the Tailor and Ansty were safely dead, the government unbanned the book. But ignorant respectability had triumphed once more over peasant wisdom. Nothing could make up for the desecration of the magic hearth and the shame of the old couple's final days.

The Blaskets from Slea Head, Co. Kerry. Irish Tourist Board

3.
WINE IN
ONE'S TEETH

◇◇◇

County Kerry

KERRY MUST BE approached with the proper respect, or it may overwhelm or elude you. Nowhere else does physiognomy correspond so closely to geography. Kerry people seem to have sprung from Kerry earth—massive, dark, and rough—but from their white-blue eyes, "cold as the March wind," shines the same astonishing luminosity that is refracted through Kerry air. The most lumbering, commonplace farmer will look at you suddenly with a gaze so clear that you feel faced by a primordial being—whether angel or serpent is hard to tell. If you go quickly through Kerry, you may miss everything; if you go carelessly, you may never get out.

Kerry has two and a half extraordinary peninsulas: Dingle in the north, Iveragh in the middle, and Beare, which it shares on the south with Cork. Glengarriff, the County

Cork gateway to Beare, is the name of a valley of ancient woods as well as a harbor in Bantry Bay. Because the Gulf Stream warms the coastal soil, Mediterranean flowers sprout in nooks of the valley and display themselves in abundance in the formal gardens of Garnish Island, which guards the harbor in the island-studded bay. From Adrigole the Tim Healy Pass snakes through the Caha Mountains into Kerry. But on Beare, as on the other peninsulas, any road is worth your while.

Beare has timeless associations with one of the manifestations of the Irish fertility goddess. In "The Hag of Beare," an eighth-century poem, the goddess, grown old, awaits her end in prayer and poverty, though her mind keeps wandering through memories of youthful exaltation. The Old Woman's vacillation between two worlds—penitential age and lusty youth—parallels perfectly the Irish vacillation between the Christianity of the present and the paganism of the past. In his translation (there are several good translations variously titled) the contemporary Irish poet John Montague gives full expression to a love of the natural world that the Beare Peninsula cannot help but stir up:

> Ebb tide has come for me:
> My life drifts downwards
> Like a retreating sea
> With no tidal turn.
>
> I am the Hag of Beare,
> Fine petticoats I used to wear,
> Today, gaunt with poverty,
> I hunt for rags to cover me.

Girls nowadays
Dream only of money—
When we were young
We cared more for our men.

. . . .

These arms, now bony, thin
And useless to younger men,
Once caressed with skill
The limbs of princes!

Sadly my body seeks to join
Them soon in their dark home—
When God wishes to claim it,
He can have back his deposit.

. . . .

Why should I care?
Many's the bright scarf
Adorned my hair in the days
When I drank with the gentry.

So God be praised
That I misspent my days!
Whether the plunge be bold
Or timid, the blood runs cold.

After spring and autumn
Come age's frost and body's chill:
Even in bright sunlight
I carry my shawl.

. . . .

No storm has overthrown
The royal standing stone.
Every year the fertile plain
Bears its crop of yellow grain.

But I, who feasted royally
By candlelight, now pray
In this darkened oratory.
Instead of heady mead

And wine, high on the bench
With kings, I sup whey
In a nest of hags:
God pity me!
. . . .

Flood tide
And the ebb dwindling on the sand!
What the flood rides ashore
The ebb snatches from your hand. . . .

No part of Kerry is far from flowing tides that wet and salt the shores; and you will see plump, straight-backed girls, brightly scarved, as well as ancient crones, lost in great black shawls. It is no wonder that vague memories of the pagan goddess and traces of fertility rites should hang on in Kerry, for it is often as remote as Mayo, as mountainy as Donegal, and lush as the plains of Meath.

FROM KENMARE the famous Ring of Kerry, or Grand Atlantic Route, hugs the coast around the Iveragh Peninsula, running finally through Killorglin to Killarney. The road of the Ring passes through some of the world's most spectacular scenery.

About six miles outside Kenmare on the southern coast of the Iveragh Peninsula, the Castle of Dromore—a ruined stronghold of the O'Mahonys—stands to the right of the road, just one mile before the beautiful Blackwater Valley opens on the Kenmare River. "The Castle of Dromore," a haunting old lullaby much favored by the folk singers, reveals a vacillation between pagan and Christian myths similar to "The Hag of Beare."

The singer, O'Mahony's wife, takes whatever precaution she must to insure her sleeping child's safety: first she appeases the "dread spirits of Blackwater's Valley" and then invokes the Virgin Mother's sympathy. She ends with the ambiguous wish of many Irish mothers that the child will at last grow up to do great deeds but will remain a child as long as possible:

> Take time to thrive, my ray of hope,
> In the garden of Dromore.
> Take heed, young eaglet, till thy wings
> Are feathered fit to soar.
> A little rest and then the world
> Is full of work to do.
> *Sing hushaby loo, la loo, lolan,*
> *Sing hushaby loo la loo.*

When George Bernard Shaw was writing *Saint Joan* in Parknasilla, ten miles farther along the Ring road, he would occasionally take tea with Mrs. Hurley, who ran a ramshackle shop-and-pub in nearby Sneem. Mrs. Hurley's daughter, Mrs. O'Connor, presides today over the establishment, now known as Hurley & O'Connor's, and offers the same genial hospitality that attracted G.B.S.: "I was only a little girl at the time, but I remember that he was tall and thin and had glorious whiskers."

Staigue Fort, ten miles past Sneem to the right of the road, is one of the best preserved examples of an Irish ring-fort. The circular stone wall, thirteen feet thick with X-patterned stairs and two little rooms, has not been dated but is a somewhat larger version of the typical Iron Age farmstead. By night the wall sheltered the farmer's animals from stalking wolves (now extinct) and provided protection from occasional raiders. Within the enclosure would have stood one or two thatched houses, round or rectangular. This isolated domestic arrangement, which persisted almost to modern times, has a direct descendant in the thatched cottages that today speck the lonely hillsides.

Four miles farther, just outside Caherdaniel, is Derrynane, ancestral home of the O'Connells, an ancient—and shrewd—Gaelic family who in the dark days of British oppression recognized that their only opportunity lay in smuggling. And in this tucked-away corner of the world they managed to prosper, making their dent in the British trading monopoly by smuggling in embargoed goods and filling the ranks of continental armies by smuggling out Irishmen. Dark Eileen, author of *The Lament for Art O'Leary*, was an O'Connell of Derrynane. Her nephew Daniel, the Great Liberator of the Irish poor, was dubbed "King of the Beggars" by the powerful who saw him only as a threat, though Gladstone acknowledged him "the greatest popular leader the world has ever known."

The house, made ugly by restoration, is an unconsciously campy shrine of Victorian taste and Catholic piety. But Daniel O'Connell's importance will survive these relics. He defended the poor in the corrupt courts, organized "Monster Rallies"—successfully for Catholic emancipation and unsuccessfully for the repeal of the Union—and was the first Catholic Irishman to sit in Britain's Parliament. His eloquence and the respect and hatred he commanded helped rebuild the pride of his crushed people. Like Martin Luther King in the United States, he was committed to nonviolent mass action and, like King, by showing the powerless the potential power of their numbers, he paved the way; inevitably and (perhaps) unwillingly, for more militant politics. To Balzac, he was—with Napoleon and Cuvier—the greatest of nineteenth-century figures "because he incarnated in himself a whole people." So, of course, did Queen Victoria, but that's a different sort of story.

Seven miles off Bolus Head, the Skelligs rise like great stone pyramids from the Atlantic surf. Little Skellig is the seasonal home of gannets. Great Skellig, one of Europe's lofty places dedicated to the Archangel Michael, was the home of sixth-century anchorites. Their monastery, perched on narrow terraces, beneath one of Skellig Michael's two summits, is an astonishing collection that has survived the storms of centuries. Dry-stone beehive huts with corbelled roofs surround an oratory, shaped like an upturned boat. There is a little graveyard of austere slabs and, at the very edge of a sheer cliff, a smaller oratory. The settlement, reached by a dizzying steep of stone stairs, is a perfect terrestrial counterpart of the wild endurance and precarious spiritual balance of these ascetic builders. "No experience," said Shaw, "that the conventional tourist travel can bring you will stick in your memory so strangely; for Skellig Michael is not after the fashion of this world." Boats sail out early on calm summer days from a number of coastal piers, including Portmagee (Kerry Boats) and Cahersiveen (Patrick McGuire, Main Street; J. B. Healy, Main Street; James O'Connor, Quay Street). Arrangements should be made at least a day in advance.

OUTSIDE CAHERSIVEEN on the northern arc of the Ring road, the peak of Knocknadober looms up between the road and the sea. In pagan days Lughnasa, the harvest festival, was celebrated on its summit. In Christian times the mountain's sacred well was dedicated to Fursa, an Irish saint of visions, and became a place of pilgrimage. Just before Glenbeigh the Ring passes through Mountain Stage, where Synge stayed in Philly Harris' cottage, and then runs on to Killorglin.

Once a year, not long before the harvest, Puck Fair happens in Killorglin. Men of the town set out for MacGillycuddy's Reeks, the magnificent range to the south, one of whose peaks—Carrantuohill, "the Left-handed Reaping Hook"—is the highest in Ireland. They snare the largest, handsomest he-goat they can find and bear him back, rearing, charging, kicking, but unharmed, to Killorglin.

By late afternoon of "Gathering Day" (usually August 10), the narrow, old-world streets are achingly full, mottled crowds streaming back and forth, catching sparks of rising anticipation. Expatriate children from England and America stride by, their foreign finery a show of success. Itinerant fiddlers and blind balladeers from all over Ireland pass the hat at every corner. Men with swift, trembling hands encourage you to choose a card, any card, from an ancient deck. The tinkers, the people of the roads, are here, for above all this is their festival: the women, each wrapped in a plaid shawl which hides a bundle or a baby, sell their trinkets and beg for the price of a loaf or a bottle of stout; the men display young horses and old furniture, and haggle with Kerry farmers; the children, ragged and wary, supplement their parents' income by keeping an eye out for accessible pockets and handbags. The Pecker Dunn, the bard of the Travelling People (as the tinkers call themselves), will almost certainly be here. A great, swarthy man, a ferocious gypsy, he will play his fiddle over his head and behind his back, and sing in a voice to make you shiver. His delicate, beautiful wife will pass a tankard that will quickly fill with silver. She is no gypsy, they will whisper in the audience, but a girl from good stock with a university degree and whatever you please. She left all to follow the gypsy rover.

"A crowd is as exciting as champagne to these lonely people, who live in long glens among the mountains," Synge wrote after visiting Puck. Despite the patches of nylon and vinyl, the scene still belongs to a much earlier age when the tribes of Europe could sweep away Christian order for a few days and revel in the unregenerate mire, and the priests stayed out of the way. The visitor may be frightened by these ancient visages and made sick by the spreading excrement; but if he stays on, he may lose himself in the alien vigor of another age. For Puck Fair is one of the last vestiges in Europe of pagan fertility rites, its origins lost in prehistory.

As the sky darkens, the procession begins with the whine

of bagpipes. Bands of kilted young men—pipers, drummers, and flutists—ramrod straight, ascend the hill to the square, high at the top of the town. The dense crowd presses forward, young girls jostling for the front line. Carts of children, costumed as Celtic courtiers, follow the musicians. In the last cart the goat, King Puck, is bound, a red and gold mantle over his back, green ribbons spiralling about his impressive horns. When the parade has reached the summit, a girl on the cusp of puberty—the necessary virgin of all fertility rites—steps forward from the costumed children and crowns the goat amid loud cheering. In the center of the square a three-tiered, fifty-two-foot platform has been erected. As King Puck is gradually elevated to the top of this by a manual pulley-system, the raucous crowd—they could not be pressed more closely—is swept by waves of heightening excitement. When Puck has reached the top, dancing breaks out in the square and it continues for three nights. The pubs, too, are open round the clock to fuel the dancing and a dozen other activities. At sunset of the third day ("Scattering Day"), the Puck is dethroned and set free, but the revellers continue energetically till daybreak. *Oh, the days of the Kerry dancing!*

The simplicity and tackiness of Puck Fair may disappoint you. The primitive haggling (this is "the world's oldest business event"), the violent fights between tinkers and publicans, the drunks sliding on the fine coat of dung that spreads everywhere, may dismay you. Even the centerpiece, the Exaltation of the Goat, has no liturgical purity about it. (Folk culture is always undiscriminating: an enormous streamer advertising Guinness stout flaps from the platform.) Nor will the revellers for one second take seriously an analysis of Puck as a fertility festival. They are there only to spend themselves in celebration, and mercilessly ridicule any sort of seriousness that does not have to do with buying and selling or the arrangement of marriages. But this is because they move within an ancient wisdom lost to us: the life process must be ritualized, but never desecrated by mere verbal abstractions; to attempt to analyze the mystery of this force could only make for impotence.

A few find or lose their souls—or some lesser valuable—at Puck. There are those who have plunged into the raggle-taggle and found themselves touching for a moment the deepest movements of human life. Padraic Colum's song about an Irish fair taps one of these underground currents:

> My young love said to me, "My brothers won't mind,
> And my parents won't slight you for your lack of kind."
> Then she stepped away from me, and this she did say
> "It will not be long, love, till our wedding day."
>
> She stepped away from me and she moved through the fair,
> And fondly I watched her go here and go there,
> Then she went her way homeward with one star awake,
> As the swan in the evening moves over the lake.
>
> The people were saying no two were e'er wed
> But one had a sorrow that never was said,
> And I smiled as she passed with her goods and her gear,
> And that was the last that I saw of my dear.

I dreamt it last night that my young love came in,
So softly she entered, her feet made no din;
She came close beside me, and this she did say
"It will not be long, love, till our wedding day."

One American visitor, Muriel Rukeyser, wrote a romantic book about Puck Fair, *The Orgy*, which finishes with a poem called "The Balls of the Goat":

Torrent that rushes down
Knocknadober
Make the channel deeper
Where I ferry home;

Winds go west over
Left Handed Reaper,
Mountain that gathered me
Out of my shame—

Your white beard streaming,
Puck of Summertime,
At last gave me
My woman's name.

Do NOT LINGER over Killarney Town, made ugly by greed and Victorian tourists. The Killarney you have heard of— the lakes and fells, em'rald isles, winding bays, mountain paths, woodland dells, and so forth—lies southwest of the town where the mountains shelter three connecting lakes. It *is* lovely; and you can see why the Victorians would prefer it to the wild peninsulas. Bundled in cloaks and lap robes, they maintained their bearing in the rickety horse-drawn carts and boats that still carry tourists round Killarney's "beauty spots." The guides that drive the carts and paddle the boats are no different now than they were then, Irish Step-'n'-Fetchits, the last surviving victims of colonial heydays. Stage Irishmen to their grimy finger tips, they will manufacture from thin air whatever story they think you might like to hear.

Since those days a favorite outing has been to the Gap of Dunloe, where the grey Victorians would sip poteen (O titillating naughtiness!), the illegally distilled whiskey Kate Kearney served up in her cottage at the entrance to the misty Gap. Thus unbraced, they would wander through the four-mile defile between MacGillycuddy's Reeks and the Purple Mountains, hallooing the echo as they went and screening the terrain of nature with the fantasies of Victorian imagination.

From Lord Brandon's Cottage at the head of the Gap, the holiday-makers would venture to the shore of the Upper Lake, and picnic before setting out in boats. Victorian fancy glimmers yet in Killarney place names: the Eagle's Nest overhanging the Long Range, the strait that connects the Upper and Middle Lakes; Devil's Island in the Middle Lake, as well as Danny Mann's Cottage, the Colleen Bawn Rock, and the Colleen Bawn Caves—all allusions to Gerald Griffin's novel, *The Collegians*, the story of an Irish love-murder that thrilled Victoria's subjects. (They could not hear of it too often: Boucicault retold it as a play, *The Colleen Bawn*, and Benedict as an opera, *The Lily of Killarney*, but the actual events took place in Limerick and Clare.) To the Middle Lake "the wild cataract" of Torc Waterfall descends, bringing down the waters of the Devil's Punchbowl from Mangerton Mountain.

At Ross Castle in the Lower Lake, not far from Tom Moore's now-denuded "fairy isle" of Innisfallen, they would disembark and take the waiting jaunting cars back to town. Before leaving, though, someone inevitably would recite from memory the lines Tennyson was inspired to write for *The Princess* when he first saw the ruins of Ross Castle:

> The splendour falls on castle walls
>   And snowy summits old in story:
> The long light shakes across the lakes,
>   And the wild cataract leaps in glory.
> Blow, bugle, blow, set the wild echoes flying,
> Blow, bugle; answer, echoes, dying, dying, dying.
>
> O hark, O hear! how thin and clear,
>   And thinner, clearer, farther going!
> O sweet and far from cliff and scar
>   The horns of Elfland faintly blowing!
> Blow, let us hear the purple glens replying:
> Blow, bugle; answer, echoes, dying, dying, dying. . . .

THERE IS ONE GEM amid the clutter of Killarney Town, Seamus Murphy's statue of the Sky-Woman of Kerry. She stands ignored in College Street, framed by the distant peaks, savage and irregular, which are heaped about Carrantuohill, its head swathed in sheets of shimmering white satin. She stares straight ahead with single-minded intensity, her body taut with suppressed fury. Her left hand over her heart, the harp in her right, she is the ancient Irish muse, simple and severe, calling on the poets to worship only her —the body and the nation, ecstasy and endurance. Beneath her feet are inscribed the names of the great Kerry poets of the seventeenth and eighteenth centuries: Pierce Ferriter of Dingle, Geoffrey O'Donoghue of the Glen, Egan O'Rahilly, Owen Roe O'Sullivan.

The statue, in its haphazard setting at the side of an undistinguished street, is an exquisite visual equivalent of an Irish poetic form, the *Aisling* or Vision poem, in which the poet describes a young woman who appears unexpectedly before him. Her beauty overwhelms him with excitement and terror, as he realizes that she is the spirit of oppressed Ireland, the proud beauty underneath the garments of age, poverty, and shame. She is the Hag of Beare grown young again, the pledge of resurrected life, the pulsating glory of the pagan past promising to break through the dreary present and flower again. The woman usually prophesies the advent of a great king, her rightful lover, who will restore the Gaelic order. Through much of the eighteenth century, the bards travelled from market to hovel, reciting their visions, while the listeners hoped in secret and in vain for the coming of Bonnie Prince Charlie.

The Vision has not been entirely forgotten. In out-of-the-way Kerry places you will still find those whose voices rise to thrilling incantation as they recite in Irish an *Aisling* two and a half centuries old. The greatest is "Gile na Gile," a marvel of rustling elusiveness by Egan O'Rahilly, one of the poets named beneath the Sky-Woman's feet. Frank O'Connor attempted the impossible and translated it:

/ 79

Brightness of brightness lonely met me where I wan-
  dered,
 Crystal of crystal only by her eyes were splendid,
Sweetness of sweetness lightly in her speech she
  squandered,
  Rose-red and lily-glow brightly in her cheeks con-
    tended. . . .

In a pub one night a dignified gentleman confided to us
an experience he had kept to himself for many years. One
morning at dawn during his student days, in a dingy Dublin
street, a woman covered in a black shawl came toward him.
Taking no notice, he presumed her to be an old crone, till
suddenly she pulled the shawl from her head and startled
him with her red hair and beauty. As she walked by, her
bare feet seemed not to touch the ground. He was terror-
struck; his hair stood up on his head. Then she vanished.
Perhaps this Vision has still the power to confer the gifts of
poetry, for the man was Sean O'Riada, until his recent, un-
timely death Ireland's foremost composer and an eloquent
voice against the death of Gaelic culture.

Between the town and the Lower Lake sprawls the Kenmare demesne, till lately the seat of the Brownes, Earls of
Kenmare. (One entrance is from New Street on the way to
Killorglin where the road bends to the right.) Once the
lands of a Gaelic chieftain, they fell finally into the clutches
of Valentine Browne, a crafty English undertaker. To Sir
Valentine proud O'Rahilly—one of the last of the Gaelic
bards—had to make his supplication. Whereas once the
poets had been unstintingly maintained by princes of an-

cient lineage, O'Rahilly is forced to beg small favors from a
pretentious merchant with a ridiculous name:

> That royal Cashel is bare of house and guest,
> That Brian's turreted home is the otter's nest,
> That the kings of the land have neither land nor
> crown
> Has made me a beggar before you, Valentine Brown.

Had it not been for the English planters, O'Rahilly would
have had for his patron MacCarthy Mor, whose estate once
encompassed much of Lough Leane (the Lower Lake).
O'Rahilly's remains are thought to lie in Muckross Abbey
in elegant Muckross demesne by the east shore of Lough
Leane. Around him are the graves of his fellow Kerry poets,
of great Gaelic patrons—MacCarthys, O'Donoghues, and
O'Sullivans—and of their usurpers. In Gaelic society, poets
—called *fili*, which means "seers"—had enjoyed a central
position and retained much of the priestly aura of the pagan
druids. Every noble family maintained a hereditary family
of poets. The magic of the *fili*'s satires could kill and their
praise was sought by princes. O'Rahilly never forgot the
proud antiquity of his roots, that for centuries past his for-
bears had been treated with reverence by heroic lords, and
that he had been robbed of his inheritance. His "Last Lines"
were loved by Yeats:

> Now I shall cease, death comes, and I must not delay
> By Laune and Laine and Lee, diminished of their
> pride,
> I shall go after the heroes, ay, into the clay—
> My fathers followed theirs before Christ was cru-
> cified.

Taken together, the works of O'Rahilly, who died in 1728, and Owen Roe O'Sullivan, born in 1748 and buried at Muckross Abbey in 1784, show the gradual degradation of the Gaelic poets throughout the eighteenth century, O'Rahilly clinging with his last ounce of strength to his shredded dignity, and O'Sullivan a rakish adventurer and penny balladeer. They are the last and most famous sons of the Slieve Luachra school of poetry, which takes its name from the mountainous region that stretches north along the eastern border of Kerry. The "Hidden Ireland" of east Kerry, even more than the peninsulas, is a no man's land, a tracery of unmapped paths, and a last, poor refuge for the dispossessed poets. Almost directly east from Killarney, in the unmarked townland of Scrahanaville not far from Gneevgullia, the farmers who eke out their living there will point with earth-stained hands to a stone wall and a laurel tree, the spot where O'Rahilly was born. In nearby Meentogues, another unmarked townland, the handful of fire-cheeked residents will direct you to a hearthstone in an empty field, all that remains of the birthplace of Owen Roe O'Sullivan. If the Tourist Office in Killarney has neglected to post signs, the people have not forgotten their poets.

The countryside that lies around Owen Roe's hearthstone is dominated entirely by an astounding geographical feature: Da Chich Anann, called in English "the Paps." These are twin mountains, the Two Breasts of the Goddess Dana, and they mass over the landscape like the full breasts of a recumbent giantess, each mound crowned by the erect nipple of a stone-age cairn. Kerry holds the strongest memories of the mother-goddess—Beare, Puck Fair, the Sky-

Woman, the Mish Mountains of Dingle—but here is the most primitive testimony to the wedding of ancient Celt with Irish earth.

Born from the bowels of Dana, Owen Roe O'Sullivan imbibed what trickle he could from a depressed culture fast losing contact with its sources. The grown man was no heroic figure, but a "bold playboy," which is close to euphemism for a whoring drunk. Though Kerrymen smile slyly at the very mention of Owen Roe's name, they will recite none of his verses (almost none of which have been translated) or tell any tales about him, till they are certain you are sympathetic with his circumstances, that you understand that his tattered triumph was in spitting joyfully in society's face. He died at Knocknagree, in the shadows of Dana, having been savaged by the retainers of a certain Colonel Cronin, about whom he had written a satire.

CITY-SICK TRAVELLERS able to spend only a few days in Ireland should go straight to the Dingle Peninsula. Immaculate, peopleless beaches and jagged mountain climbs, ancient architecture, myth and folklore, singing and dancing, and the haunts of writers—Dingle is rich in Ireland's most arresting features. The fair Lady Banba, another manifestation of the mother-goddess, dwells forever in the mountains of Slieve Mish and breeds a wild restlessness through these hills. If you make the exhilirating climb up steep Caherconree in the Mish range, you will come to the fortress wall of the chieftain Curoi, who carried off Blathnad, the mistress of the mythical hero Cuchulainn, and made her his wife. Blathnad poured milk into the nearby stream, turning it white, as a signal to her old lover that Curoi lay within the fortress asleep and unarmed. It was Curoi's final sleep.

Inch Strand, a few miles west of Aughlis, is a place to be alone. White and almost endless, it unfurls beneath the high violet altars of the Kerry mountains and is met by the wide blue arc of Dingle Bay. Farther west another strand, Ventry, was the scene of primeval warfare. Daire Doon, the King of the World, landed with his vassal monarchs to invade Ireland and was defeated on the beachhead by the giant Finn MacCool and his warriors, the Fianna.

Along the route from Ventry around Slea Head you will feel dangerously close to the immortals. In the sudden squalls that thrash up from the sea and down from the slopes of Mount Eagle, your small car may sway precariously close to the cliff's edge. Dunbeg Fort, a magnificent complex, is perched at the edge of a perilous cliff outside Fahan. Sprinkled along the route is an abundance of forts, souterrains, crosses, and stone clochans—the beehive-shaped cells of early hermits and the homes of herdsmen down almost to the present day. One cluster of beehive huts commands the hillside to the right of the road on the bend to the north. Synge walked this way; and in his essay "In West Kerry," he describes the mingling of exterior and interior landscapes:

I wandered round the wonderful forts of Fahan. The blueness of the sea and the hills from Carrantuohill to the Skelligs, the singular loneliness of the hillside I was on, with a few choughs and gulls in sight only, had a splendour that was almost a grief in the mind.

The litter of the Blasket Islands, the most westerly land in Europe, sits in the Atlantic off Slea's black snout. Beyond, in the twilight flood of red and orange and first or last stars, lies Tir-na-nOg, the Land of Perpetual Youth, the Celtic Otherworld. Ancient poems like *The Voyage of Bran* describe the happy place to the wishful voyager:

> There is a distant isle, around which sea-horses
>   glisten,
> a fair course on which the white wave surges,
> four pedestals uphold it. . . .
>
> Unknown is wailing or treachery in the happy
>   familiar land;
> no sound there rough or harsh,
> only sweet music striking on the ear. . . .
> There, there is neither "mine" nor "thine";
> white are teeth there, dark the brows . . .
> a wondrous land is the land I tell of,
> youth does not give way to age there.*

Three superb miles north in the tiny cliff-top village of Dunquin, currachs can be hired for a real voyage to the Great Blasket, inhabited until 1953 and ruled by a hereditary king, whom Synge visited. Life on the Blaskets has been lovingly described by islanders Maurice O'Sullivan in *Twenty Years A-Growing*, Thomas O'Criffan in *The Islander*, and Peig Sayers in *Peig*—a surprising cascade of literary enterprise for a place so small and remote. When the people were moved to the mainland, many settled in Dunquin, where you will find them of an evening, singing.

* Translation by Proinsias MacCana, *Celtic Mythology*.

dancing, and spinning tales at Kruger's pub, where the casts and crews of films like *Ryan's Daughter* have often done their drinking. It was in outposts like Dunquin that Synge heard from the mouths of bilingual Kerrymen the harsh poetry he would later set down almost verbatim as dialogue for *The Playboy of The Western World*.

Two miles west of Ballyferriter, off the main road, you will find Dun an Oir—not the ruined fort of the same name but a good hotel run by the government especially for guests learning Irish. (Advance booking recommended.) Across from the hotel and dwarfed by the stern slopes of Croagh Martin is the last standing corner of Ferriter's Castle, the family home of the seventeenth-century Kerry poet Pierce Ferriter, a leader of the Munster resistance to Cromwell. The ghost of his beloved Sybil Lynch is said to walk near the castle, where the two had lived together after he had stolen her away from her family. When her kinsmen surrounded the castle, Ferriter hid her—out of harm's way, he thought—in a cave by the sea, only to find later that she'd been drowned by the rising tide. Synge walked here, too:

I go out often in the mornings to the site of Sybil Ferriter's Castle, on a little headland reached by a narrow strip of rocks. As I lie there I can watch whole flights of cormorants and choughs and seagulls that fly about under the cliffs. . . . Further on there are Sybil Head and three rocky points, the Three Sisters; then Smerwick Harbour and Brandon far away, usually covered with white airy clouds.

Across the way "on the side of a magnificently wild road

under Croagh Martin, where I could see the Blasket Islands," he felt vibrations of tragedy,

the pang of emotion one meets everywhere in Ireland—an emotion that is partly local and patriotic, and partly a share of the desolation that is mixed everywhere with the supreme beauty of the world.

From the castle you can climb to the top of Sybil Head and look out over the little adjoining peaks of the Three Sisters and northeast to Mount Brandon, a mighty throne of clouds and rock set high over Smerwick Harbor, where Edmund Spenser and Walter Raleigh watched Lord Grey massacre six hundred insurgent soldiers at Dun an Oir fort. But at the summit of Sybil Head Synge's words and this place meld together, dispelling the horrors of history with the healing language of benediction:

I walked up this morning along the slope from the east to the top of Sybil Head, where one comes out suddenly on the brow of a cliff with a straight fall of many hundred feet into the sea. It is a place of indescribable grandeur, where one can see Carrantuohill and the Skelligs and Loop Head and the full sweep of the Atlantic, and, over all, the wonderfully tender and searching light that is seen only in Kerry. Looking down the drop of five or six hundred feet, the height is so great that the gannets flying close over the sea look like white butterflies, and the choughs like flies fluttering behind them. One wonders in these places why anyone is left in Dublin, or London, or Paris, when it would be better, one would think, to live in a tent or hut with this magnificent sea and sky, and to breathe this wonderful air, which is like wine in one's teeth.

We go in peace, high on the liturgy of his words and world.

For thousands of years Dingle has inspired artists—pagan Celts and Christian monks—to worship the natural universe. Going counterclockwise around Smerwick Harbor from Ballyferriter, you will reach the field of the little Gallarus Oratory, an upturned boat of unmortared stones, still water tight after thirteen hundred years, its shape and color almost closer to nature's ways than to man's. Here is an image of the early Irish Church, decentralized, anarchic, before it was finally swallowed up in the organizational discipline of imperial Rome. Independent and ascetic, Gallarus is inspired by its environment, not by institutional pride. To a lesser degree, the same is true of nearby Kilmalkedar (on the northeast loop between Ballynana and Murreagh), an understated twelfth-century church with a wonderful sundial and alphabet stone. One can picture the monks of Dingle, going about their humble routines in the awesome shadow of Brandon, convinced that the world is a sacrament, sharing the heresy of the great Irish theologian, John Scotus Eriugena, who speculated that the divine body of Christ is not the Church but the World.

When at last you must leave these little roads at the edge of the western world, make your departure from Dunquin. The Dingle Peninsula's final movement is a sustained crescendo of grandeur, beginning on the Dunquin-Ventry mountain road between Croagh Martin and Mount Eagle and, after Dingle Town, climbing high and wild through Connor Pass.

FROM TRALEE (where they crown the Rose amid much

drinking and good ballad-singing early in September) head for Clare. The roads in between, a bit uneventful, have a bright patch or two. The town of Listowel has fostered an assortment of writers, such as George Fitzmaurice, a solitary who wrote for the early Abbey Theatre, and Maurice Walsh, best remembered for his short story "The Quiet Man." Bryan MacMahon (*Children of the Rainbow*, *The Red Petticoat*) is the local schoolteacher; and John B. Keane, whose plays (*Sive*, *Big Maggie*) give pleasure to plain people throughout the country, is often to be found listening carefully to the conversation in his congenial pub. Eight miles north the road leading to the scenic route along the Shannon passes through Ballylongford, the childhood home of the young Kerry poet Brendan Kennelly, and past "green Lislaughtin," a Franciscan Abbey on a Shannon inlet, where "The Shannon moves with ease/Towards a mighty union with/Atlantic mysteries." Sean O'Faolain set his novel *A Nest of Simple Folk* farther east in Rathkeale, County Limerick (where his mother came from), and throughout these sleepy flatlands, a fertile web of Shannon rivulets.

The charming village of Adare was given its present appearance in the nineteenth century by the third Earl of Dunraven, whose demesne is now open to the public. The eighteenth-century poet Sean O'Tuomy kept hens here for Mrs. Windham Quin, then lady of the manor, whose imperious ways inspired him to satire. O'Tuomy had come to penury through openhandedness. He had once kept a pub in nearby Croom on the River Maigue, and advertised free tankards of ale for any fellow poet. There was an abundance of poets in those days, and Croom, County Limerick, became a great center of literary pilgrimage. Penniless, Sean had to close down, but not before he and his learned clientele had perfected that now-pervasive literary form: the limerick. Each year in May Croom holds a limerick contest, and Mrs. Quin has been immortalized several times over.

Limerick City is a respectable city—self-righteous, bigoted, and prim. Rather than find out at first hand, drop in at one of the bookshops in O'Connell Street, pick up a novel (such as *Without My Cloak*) by Kate O'Brien, a native daughter who now lives in London, and move on.

On T. 11 just before Shannon Airport in County Clare is the splendid Bunratty Castle, a handsomely restored fifteenth-century keep that houses one of the best collections of late medieval furnishings in these islands. Beside the castle is Bunratty Folk Park, a reconstruction of a traditional village. The most popular of Ireland's medieval banquets is held nightly at the castle. (We recommend, rather, the literary banquet at Dun Guaire in County Galway.) In the south wall of the lower hall is a small, crude relief the Irish call a "sheela-na-gig"—a woman with a huge open mouth, who displays her distended genitals; she is skeletal at top, gigantic below. Here again we have the grotesque goddess of Irish sexuality, half witch of destruction, half mother of creation, occasion for humor and source of terror.

Thoor Ballylee, Gort, Co. Galway. Irish Tourist Board

4.

COLD CLARE ROCK AND GALWAY ROCK AND THORN

Counties Clare, Galway, Offaly, Westmeath, and Longford

We dreamed that a great painter had been born
To cold Clare rock and Galway rock and thorn,
To that stern colour and that delicate line
That are our secret discipline
Wherein the gazing heart doubles her might.

W. B. YEATS, "IN MEMORY OF MAJOR ROBERT GREGORY"

AS YOU HEAD NORTH past Shannon Airport's space-age comforts, you quickly get caught in the Irish time machine, whirling you back into the monastic, feudal centuries of petty kings and rival friaries, and further back to sacred hills and grim prehistoric figures balancing mysterious configurations of stone. The time machine will then take you forward, just as unexpectedly, to uncover the favorite lake of Brian Merriman, an eighteenth-century bard; Coole Park where the writers of the Revival met; and Yeats's grey Norman tower, which Sylvia Plath called "the most beautiful and peaceful place in the world." Our route loops in and out of the barony of ancient Thomond—modern Clare—through southern Galway and the Midlands. Since the Irish were never too careful about these boundaries, we won't be either.

The first right turn after Newmarket-on-Fergus on the Limerick-Ennis road brings you to the village of Quin by the pleasant River Clune. Three miles before the village, the old MacNamara stronghold of Knappogue Castle rises on the left, its pennants flapping merrily. Here you may enjoy a medieval banquet and a historical pageant by Bryan Mac-Mahan, the Kerry writer. Tickets may be had from Tourist Information offices.

In the fields beyond the village stands Quin Abbey, an abandoned but almost perfect fifteenth-century Franciscan friary. (In Ireland ruined friaries are invariably called abbeys.) The Franciscans were driven out in the sixteenth century and again in the seventeenth, but they lingered in the district till John Hogan, the last member of the community, died about one hundred fifty years ago and was buried in the cloisters.

Among the small rooms and open spaces you will find the old kitchens, refectory, and chapter room; the cloisters, among the best preserved in the country, with their contrasting tributes to light and darkness; above these, to the south the remains of a dormitory; the church with its fine windows. The country people use these abandoned foundations as burial places; and all about are tombstones, which tell their own stories, from the grave of a fifteenth-century MacNamara overlord to a twentieth-century Clune rebel. To the left of the high altar is the tomb of Fireball MacNamara, who died about 1500. The victor of forty-five duels, he called his pistols "Bas Gan Sagart"—"Death without the Priest."

By all means, climb the tower's spiral stairway of narrow stones to the top. If you arrive in the bright arc of twilight on a summer's evening the countryside will be bathed in a joyously unearthly light. The low sun lengthens every shadow to its utmost, and from the tower's height the least blade of grass seems quietly important.

The monastic foundations grew from small lonely hermitages (such as the beehive huts of Kerry) to centers of great power and learning. Around Quin Friary a "city" sprouted—with scholars from distant parts, farmers dependent on the friars' protection, and craftsmen dependent on their patronage. The impulse towards the holy life turned quickly enough into the thrust towards cultural and political expansion. The Prior of Quin, viewing his city from the tower, might have echoed the words of the anonymous medieval hermit (in Frank O'Connor's translation, "The Hermitage") who begins by asking God only for "a small hut," but then refines his request. In a kind of telescoping of Irish monastic history, the poet's expectations grow. The hut becomes a church with a choir of monks and "a *little* house where *all* may dwell"—and, finally, a laborless Eden. The Irish have long had the knack of wheedling favors small and large, and are apparently not averse to trying the method out on God. One of their verbal twists is to make the large or important or imposing seem small and insignificant and familiar, which is what the hermit does in minimizing his request. If you stop an old-timer in this district and ask him directions, he will tell you to put away your map-*een,* the poor useless auld t'ing, and turn right at the little house-*een,* and keep to the wee *boreen* (road) till you see the lights of Ennis, a fine big town.

Surely, the holy poet could not have found a "choice of men" more to his liking than the people of Quin. The elderly residents will tell you stories of the dark days when O'Brien, Lord Inchiquin, ruled from nearby Dromoland Castle. To the left of the Abbey is the Marlboroughs' most hospitable guesthouse.

From Ennis (neither big nor fine) a road will take you to Kilrush, where you may hire a boat to Scattery Island in the Shannon estuary. Here Saint Senan—really the Shannon river god christened up—dispatched Scattery's sole occupant, a local dragon, and established a female-free foundation from which cows, sows, ewes, and ladies were banned. Harsh fellows these pagan deities, even after they had been turned into saints. The island is dominated by a roughly built round tower, unusual for its ground-level entrance. Unlike Quin, Senan's monastery has no feeling of gracious and easeful community life. The oldest remains are pre-Romanesque sixth-century chapels, the private oratories of gaunt, hooded cenobites with hard, glittering eyes, men who wanted no company but had banded together from necessity. They would much prefer the testing ground of a lonely island to Quin's soft fields. The apocalyptic hermit had not yet yielded to the well-fed friar. Pick up a stone: it will keep the boat afloat on the way back.

KILKEE'S SEASIDE RESORT is usually host to the Merriman Summer School, which assembles in September to honor Brian Merriman, Clare's most famous poet, and the Irish language in which he wrote. Only the hardy and puncture-proof should include this junket in their itinerary. The session is a week-long Celtic drinking bout replete with the thrusts and parries of slashing wit, traditional music and song, late-night liaisons, and sunrise swimming in cold pools scooped out of the lava cliffs. As with Senan's monks, endurance is paramount. The revellers are not lords and ladies ornamented in gold torq collars and colored capes, but writers, professors, media people, and a handful of intellectual politicians. But in a country where few traditions ever really die, this assembly has gladly assumed the old mantle of unregenerate aristocracy, and Club Merriman is probably as close as any ordinary, twentieth-century mortal can come to the pagan pride, liveliness, and treachery of the old Gaelic order. There are usually one or two excellent lectures, but the seminars are conducted by D. Phil.'s who fling their pearls while trying to get their heads together from the night before. Talk is the holy experience and, though Irish is reverenced, English is the usual vehicle for verbal pyrotechnics. It is possible to register on arrival, but if you go, go prepared. The Irish elite, like the Chinese, has always been sure of the stranger's unworthiness.

Sixteen miles north is the village of Quilty, where the Merriman people join with the fisherfolk for an afternoon of jigs and reels in the good, plain pubs to the accompaniment of fiddles, concertinas, and *uileann* pipes played by huge, gnarled hands. Hulking, silent fishermen and their weathered wives move with silken grace through set after set, their quick feet seeming never to touch ground. Quilty is also the entrance to a scenic stretch of coast culminating in the Cliffs of Moher, which like a dizzying symphonic climax rise sheer from the sea to a height of nearly seven hundred feet. The best view is from the promontory of O'Brien's Tower. Look north to Galway Bay and northwest, where the sea-beasts of Aran sit. Dare to lie on your belly, head over the edge, and look south along the miles of cliff as the sea reaches multiple ecstasies against the rocks and seems to release wild sea-birds that glide effortlessly through the great hollows. These cliffs moved the American poet, Wallace Stevens, to a meditation on origins:

> Who is my father in this world, in this house,
> At the spirit's base?
>
> My father's father, his father's father, his—
> Shadows like winds
>
> Go back to a parent before thought, before speech,
> At the head of the past.
>
> They go to the cliffs of Moher rising out of the mist,
> Above the real,

Rising out of present time and place, above
The wet, green grass.

This is not landscape, full of the somnambulations
Of poetry

And the sea. This is my father or, maybe,
It is as he was,

A likeness, one of the race of fathers: earth
And sea and air.

Seven miles northeast of the Cliffs of Moher is Lisdoonvarna, popular for its dances and sulphur springs. North of
Lisdoonvarna lie the low hills of the Burren, a moonscape of
jagged limestone where in spring delicate wildflowers break
out between the rocks to celebrate Lisdoonvarna's mating
season. At other times the Burren is a science-fiction wasteland, but even then, in the glistening aftereffects of a
shower, the cold Clare greys will separate into the colors of
an evanescent spectrum. In "Sunday in Ireland" John Betje-
man is struck by the connection between the stark landscape and the minds of its inhabitants:

Stony seaboard, far and foreign,
  Stony hills poured over space,
Stony outcrop of the Burren,
  Stones in every fertile place,
Little fields with boulders dotted,
Grey-stone shoulders saffron-spotted,
Stone-walled cabins thatched with reeds,
Where a Stone Age people breeds
  The last of Europe's stone age race.

The hills seem quite inhospitable to life; but, as your eyes begin to adjust, remarkable sights reveal themselves. From Lisdoonvarna the road winds over Corkscrew Hill, aptly named, to Ballyvaughan. On the right along the way is a mound called Cahermacnaughten, where a ring of stones encloses some rectangular foundations—all that is left of O'Davoren's Town, medieval Ireland's most famous school of Brehon law (the old Gaelic code of justice abolished under James I). The well-appointed tourist cottages at Ballyvaughan on the edge of Galway Bay are supervised by a descendant of the O'Loughlins, who once vied with the O'Davorens for lordship of the Burren. As quietly gracious as any of his blood-proud line, he loves to visit the ruined castles of his ancestors and imagine the sounds of feasting and the fires of hospitality that once dispelled the loneliness of the Burren night. One of these castles, Gleninagh, with its ample fireplace, stands by the shore towards Black Head. It was abandoned only a generation ago.

The Burren is littered with prehistoric constructions, which at a distance blend with nature's work. Less than five miles south of Ballyvaughan on the road to Corofin, the Poulnabrone Dolmen sits a hundred yards to the left of the road in a camouflaging field of stone. (The only indicator is a stile, by the field's wall, next to an iron gate.) It is a tilted stone table, the grave-memorial of an unknown human, a barbaric abstraction built by a lost civilization four thousand years ago. In later times the dolmens were taken to be the altars of druids. This one could assume its place in the best gallery of modern art. Opposite the dolmen is a small standing stone, placed there by human hands or cast up by geological changes. On it the weather has sketched a puffed, exhausted face, the mourner of some nameless, ancient tragedy. The Burren is full of such troubling things, where the work of man has become a part of nature's body and the work of nature seems the deliberate symbol of some dim intellect.

Farther south towards Corofin is Lemaneh, a fifteenth-century O'Brien tower adjoined to an early seventeenth-century fortress-house. Here lived Maire Rua, or Red Mary, one of the great iron-breasted women of Irish legend. When her husband died of wounds inflicted by the Cromwellians, she promptly married one of his attackers in order to save the O'Brien lands for her infant son, then three days later kicked her new husband out a top window. Just inside the tower entrance a "murder hole" is carved out of the ceiling, a convenient device for halting unwelcome visitors.

Not far from Ballyvaughan on the way to Kinvara, Yeats set the action for *The Dreaming of the Bones* in the hills around Corcomroe Abbey, a twelfth-century Cistercian foundation. Its old name was St. Mary-of-the-Fertile-Rock, for it stands in a lush green cavity between two limestone mountains. The church—the only building left standing—has a delicately vaulted choir, with a pyramid of narrow lancet windows in the east wall, a sprightly abbot in low relief, and the placid effigy of a thirteenth-century O'Brien. The capitals of the choir and transept chapels are carved with human masks as well as with leaves, berries, and acorns in celebration of Corcomroe's fertility. In Yeats's play, a modern revolutionary meets the ghosts of Dervorgilla O'Rourke and Dermot MacMurrough, a twelfth-century king of Leinster. When Dermot eloped with Dervorgilla—the wife of his host, O'Rourke of Breffni—he was outlawed by the other Irish chieftains and so sought allies in England. Aid came to him in the person of Strongbow, who initiated the Norman invasion of Ireland and the seven centuries of foreign domination which followed. In order to be reunited, Dermot and Dervorgilla must be forgiven their sin by a member of their own race, but the revolutionary soldier cannot bring himself to it. Come at dusk, and you will know why Yeats saw these two, dancing with anguished longing through endless time.

Yeats came to the Burren as the guest of Lady Gregory, whose summer house, Mount Vernon Lodge, overlooking an inlet of Galway Bay, is in the townland of New Quay, a bit farther north along the coast. (When you reach a cluster of houses with a Post Office marked "Burren," ask for directions.) The Lodge is unexciting, but you will also see "Burrin pier," where G. B. Shaw, another of Lady Gregory's guests, set Part IV, Act I, of *Back to Methuselah*—"in the year 3000 A.D." With tongue firmly in cheek, Shaw envisions Ireland as the most advanced country in the world, and superhumans tread the desolate Burren hills.

JUST BEFORE KINVARA, a signposted left turn takes you to Parkmore Strand and the youth hostel, Duras House, formerly the home of Count Florimond de Basterot, where Yeats and Lady Gregory first discussed the possibility of creating a national theatre. In this historic conversation the seed of the Abbey Theatre was planted, as the poet and the lady walked the garden and then retired to a room, today decorated with informative quotations from the two participants. On the pier at Kinvara, Lady Gregory set her most famous one-acter, *The Rising of the Moon*, in which a hunted rebel, disguised as a ballad singer, stirs the latent patriotism of a policeman, who lets him escape to a waiting boat below. Just beyond Kinvara at the moated, lilliputian Dun Guaire Castle, the best of the medieval banquets is held. It includes a fine assemblage of literature inspired by the district and performed with spirit. King Guaire, for whom the place is named, was a sixth-century marvel of largesse: he provided Saint Colman with the monastery of Kilmacduagh and feasted a haughty poet's huge retinue for years. (But, then, you don't treat Irish poets lightly if you know what's good for you.) Yeats used the legend of the king's patronage of the saint in his play *The King's Threshold*. (If after attending the banquet you feel the night should not yet be over, visit Moran's-on-the-Weir, where they serve the most succulent oysters and fresh salmon on wheaten bread, to be washed down with drafts of brown stout. Drive eight miles north on T. 69 to Kilcolgan, where signs will direct you westwards to Moran's.)

A little way inland east of Ardrahan, Edward Martyn lived at Tulira Castle. He was a cousin of George Moore's, an early patron of Yeats and Lady Gregory's theatre, and contributor of some slight plays. It was here that Yeats and Lady Gregory first met, and Tulira was the scene of several planning sessions for the proposed theatre. Because of Martyn's fierce Catholicism—Tulira's stained-glass chapel is its monument—he threatened to withdraw his patronage when

/ *103*

the archbishop of Dublin attacked the theatre on theological grounds. Tulira is not open to the public (but you can take a peek in).

South of Ardrahan on the way to Gort a sign to the left of the road directs you to Thoor Ballylee, one of the most important symbols in Ireland's literary landscape. Yeats, who has described his early visits to the townland of Ballylee in the essay " 'Dust Hath Closed Helen's Eye,' " first came here to discover what the witch Biddy Early (*see* Feakle) meant when she said: "There is a cure for all evil between the two millwheels of Ballylee." Though Yeats never located the cure, the district's imaginative associations held him. He restored its tower, called it Thoor Ballylee, and sometimes resided here in summer. He was here for part of the Civil War. But he did more than make this tower habitable again: he transformed it into a many-layered image and wove it through the fabric of his poetry.

The tower is a square, four-storey Norman keep, sheltering two humble thatched cottages—peasant dwellings protected by the lord of the castle. The contrast appealed to the poet, who believed in hierarchic roles and saw himself as recipient of both aristocratic and folk traditions: "We shall live on the road like a country man, our white walled cottage with its border of flowers like any country cottage— and then the gaunt castle." A walled rose garden adjoins the cottages, and a stream flows under a bridge and past the islanded tower. The interior is painted white, though the walls were piercing blue and the ceilings multicolored when Yeats lived here. He had a local carpenter construct a few pieces of simple, massive furniture from unpolished elm and oak. The rooms have been turned somewhat from their original simplicity by the unfortunate addition of large metal heaters; and some of the furnishings have disappeared, including Yeats's substantial bed, the wall-length draperies, and the brass candlesticks, tall as a man, that once stood in the living room before the great hearth.

Here Yeats thought to preside over a cultural flowering: "I am making a setting for my old age, a place to influence lawless youth with its severity and antiquity." Then, with more wishfulness than realism, he adds: "If I had this tower when Joyce began I might have been of use, have got him to meet those who might have helped him." A stone bearing Yeats's own inscription was placed on the front wall after his death:

> I, the poet William Yeats,
> With old millboards and sea-green slates,
> And smithy work from the Gort forge,
> Restored this tower for my wife George;
> And may these characters remain
> When all is ruin once again.

Though he hardly restored the tower for George alone, it answered his need for a rooted place. Everything about it—from the great oak doors to the profusion of flowers—was to be at once humble and exalted. In his "Prayer on Going into My House," Yeats specifies:

> No table or chair or stool not simple enough
> For shepherd lads in Galilee, and grant
> That I myself for portions of the year
> May handle nothing and set eyes on nothing

> But what the great and passionate have used
> Throughout so many varying centuries. . . .

So too, everything—from *"My Table"* to *"The Road At My Door"*—was to be emblematic. In "Meditations in Time of Civil War" he considers these enduring elements amid the turbulence of the times:

> An ancient bridge, and a more ancient tower,
> A farmhouse that is sheltered by its wall,
> An acre of stony ground,
> Where the symbolic rose can break in flower,
> Old ragged elms, old thorns innumerable,
> The sound of the rain or sound
> Of every wind that blows . . .
> A winding stair, a chamber arched with stone,
> A grey stone fireplace with an open hearth,
> A candle and written page.

Like some half-pagan bard casting maledictions, he prays fiercely that, in this era of upheaval, no one shall alter the unchanging countryside:

> . . . and should some limb of the Devil
> Destroy the view by cutting down an ash
> That shades the road, or setting up a cottage
> Planned in a government office, shorten his life,
> Manacle his soul upon the Red Sea bottom.

One night, as he plies his "sedentary trade" (in "The Phases of the Moon"), Aherne and Robartes, the characters he has created as his masks, discuss their author:

> We are on the bridge; that shadow is the tower,
> And the light proves that he is reading still.

He has found, after the manner of his kind,
Mere images; chosen this place to live in . . .
And now he seeks in book or manuscript
What he shall never find.

In one of the tower's large and pleasant rooms the poet
composes "A Prayer for My Daughter," who sleeps in her
cradle, an innocent born in the disruptive storm of modern
events:

I have walked and prayed for this young child an hour
And heard the sea-wind scream upon the tower,
And under the arches of the bridge, and scream
In the elms above the flooded stream. . . .

He brings quiet to the storm without and within by finding
salvation for his daughter in the traditions of the aristocratic
past:

And may her bridegroom bring her to a house
Where all's accustomed, ceremonious . . .
How but in custom and in ceremony
Are innocence and beauty born?

In "The Tower" he recalls the nameless medieval lord,
"an ancient bankrupt master of this house," who owned the
tower when it was sacked by enemies. He looks further
back to the time when

Before that ruin came, for centuries,
Rough men-at-arms, cross-gartered to the knees
Or shod in iron, climbed the narrow stairs. . . .

The winding stone stairs become symbolic of the tortuous circuits of history, of the men who contributed to Irish traditions, and of the intricate strains that the poet finds within himself in his own ascent to wisdom. In "Blood and the Moon" Yeats summons his personal ghosts:

> I declare this tower is my symbol; I declare
> This winding, gyring, spiring treadmill of a stair is
>   my ancestral stair;
> That Goldsmith and the Dean, Berkeley and Burke
>   have travelled there.

But the tower is good and bad, past and present:

> Blessed be this place,
> More blessed still this tower;
> A bloody, arrogant power
> Rose out of the race
> Uttering, mastering it,
> Rose like these walls from these
> Storm-beaten cottages—
> In mockery I have set
> A powerful emblem up,
> And sing it rhyme upon rhyme
> In mockery of a time
> Half dead at the top. . . .
> Is every modern nation like the tower,
> Half dead at the top? . . .

The tower mocks not only the time but the aging poet himself. For as Yeats (in "The Tower") paces upon the battlements, he is troubled by approaching decrepitude, which he calls "this absurdity," "this caricature," "a sort of battered kettle at the heel":

> Did all old men and women, rich and poor,
> Who trod upon these rocks or passed this door,
> Whether in public or in secret rage
> As I do now against old age?

The erect phallus of the tower is as much a mockery of Yeats's waning powers as it is the enduring monument to his work and to the ageless perfection of all art. But the dwelling is female, as well as male; and the winding stair is the bloody passage of birth, the vaginal passage of love.

He is haunted by his unrequited love for Maud Gonne, the most beautiful woman in Ireland, whose unswerving dedication to bloody revolution he could not emulate. Sometimes she appears as Helen, whose beauty—sung by the aged blind poet, Homer—brought down the towered walls of Troy. Sometimes she is Leda, whose union with the swan unleashed turbulence upon the world:

> A shudder in the loins engenders there
> The broken wall, the burning roof and tower
> And Agamemnon dead.

The tower of Ballylee, then, is the symbol of the conflicts and oppositions within Yeats himself.

There is a fine view from the battlements; and you can see the place, called "Raftery's Cellars," where the river vanishes underground and takes its subterranean course westward to Coole Park. Anthony Raftery was a blind Irish-speaking bard who wandered through this area in the eighteenth century. His poetry was not written down, but memorized by generations of country folk. Yeats felt a kinship with Raftery, as he did with Homer, especially since both blind poets had sung of a beautiful woman. Nearby, Raftery met Mary Hynes. Her beauty was still remembered in Yeats's day by the local people, who thought it cause for pride and fear, for great beauty was often of the Faery. But Raftery had no such fears:

> My conversation was smooth and easy,
>   And graciously she answered me
> "Raftery dear, 'tis yourself that's welcome,
>   So step beside me to Ballylee." . . .

The village beauty never married the wandering beggar, though he proposed to her in his mind as he worried about the unnavigable roads. "Mary Hynes" is playful and light, but Yeats, responding personally, saw these two as "perfect symbols of the sorrow of beauty and the magnificence and penury of dreams." Bear west past the tower along the unmarked roads. At the first fork take a right; at the second, a left. You may get lost for awhile, but the low, rolling countryside is a miracle of dark green cut by innumerable rivulets. Here, in the barony of Kiltartan, Lady Gregory visited the cottagers, listened carefully, and collected the material for her plays and redactions of Irish legend. If you take this drive just after sunset, you are sure to see what Yeats saw when he was young and in love with Maud Gonne:

> Had I the heavens' embroidered cloths,
> Enwrought with golden and silver light,
> The blue and the dim and the dark cloths
> Of night and light and the half-light,
> I would spread the cloths under your feet:
> But I, being poor, have only my dreams;

I have spread my dreams under your feet;
Tread softly because you tread on my dreams.

On the main road a mile before Gort, a sign points to
Coole Park, Lady Gregory's demesne, once a well-land-
scaped tract in whose Seven Woods Yeats found much
peace:

I have heard the pigeons of the Seven Woods
Make their faint thunder, and the garden bees
Hum in the lime-tree flowers; and put away
The unavailing outcries and the old bitterness
That empty the heart. . . .

In Lady Gregory's day Coole was Ireland's principal literary refuge, and many famous figures found refreshment
here. On the trunk of the great copper beach they carved
their initials for us to identify today: JMS, SO'C, WBY,
JBY (the poet's painter-brother, Jack), Æ in a triangle,
KTH (Katherine Tynan Hinkson), VM (Violet Martin,
the "Ross" of Somerville and Ross), AG and RG (Lady
Augusta Gregory and her son, Robert), and high up in a
great sweep of ego, GBS.

Lady Gregory's hospitality, encouragement, perceptive-
ness, and hard-working commitment were essential ingredi-
ents of the Irish Literary Revival. But to none was the atmosphere of Coole more nourishing than to William Butler
Yeats, who made his first long visit here at a time when he
was physically and psychologically depleted. Lady Gregory
nursed him back to health, and for some twenty years he
practically made Coole his home. Much of the poetry of his
middle period (*In the Seven Woods, The Green Helmet, Re-*

sponsibilities, The Wild Swans at Coole, and later *The Winding Stair*) is flavored with images of Coole Park and its gracious owner. Like a painter who returns again and again to the same subject, his descriptions of Coole record the changes of time and seasons and the changes within the artist-observer.

A small house hidden away on the estate belongs to Old Tom O'Loughlin, a gaunt, straight-backed man in his late eighties with enormous hands and long white hair, whose father kept Lady Gregory's stables. He saw the great ones come and go, but from the dispassionate vantage point of the cottager, and his word-sketches have the cool, metallic ring of the valet's truth. "A sober dope," he described Edward Martyn to us, "he should have gone for the church. Not that I mean he'd have made a good priest, for he wouldn't give a rotten stick from a dead tree to a poor divil to light a fire to heat a kettle." Of Lady Gregory: "She could run with the hare or hunt with the hounds." To illustrate what he meant he told us how his patroness—whose imaginative debt to peasants like himself was immeasurable—would pay him six pence (old currency) to weed her plum and strawberry garden. " 'Mind you don't eat any, Tom,' she would warn me, 'for they are poison.' Of course I believed her, for I had never seen a plum or strawberry before." To Old Tom, Robert Gregory was "a peevish man, too much under the petticoat government."

If you can find Tom's house (it is impossible to give directions), he will welcome a baby bottle of Power's and perhaps tell stories of how G. B. Shaw got lost till 2 A.M. one night in Coole Park, of how Colonel William Gregory, a

gambling man, once shot a horse for losing a race and another time lost five hundred acres on a bet, of how Tom
played football with Maud Gonne's son while she lay on the
grass, and of how people like himself survived in those days:
"But we were content. You could trust people then." He
remembers most fondly Jack Yeats, who liked to talk to
tinkers, was at his ease among the humble folk and generous
with tips. W.B., on the other hand, Tom thought "crazy,"
for he never acknowledged a greeting, but stared ahead, abstracted utterly. "He would listen only if you talked of
Faeries."

For Yeats, the insider, Coole's reality lay elsewhere:

> Great works constructed there in nature's spite
> For scholars and for poets after us,
> Thoughts long knitted into a single thought,
> A dance-like glory that those walls begot.

The walls were pulled down in 1941 and only their de-
bris remains. Yeats foresaw this in the final stanza of "Coole
Park, 1929," a tribute to Lady Gregory:

> Here, traveller, scholar, poet take your stand
> When all these rooms and passages are gone,
> When nettles wave upon a shapeless mound
> And saplings root among the broken stone,
> And dedicate—eyes bent upon the ground,
> Back turned upon the brightness of the sun
> And all the sensuality of the shade—
> A moment's memory to that laurelled head.

A path to the west brings you to a small lake and stream,

a place of mesmerizing stillness. These are the same waters that vanish through Raftery's Cellar at Ballylee, then

> Run underground, rise in a rocky place
> In Coole demesne, and there to finish up
> Spread to a lake and drop into a hole.
> What's water but the generated soul?

The water, therefore, connects Yeats's Tower to Lady Gregory's house and represents their deep bond, which Yeats found so restorative. In a kindred thought, he sees the underground waterway as the hidden passage of the soul's regeneration.

In addition to the emblems he finds at Coole, Yeats reserves for it his richest nostalgia. Coole is the demesne of classical friendship and the fading tradition of artistic patronage, the idyl of great minds and hearts, a place rooted in the people, the sad symbol of the old order's destruction. Thus, he closes his last Coole poem, "Coole Park and Ballylee, 1931," as Lady Gregory lay dying, a tenant on her former estate:

> We were the last romantics—chose for theme
> Traditional sanctity and loveliness;
> Whatever's written in what poets name
> The book of the people; whatever most can bless
> The mind of man or elevate a rhyme;
> But all is changed, that high horse riderless,
> Though mounted in that saddle Homer rode
> Where the swan drifts upon a darkening flood.

Coole Park is still full of Yeats's emblems: the ruined

house; the ancestral trees and woodland paths; the brimming water, mirroring a sky whose stillness is broken only by the clamorous wings of the seasonal swans, "mysterious, beautiful," and immortal:

> Unwearied still, lover by lover,
> They paddle in the cold
> Companionable streams or climb the air;
> Their hearts have not grown old. . . .

IF YOU HEAD SOUTH from Gort along T. 11 and take the first small road leading eastward, you will come to the banks of Lough Graney and the settings of *The Midnight Court*. This long poem, written in Irish, is the sole work from the pen of Brian Merriman, an eighteenth-century schoolmaster, whose only other entry in the historical record is a prize for growing flax. His name, though, hints at a further biographical possibility: the bastard sons of priests were often surnamed "Merryman."

Just beyond the minuscule village of Caher, the first small path to the left past the bridge brings you to Hanlon's Wood and the south shore of grey Lough Graney, where, "in the river meadows/ In the thick of the dew and the morning shadows," *The Midnight Court* begins. Merriman's pastoral opening, however, is a deliberate, lulling deception, for this is hardly a formulaic nature poem. Frank O'Connor's lively translation of *The Midnight Court* is the only verse work ever to have been banned in Ireland; and though every schoolchild can recite by rote the first stanzas in Irish, none can tell you what happens after line 30.

The poet is shaken roughly from his bucolic reverie and whisked off to stand trial in a surreal court, where the Queen of the Faeries sits in judgment. In the eyes of the court he is the typical Irish male and his crime is bachelorhood, for he has fallen victim to a peculiarly Irish disease, fear of marriage. One maiden *malgré lui* displays ample proofs of her desirability in testifying against the chaste men of Ireland. An old codger rises to the defense, marshalls his anecdotes of why women are not to be trusted, but ends by advocating free love:

> Let lovers in every lane extended
> Struggle and strain as God intended
> And locked in frenzy bring to birth
> The morning glory of the earth. . . .

The maiden counters by describing the vain exertions of the old man's young bride on their wedding night ("But she'd nothing to show for all her labour;/ There wasn't a jump in the old deceiver") and goes on to bemoan all the "primest beef" that is lost to priestly celibacy:

> Backs erect and huge hind-quarters,
> Hot-blooded men, the best of partners,
> Freshness and charm, youth and good looks
> And nothing to ease their mind but books!

Yet, she admits (and here Merriman may be drawing on his own family history):

> Many a girl filled byre and stall
> And furnished her house through a clerical call.

The Queen of the Faeries passes appropriate sentences on the varieties of Irish males who scorn "the old delight" of carnal love; and, as the women move in on the poet to strip him for inspection and punishment, he wakes from his nightmare.

The poem's ribald points are as applicable today as they were two centuries ago in a countryside where "a young fellow" means any eligible male under fifty. Irish Jansenism and Victorian prudery may not be so responsible for all this voluntary virginity as the more ancient fear of property diminishment through impoverishing alliances. When marriages do take place, the talk is of the bride's heifers and fields, not of her personal endowments. *The Midnight Court* shows its County Clare breeding in the whip of its couplets and the sleight-of-hand ability of the speakers to change instantly the ground of argument to suit themselves. But Merriman also cut through a conservative rigidity that was epitomized for us by a farmer we hailed on the road by Lough Graney. We were looking for the home of a local authority on Merriman. "Ah," said the farmer, "he doesn't know anything a-tall. He's a Tipperary man. He's only passing through." The Tipperary man, it turned out, had lived by Lough Graney for thirty-five years.

Merriman lies in an unidentified grave in the old churchyard at Feakle, where his dream court met at midnight. One and a half miles farther south on the Limerick road, a whitewashed, one-storey cottage crowns a steep hillock of lichen, thorn, and ash. It is a witch's eyrie, for here Biddy Early lived, told fortunes from her magic bottle, and cured the dying more than a century ago. Well-known to readers of

Yeats and Lady Gregory, she was a small red-haired woman with red eyes, who buried three husbands and, when she was over eighty, married a fourth—"a fine young man, named Pat O'Brien." In her later years, she was visited by people travelling from the corners of Ireland to be cured of their ills or find out who had stolen their cattle. Her powers of healing and prophecy seem to have been real enough to provoke vehement denunciations from the clergy. But the priests were poor competition before Biddy's white witchery. She never accepted money for her services—only food and whiskey—and her clients would stay on at her cottage well into the morning hours, enjoying their new health. The cottage was recently restored and several of Biddy's unpretentious belongings are on view. In the end, her sixth sense must have deserted her, for on her deathbed she entrusted her magic bottle to the anointing priest, who promptly threw it into the tarn of Kilbarron, where it lies to this day. The pond, visible from the hillock, may tempt serious students of parapsychology.

To the east is Tuamgraney, Edna O'Brien's dreary landscape, and Lough Derg, the most spectacular of the Shannon lakes. C.I.E., the national bus company, runs cruises from Portumna, on the north shore, and Killaloe, on the south. Craglea, three and a half miles north of Portumna, commands a splendid view of Lough Derg and is the mountain home of Eevul, Faery Queen of Munster and presiding judge of *The Midnight Court*. From Mountshannon, on the west shore, boats can sometimes be hired to Holy Island, seldom visited but now under excavation, with its ancient graveyard and extensive, early monastic remains.

UPPER LOUGH DERG IS as good a starting point as any for exploring the less accessible reaches of the Midlands. Because Ireland is a geophysical saucer, with a rim of cliffs and mountains and a flat, uniform interior, the scenically undramatic Midlands get little tourist traffic. But the central plains and bogs have hidden treasures, well worth a detour.

Fifteen miles east of Portumna is Birr, the Irish seat of the Earls of Rosse, who laid out the town with simple elegance around a formal square. The architecture is an unusually pleasing collage of Georgian and early Victorian. Birr Castle's ornamental gardens are open on summer afternoons, and in the park is the shell of the Great Telescope through which the Third Earl did his stargazing. On the road northwest from Birr to Clonfert, you pass Banagher, where Anthony Trollope worked as a clerk for the Post Office Surveyor and wrote his first two novels, *The Kellys and the O'Kellys* and *The MacDermots of Ballycloran*, both set in the Midlands. Just a few months before her death Charlotte Brontë honeymooned in Banagher with her husband, Arthur Bell Nicholls, Rector of Birr.

The doorway of Clonfert Cathedral is the most glorious Romanesque display to survive in the land and one of the best examples of how this continental style was altered when planted in Irish soil. At a distance Clonfert has the usual squat charm of any small medieval parish church. (By European standards "cathedral" is far too grand a title. As Clonfert was never a populous place, the site was chosen for its ancient sacral associations.) But at close range the doorway becomes a maw from which issues a sepulchral wind out of the barbaric past. The entrance is an archway of six orders intricately carved with foliage and human and animal heads. (The innermost order is a later addition, replacing the original order of decorated chevrons, now built into the wall inside the door.) Above the archway rises a pointed hood containing an ornamental arcade and, higher up, a pyramid of inverted triangles. Hanging from each little arch and sitting in the niche of each triangle is a severed human head.

The doorway is full of heads, shrunken, mongoloid, strangled by leaves, the expressionless trophies of head-hunters. In the spaces between the outer order and the arcade more heads are sandwiched in. Though Confert was built as a house of Christian worship, one searches the entrance in vain for the least symbol of its Christian identity. The carvings date from the twelfth century—seven hundred years after the conversion of the Irish tribes to the Gospel—but they are the unredeemed work of pagan feeling.

When the Celtic peoples of Europe make their first appearance in prehistory, we find at the center of their mythology the cult of the severed head. Heads hang from their belts and sit on their tables as gilded drinking goblets. Their temples give pride of place to niches for real skulls and stone representations. Some heads are two-faced, others—in fulfillment of the great magic number—are three-faced, like the Corleck Hill Tricephalos now in the National Museum, Dublin. The hero Cuchulainn brandishes "nine heads in one hand and ten in the other" at the hosts of his enemy to strike them with terror. The head is the evil-averting talisman, the seat of the soul and magical truth; it is the essence of being, and can continue to live after the body's death. Severed heads tell the future. A human head presides over the Otherworld Feast, entertaining and telling tales. In the Celts, the veneration of the godhead finds its most concrete expression.

So long after the supposed success of the Christian missionaries and the apparent destruction of the Druidic order, comes the startling anachronism of Clonfert Cathedral. The stylized riot of foliage in the six orders of the arch cannot be interpreted—as it can in other stonework—as a pledge of Christ's resurrection. The leaves and heads form an unbaptized arrangement, originating in a lost world-view and joining hands across seventeen centuries with its earliest models—the great Celtic sanctuaries at la Têne, Entremont, and Roquepertuse. In the face of this incredible testimony to the sturdiness of Irish pagan tradition, you are left to wonder what other barbaric attitudes—since ideas are more durable than images—survived whole into Christian society.

The original single-chamber church was altered in each succeeding age and contains a good deal of Victorian clutter. The playfully Franciscan spirit of the fifteenth-century chancel arch seems light years removed from the head-niches of the entrance: there are good-natured angels with smiling Irish faces, and a mermaid who holds a mirror.

From Clonfert, return to Banagher and continue east to Cloghan where T. 32 takes you north toward Athlone. Thirteen miles south of Athlone a left turn leads to Clonmacnois, perhaps Ireland's least accessible place and once its greatest monastery. Today it is its most historic graveyard, with memorials dating from the eighth century to the present. A great number of the earliest grave slabs have been re-erected on a long wall to the left of the entrance. Placed in their approximate historical order, these grey and reddish stones show the evolution from pagan standing stone to medieval high cross. The first ones bear Ogham marks—the characters of the pagan alphabet, formed by lines of varying lengths cut into the corner of a stone pillar—or are decorated with simple pinwheels. But soon the pinwheels become crosses, cut into the slabs, plain at first, then ever more elaborate with delightful spirals, interlacings, and festoons. Along the way, short vertical messages start to appear under the arms of the crosses. They invariably begin with the request in Irish, OR DO . . . ("A prayer for . . ."), and end with a man's name. It would seem that even the most prosaic chieftain wished to be buried in Clonmacnois, "St. Kieran's city fair," though T. W. Rolleston puts it more majestically in "The Dead at Clonmacnois," his rendering of a Gaelic lyric:

> There beneath the dewy hillside sleep the noblest
> Of the clan of Conn,
> Each below his stone with name in branching Ogham
> And the sacred knot thereon.
> There they laid to rest the seven kings of Tara,
> There the sons of Cairbre sleep—
> Battle-banners of the Gael that in Kieran's plain of
> crosses
> Now their final hosting keep.

The warring chieftains of the rattling hosts must have been attracted to the stillness of Clonmacnois, set in the middle of the uneventful Shannon bog, and to the monks who—to judge by what they left behind—were reaching for a gentleness that eluded the builders of Clonfert. In front of the cathedral stands the monumental Cross of the Scriptures, the sculptural flowering of the two-dimensional grave slabs. Around the base are hunters and their prey. The west face depicts the events of Christ's Passion with bottom panels of his betrayal by Judas' kiss, his arrest, and Roman soldiers guarding his tomb. Above these in the stone ring, which surrounds the joint of the crossbars and gives Celtic crosses their distinctive feature, is Christ crucified. On the east face, the High King Dermot helps Saint Kieran to set the foundation's first cornerpost and, in the ring, Christ sits on Judgment Day with the good souls on his right happily making music and the bad souls on his left going to hell. On the south face is a bishop and King David playing his harp; on the north, another bishop, and Pan playing his pipes.

The Cross of the Scriptures, sculpted in the first half of the tenth century for the edification of the faithful, exhibits to a remarkable degree the integration of Irish life with Christian belief. (A little to the south is a ninth-century ancestor, showing the first tentative attempts at high-cross relief.) The story of salvation is seen as a many-sided unity: on one side, Christ redeems sinners by his death; on another side, redeemed sinners—a good king and a holy monk—continue the work of sanctifying the earth in anticipation of the Final Day of Christ's Glory. An Old Testament king and a pagan demigod are both seen as precursors of the Christian order, which grows out of the lives of ordinary men—the Irish hunters around the base.

The little figures who act out this vision of history are

thoroughly human and unmagical, reflecting a world-view quite different from the severed heads of Clonfert. In the tiny, decentralized communities of early medieval Ireland such opposites could exist side by side. Still, Clonmacnois was special, in its day the Irish Oxford, and here a great many important manuscripts, such as *The Book of the Dun Cow*, were compiled. The monks were eloquently aware of the significance of their role in transforming landscape and mores, as in the introduction to the *Festology of Aengus, Spouse of God*:

> Heathendom has gone down
>> Though it was everywhere;
> God the Father's kingdom
>> Fills heaven and earth and air.
>
> . . . .
>
> All the hills of evil,
>> Level now they lie;
> All the quiet valleys
>> Tossed up to the sky.

This claim to complete victory is a proud overstatement, for in its very triumphal thrill the old pagan lustiness still sings out; and the Spouses of God remained unregenerate enough to house their wives at Clonmacnois, where the bishopric passed from father to son.

Over the north doorway of the Cathedral—where the last high kings are buried—is a friendly Saint Patrick, flanked by the merry mendicants, Saints Dominic and Francis. In marked contrast is the Nun's Church, outside the western wall of the enclosure and adorned with monsters. Here the penitant Dervorgilla, Ireland's Helen of Troy, spent her waning days.

FROM CLONMACNOIS wind northwards through Athlone. (The quicker you're through Athlone the better—except for the Bonne Bouche Restaurant, which has especially good cold board.) Fourteen miles east of Athlone on the Mullingar road is the legendary center of Ireland, the Hill of Ushnagh, which stretches out over five townlands. This is one of "the hills of evil," levelled by Christ's kingdom in the *Festology of Aengus*. Because of its breadth, it is easy to lose direction on the slopes, though this may be just what you want in order to explore the flickering signs of prehistoric habitation—earthworks, ring-forts, stones, and tumuli—scattered over the hilltop. Here was the home of the bold Sons of Ushnagh, "the three bright candles of the Gael," who figure in the Ulster Cycle of mythological tales. One of them, Naisi, was the fated lover of Deirdre of the Sorrows, whose tragedy has been retold by several Abbey playwrights, Synge most notably. By eloping with Naisi, Deirdre provoked the wrath of her betrothed, the aging High King Conchubar MacNessa, who betrayed and killed the Sons of Ushnagh. Tom Moore's song, "Avenging and Bright," celebrates the downfall of the jealous tyrant.

From earliest times Ushnagh was sacred, the seat of Bealtaine, the pagan May Day fire festival. On the southwest slope is a large natural rock formation, named locally "The Catstone" because it resembles a cat watching a mouse. The ancient tribes called it the Rock of the Divisions, and it marked the midland boundaries of the five original provinces. Streams tumble down Ushnagh from spring wells, and here—"near to a fountain that clearly ran"—the anonymous author of "The Rights of Man" imagined the Irish nation assembling without fear to assert its political rights: This song, written more than two hundred fifty years ago, is one of the most stirring popular demands for justice to come out of Ireland.

"The Goldsmith Country"—the area around Lissoy, nine miles north of Athlone on T. 31—has little to show for the pains of the Goldsmith Society, who posted little signs all about that are becoming gradually illegible with wet weather. Lissoy's alias is

> Sweet Auburn! loveliest village of the plain,
> Where health and plenty cheered the labouring
>   swain,
> Where smiling spring its earliest visit paid,
> And parting summer's lingering blooms delayed . . .

Here is the setting for Oliver Goldsmith's *The Deserted Village*, a poem inspired by the Enclosure Acts that drove the peasants from the land:

> But a bold peasantry, their country's pride,
> When once destroyed, can never be supplied.

Lissoy is as desolate today as it is in Goldsmith's description of his return to this, his native village:

> No more thy glassy brook reflects the day,
> But choked with sedges works its weedy way;
> Along thy glades, a solitary guest,

> The hollow-sounding bittern guards its nest;
> Amidst thy desert walks the lapwing flies,
> And tires their echoes with unvaried cries.
> Sunk are thy bowers in shapeless ruin all,
> And the long grass o'ertops the moldering wall . . .

The little signs direct you to the scant remains of Goldsmith's gauzily remembered childhood: a wall of his father's house ("the village preacher's modest mansion"); the site of the "busy mill"; the shell of a church in Kilkenny West ("the decent church upon the hill"). Since there is almost nothing to see, your only recourse is to try the Three Jolly Pigeons, which is *not* the place mentioned in Goldsmith's poem, but an eighteenth-century alehouse nonetheless. Here the locals still gather, as they did in Oliver's day, when

> . . . village statesmen talk'd with looks profound
> And news much older than their ale went round.

Though they won't care much about Goldsmith, they may have a good story or two.

A slightly more rewarding Goldsmith locus is the plain white Georgian house, now a convent school, that dominates the little village of Ardagh to the north. One cold night in 1744 Goldsmith mistook Ardagh House for an inn and began to order its dowdy proprietor about, a man named Fetherstone. Goldsmith expanded the incident into a brilliant comedy, *She Stoops To Conquer, or The Mistakes of a Night.*

Farther north is Edgeworthstown, home of Maria Edgeworth, author of *Castle Rackrent.* She was a pioneer: the first

woman writing in English to crash the male preserve of literature and originator of the regional novel, with its careful
attention to provincial accents. To her inspiration Walter
Scott owed his Highland novels, and Turgenev said that,
but for her stories of peasants and squires, he would never
have found his own subject matter. Scott and Wordsworth
visited her at Edgeworthstown House, now a hospital. A retiring spinster, dominated by her father—one of the few hu-
mane landlords—she understood the Irish, lords and cottiers,
far better than did most of her contemporaries. The month
she died, she wrote:

> Ireland, with all thy faults, thy follies, too,
> I love thee still, still with a candid eye must view
> Thy wit too quick, still blundering into sense,
> Thy reckless humor, and improvidence,
> And even what sober judges follies call . . .
> I, looking at the Heart, forget them all.

Cliffs, Aran Islands. Irish Tourist Board

5.
RIDERS TO
THE SEA

◇◇◇

Counties Galway and Mayo

GALWAY CITY, geographically Ireland's San Francisco, is actually a has-been port the Irish call "the principal city of Connacht," but a wonderful town for simple, sensuous pleasures had for a song. A delightful evening could begin with a succulent meal at The Tavern in Eyre Square, move on through the Spanish Arch to the piers and moon-wet bay, once alive with the traffic of Galway's trade with Spain, then proceed to a good singing pub, The Cottage in Salthill, and end comfortably in the Odeon Hotel in a room overlooking the Square. In the morning you can watch the red-socked children playing ball on the green below, against the background of Galway Bay; and once outside, take a daylight look at the Square's elflike statue of Padraig O Conaire, a popular Gaelic storyteller who moved through these parts, and the Browne Doorway,

/   131

one of several architectural remnants of Spanish influence to be seen around town. Browsing in Kenny's Bookshop in Shop Street, which has a surprisingly rich selection of books and prints for this part of the world, can wreck your luggage limit in no time flat, but stopping to stare at the River Corrib from the Salmon Weir Bridge for as long as you like can set you rapturously carefree.

James Joyce loved Galway, town and county, for its powerful simplicity reminded him of Nora Barnacle, the Galway girl who became his lifetime companion, the mother of their two children, and a model for his passionate women characters, Gretta Conroy of "The Dead," Molly Bloom of *Ulysses*, and Anna Livia Plurabelle of *Finnegans Wake*. He visited the home where she was born, a still-occupied two-room cottage at No. 8 Bowling Green, a few hundred yards from the fourteenth-century Church of St. Nicholas, where, the Galwegians claim, Columbus prayed before sailing to America. Joyce's passion renewed by Nora's unpretentious neighborhood and family, he wrote to his Galway Muse, who had stayed at home in Trieste:

Guide me, my saint, my angel. Lead me forward. *Everything* that is noble and exalted and deep and true and moving in what I write comes, I believe, from you. Take me into your soul of souls and then I will become indeed the poet of my race.

What Maud Gonne was to Yeats, a girl from the West of Ireland was to Joyce. He said that she made him a man.

His writing also draws upon her neighborhood and its lore. At the top of Bowling Green he saw the memorial to Galway's Mayor Lynch, who in 1493 executed his own son,

a convicted murderer, and thus launched the verb "lynch";
in *Ulysses* Joyce, mindful of this legend of human solidarity
betrayed, gives the name "Lynch" to a character based on a
treacherous "friend" of his university years. He visited
around the corner at No. 5 Nun's Island, the simple bungalow where Nora had lived with her grandmother, today occupied by a lady who complains that the books that is now is
only dirt and not what they used to be. In "The Dead," the
last and greatest short story in *Dubliners*, Gretta Conroy remembers the rainy night Michael Furey, the young Galway
man who died of love for her, threw gravel up against her
window in Nun's Island. The character of Michael Furey is
based on Nora Barnacle's Galway sweetheart, Michael
("Sonny") Bodkin. The rainy night before she left Galway
for Dublin, he left his sickbed to say goodby by singing to
her from under an apple tree outside No. 5 Nun's Island.
He died from exposure and lies buried in Rahoon cemetery,
about a mile and a half from here (via Bridge Street and
Shantalla Road which ends at a T-junction, at which turn
left onto the main road and then immediately right onto a
narrow road).

Across the cemetery's entrance hangs a red gate with
spear-shaped bars; in the surrounding fields thorn trees lean
into the wind, and stone crosses usurp the grassy hillside,
details Joyce remembered from his visit here in 1912 and
later used in the last paragraph of "The Dead":

. . . snow was general all over Ireland. It was falling on every
part of the dark central plain, on the treeless hills, falling softly
upon the Bog of Allen and, farther westward, softly falling into

the dark mutinous Shannon waves. It was falling, too, upon every part of the lonely churchyard on the hill where Michael Furey lay buried. It lay thickly drifted on the crooked crosses and head-stones, on the spears of the little gate, on the barren thorns. . . .

Michael Bodkin's grave, to the left of the yew-lined path beyond the gate, also figures in one of Joyce's most haunting poems, "She Weeps Over Rahoon":

> Rain on Rahoon falls softly, softly falling,
> Where my dark lover lies.
> Sad is his voice that calls me, sadly calling,
> At grey moonrise.
>
> Love, hear thou
> How soft, how sad his voice is ever calling,
> Ever unanswered, and the dark rain falling,
> Then as now.
>
> Dark too our hearts, O love, shall lie and cold
> As his sad heart has lain
> Under the moongrey nettles, the black mould
> And muttering rain.

Later, the dark lady of this western hillside, having lain with tragedy, will, in her earthy wisdom, turn away from grief; in another's arms on an eastern hill of rhododendron, she will utter the most passionate Yes in literature. For Joyce, the dark women of Rahoon and Howth come from west of the Shannon, where the holy wells of passion, having es-caped the usurper's plunder, run deep and pure in the an-cient Celtic soil.

SYNGE, TOO, struck by "the singularly spiritual expression that is so marked in . . . the West Ireland women" makes their passions the subject of his plays. He heard their stories west of Nora's Galway on the Aran Islands. It was probably in the elegant Paris of 1897 at one of the meetings of the Irish League held in Maud Gonne's apartment that Yeats urged him to go to Aran to "express a life which has never found expression." One can imagine the fiery Maud preaching the politics of Irish independence and off in the corner the famous poet counselling the younger man to travel to the islands where "the language . . . takes its vocabulary from the time of Malory and of the translators of the Bible, but its idiom and vivid metaphor from Irish." More compelled by Yeats's brand of nationalism than Maud's, Synge quit the League a few months later, explaining, "I wish to work in my own way for the cause of Ireland, and I shall never be able to do so if I get mixed up with a revolutionary and semi-military movement." A year later he made his first trip to Aran.

There are three islands: Aranmor, the north island, about nine miles long; Inishmaan, the middle island, about three miles and a half across, and nearly round in form; and the south island, Inishere—in Irish, east island,—like the middle island but slightly smaller. They lie about thirty miles from Galway, up the centre of the bay, but they are not far from the cliffs of County Clare, on the south, or the corner of Connemara on the north.

Thus Synge's simple description of the islands' geography in his preface to *The Aran Islands*, an account of his life there and a defense of its primitive culture. Citing the two

/ *135*

automobiles and tiny airport recently introduced to Aranmor (today called Inishmore), old-timers claim the place Synge knew has been destroyed utterly. But citizens from technopolis continue to be amazed by this outpost of preindustrial Europe, its limestone hills ringed by the sea and peopled by islanders with faces as unfathomable as the world around them. In summertime, three days a week, the steamer goes at 9 A.M. from Galway City pier to all three islands and returns in the evening, weather permitting; more information about the schedule and overnight accommodations is available at the Tourist Office off Eyre Square. Dramamine is recommended before sailing, for the voyage can be rocky, especially if you miss the steamer and tag along on a fishing trawler. The solemn-faced fisherman who took us aboard one October turned out to be a high-spirited stunt pilot. He raced two other randy boatmen most of the way. After huddling for three hours in a corner of the deck while the captain ploughed his wild sea-bird home, we climbed up the side of Kilronan pier, having literally tasted Synge's poetic description—"the bay full of green delirium."

Following the Kilronan-Kilmurvey road on foot, bicycle, or atop a pony trap, you can see the sites Synge explored on his first trip to Aranmor, "wandering out along the one good roadway of the island, looking over low walls on either side into small flat fields of naked rock . . . looking at the antiquities that abound in the west or north-west of the island." Beside the holy well at the Church of the Four Beautiful Persons (Ceathair Aluinn), an old man told him the story of the miraculous well which Synge transformed into the play *The Well of the Saints*. South of Kilmurvey, a short climb up a rock-strewn slope brings you to Dun Aengus, which has been called "the most magnificent barbaric monument in Europe," erected sometime between 700 and 200 B.C., supposedly by the pre-Celtic Fir Bolg—Ireland's original mythical inhabitants. Far more magnificent than the remains of the fort is its location on the edge of a cliff-wall rising three hundred feet above "the endless change and struggle of the sea." When the Fir Bolg were not busy at Dun Aengus, repelling or awaiting an invasion, they could be found to the northwest, passing their domestic pagan lives in dwellings like Clochan na Carraige, a beehive-shaped hut in perfect condition midway between Kilmurvey and The Seven Churches, a litter of monastic ruins in the vicinity of Temple Breancan. All these antiquities excited Synge as visible signs of the mingling of paganism and Christianity he sensed in Aran culture.

The grim topography speaks of tragedy as Aran's unchanging way of life. In his powerful short stories and novels Liam O'Flaherty, born and raised an Aran Islander, recreates the terror and pity of his native place. A short hike off the Kilronan-Killeany road, the perilous Black Fort (Dubh Cathair) affords a dramatic view of the kind of cliffscape described in his masterpiece, "The Wounded Cormorant." This story begins with an evocation of the cosmic pattern that Islanders know is tragic and impersonal:

Beneath the great grey cliff of Clogher Mor there was a massive square black rock, dotted with white limpets, sitting in the sea. The sea rose and fell about it frothing. Rising, the sea hoisted the

/ *137*

sea-weed that grew along the rock's rims until the long red winding strands spread like streams of blood through the white foam.
Falling, the tide sucked the strands down taut from their bulbous
roots.

Approaching Killeany, you can imagine any "crooked
stretch of limestone road, surrounded by grey crags that
were scorched by the sun" as the place where the mother in
"Going Into Exile" runs screaming "Come back, . . . come
back to me" after her two children, forced by Aran's poverty to emigrate to America. And slightly east of Killeany
village are the broken remains of the fifth-century monastery of St. Enda, images of the stony religion of Father Mo-
clair, the cruel devil of O'Flaherty's terrifying Aran novel,
Skerrett.

Synge's *Riders to the Sea*, which has often been called the
most perfect one-act play in the English language, is made
in the image and likeness of immutable Inishmaan, the middle island, its black cliffs and tides and wild keens the
sources of old Maurya's wisdom: "No man at all can be living for ever, and we must be satisfied." Patrick Mac-
Donagh's cottage, where Synge lived, is no longer thatched,
and Pat Dirane, who told him the stories he made into *In the
Shadow of the Glen* and *The Playboy of the Western World* is
long gone, but storytelling is still a living art, and the awesome walls of Dun Conor, the best-preserved stone fort in
Ireland, remain what they were for Synge, a place to enjoy
the freedom of one's imagination:

I have the black edge of the north island in front of me, Galway
Bay, too blue almost to look at, on my right, the Atlantic on my

left, a perpendicular cliff under my ankles, and over me innumerable gulls that chase each other in a white cirrus of wings. . . . As I lie here hour after hour, I seem to enter into the wild pastimes of the cliff, and to become a companion of the cormorants and crows.

Deeply conscious of the tyrannical fact of mortality, he relishes images of flight. The wild sea-birds over Dun Conor, like the tramps of Wicklow and Mayo, present to his tragic eye bold patterns of liberation.

OUT IN WEST CONNACHT, between Lough Corrib and the Atlantic, lies the paradox of Connemara, like the Irish themselves, magnificent and harsh. Along the roads unfold vistas of the sea, of sandy Connemara ponies grazing in sun-streaked valleys, of mountain ranges, their sides cradling sudden blue lakes and in June sprouting gorgeous rhododendron. But abandoned cottages and fishing villages tell the bitter truth of chronic depression and forced emigration. As a visual paradise, Connemara rivals the Dingle Peninsula and deserves a most leisured visit. As an economic wasteland, it arouses a sharp interest in why the Irish people have fared so poorly at the banquet of European history.

Twenty-five miles out of Galway City on the Spiddal Road (100) is the Gortmore turn for Rosmuc, where Patrick Pearse, leader and "martyr" of the 1916 Rising, pondered the hard lot of his race in an isolated cottage, now a national landmark open to the public, overlooking a creek of Camus Bay. A solitary student of Gaelic in Rosmuc's famous Gaeltacht (or Irish-speaking district), he dreamed of overturning the tables of history with the myth of Gaelic superiority and his own blood sacrifice. Pragmatism is not yet in style around Rosmuc. Local politics seems to consist of purging bilingual roadsigns of their "foreign" English words with a brushful of black tar. But the proud native tongue lives not on dreams alone but on every check that comes forth from the government dole. In return for preserving the language, Gaeltachts receive financial grants and unannounced visits from government linguist-workers who investigate the natives for unsubsidized slips of the tongue.

The most scenic route through Connemara (T. 71) begins at Maam Cross and leads west past the Maumturk Mountains, under the Twelve Bens—each peak magnificently visible on a clear day—and then through the alpine town of Clifden, where maps of scenic walking tours are available at Tourist Information. Northwest of Letterfrack, the Renvyle Peninsula slides down from the walls of the Twelve Bens, its northern shore distinguished by Renvyle House. In his autobiography *As I Was Going Down Sackville Street*, Oliver St. John Gogarty describes his former home, now a first-class hotel:

My house . . . stands on a lake, but it stands also on the sea. Water-lilies meet the golden seaweed. It is as if, in the faery land of Connemara at the extreme end of Europe, the incongruous flowed together at last; and the sweet and bitter blended.

Gogarty himself knew no such reconciliation. The model for the heartless Buck Mulligan in Joyce's *Ulysses*, he revered classical literature and the lofty company of Dublin's intellectual aristocracy. With great conviction he served on the national film censorship board and, upon publication of his autobiography in 1936, was sued successfully for anti-Semitic libel. (Henry Morris Sinclair, a Jewish antique dealer, charged that Gogarty had referred to him as the grandson of an old usurer who had inherited along with the antique shop his grandfather's penchant for molesting little girls behind the old highboys and Chippendale. Sinclair's counsel pleaded, "Is there a hope that a Jew will not receive justice from a Dublin jury? . . . Throughout all our chequered history one of the great traditions of our city is that it has never persecuted the Jews, and I know, members of the jury, that you will preserve that tradition." Samuel Beckett, ridiculed by Gogarty's counsel for writing a book about "Marcel Prowst," appeared as Sinclair's character witness. Gogarty's slander cost him two thousand pounds.)

While on their honeymoon, Yeats and his wife, who was a medium of sorts, visited Gogarty at Renvyle. They had a marvelous time, as Gogarty tells it, amid flickering candles and boomps in the night, conjuring up the ghost of Athelstone Blake, son of the original owners. (In her zany *Adventures in Connemara* Maria Edgeworth described visiting the Blakes.) The American Association of Ghosthunters holds seances here, a chambermaid having spotted Yeats's shade drifting through a rear hallway. You may book a haunted room in advance, either Yeats's or Athelstone's. The house was exorcised ten years ago, but having stayed one night in Athelstone's old room, we could not swear that that unhappy boy, a suicide at the age of fourteen, does not still hover about, resenting strangers in the home of his ancestors. The house has been extensively restored. During the

Civil War the I.R.A. burned everything but a few wings and chimneys because Gogarty favored signing the Anglo-Irish Treaty, a gesture of compromise the all-or-nothing I.R.A. regarded as treasonous.

IRISH COUPLES still honeymoon at Renvyle, but Connemara's most romantic and private places rise and fall to the east, through Kylemore Pass, along the mountain-flanked shore of Killary Harbor, and all over the Joyce Country, extending twenty-five miles east from Leenane around the enchantment of Lough Nafooey to the western and southern shores of Lough Mask. In summertime the mossy mountainsides of the Joyce Country seem the natural territory of lovers, breathing the tenderness of Ireland's most cherished love song, "The Coolin":

> Come with me, under my coat,
> And we will drink our fill
> Of the milk of the white goat,
> Or wine if it be thy will.
>
> And we will talk, until
> Talk is a trouble, too,
> Out on the side of the hill;
> And nothing is left to do,
>
> But an eye to look into an eye;
> And a hand in a hand to slip;
> And a sigh to answer a sigh;
> And a lip to find out a lip!
>
> What if the night be black!

Or the air on the mountain chill!
Where the goat lies down in her track,
And all but the fern is still!

Stay with me, under my coat!
And we will drink our fill
Of the milk of the white goat,
Out on the side of the hill!

This old Connacht lyric, whose title means literally "the twist of fair hair on the nape of a girl's neck," has many different versions. This translation is by James Stephens, the writer to whom James Joyce (a self-proclaimed descendent of the clan that named this part of Galway after itself) once planned to turn over the unfinished manuscript of *Finnegans Wake* for completion because their day and year of birth were the same, both were Dubliners, and Stephens' last name was the same as the one Joyce took for himself in *A Portrait of the Artist as a Young Man*. Except for their common loveliness, there are no known connections between the song and Lough Coolin on the eastern tip of the Joyce Country near Clonbur.

Beyond the borders of Connemara is another literary landmark that reveals the murderous spitefulness of Irish politics: Moore Hall on the eastern shore of Lough Carra, birthplace and ancestral home of the novelist and art critic George Moore. His novel *The Lake* celebrates this shadowy region seldom explored by tourists.

The route is scenic from Clonbur to Cong, where Ashford Castle fascinates as a nineteenth-century splurge of the Guinness family, completely out of touch with the personality of the region. The way north from Cong to Ballinrobe passes through country charged with unforgettable stillness and simplicity if you explore it along the secondary roads leading to the eastern shores of Lough Mask. The road northwest of Ballygarries cuts through dark forest yielding bright glimpses of sun and water, a fitting approach to the tragic and dignified presence of Moore Hall.

It stands today in remembrance of the handiwork of the Mayo contingent of the I.R.A. that in 1923 put the mansion to the torch. During the Civil War they burned the houses of the Imperial Irish throughout the West for a variety of reasons. Their strategy, they believed, would help the cause of land redistribution: with the owner of the shell unable or unwilling to rebuild, the demesne could be divided among the peasants. The landowners—like Gogarty at Renvyle and the Moores at Moore Hall—who supported the Free State treaty instead of the Republican cause knew it was only a matter of time before the I.R.A. took its revenge. The Mayo republicans burned, too, to get even. For they remembered the ethos of tyranny as clearly as did George Moore in his autobiography *Hail And Farewell*:

Until the 'seventies Ireland was feudal, and we looked upon our tenants as animals that lived in hovels round the bogs, whence they came twice a year with their rents. . . . And if they failed to pay their rents, the cabins they had built with their own hands were thrown down, for there was no pity for a man who failed to pay his rent. And if we thought that bullocks would pay us better we ridded our lands of them, cleaned our lands of tenants, is an expression I once heard, and I remember how they used to go away by train from Claremorris in great batches bawling like animals. There is no denying that we looked upon our tenants as animals, and that they looked on us as kings. . . .

The descendants of the tenants, who were as fanatical in their piety as in their politics, must have hurled their torches at Moore Hall with special indignation. For wasn't Mr. George Moore a lapsed Catholic, one of your agnostics (who a few years later had the cheek to predict that "by degrees the parish priest will pass away like his ancestor the Druid")? Worse, he had made Lough Carra known to the world as the setting of *The Lake*, a novel about a priest's revolt against celibacy, writing "there is a lake in every man's heart, and he listens to its monotonous whispers year after year, more and more attentive, until at last he ungirds."

In 1933 local boatmen would not unbend to row the mourners attending Moore's funeral to Lough Carra's Castle Island, where his ashes are buried beneath a cairn. It was no secret that Moore's love of Ireland did not include the Irish people. To friends who offered condolences when his house was gutted he made one of his mildest comments on the national character, "Ireland is not a gentleman's country." In his funeral oration on Castle Island Æ defined the limits and the significance of Moore's love of his native place:

If his ashes have any sentience they will feel at home here, for the colours of Carra Lake remained in his memory when many of his other affections had passed. It is possible that the artist's love of earth, rock, water and sky is an act of worship. It is possible that the faithfulness of art is an acceptable service. That worship, that service, were his.

That all sorts of mystiques have found passionate disciples in Ireland becomes understandable as you return to Leenane in Connemara along the western shore of Lough Mask and continue northwest (100) through Doolough Pass. In the quiet magic of the Celtic twilight, the Delphi Valley—where Doo Lough nestles into the Sheefry Hills—appears part of a radiant Otherworld. Farther north, overlooking Clew Bay from Croagh Patrick, Thackeray worshipped in the nineteenth-century tones of his *Irish Sketch Book*:

From an eminence, I caught sight not only of a fine view, but of the most beautiful view I ever saw in the world. . . . A miracle of beauty . . . the Bay, and the Reek, which sweeps down to the sea, and a hundred islands in it, were dressed up in gold and purple, and crimson, with the whole cloudy west in a flame. Wonderful, wonderful!

A few miles beyond Croagh Patrick, which penitents ascend on their hands and knees every July, you'll find nothing mystical or miraculous in Westport's well-designed townscapes or the stately Westport House. But that doesn't mean that the townspeople do not believe, along with their rural cousins, that the Irish hills belong to the gods.

AFTER CHRISTY MAHON "destroyed his da" down in Kerry, he hit the road and ended up in northwestern Mayo, the bleak region of Synge's *The Playboy of the Western World*. On the way he would have passed through wild country, its legends bursting with the uncowed spirit he brought to the men-starved women of Mayo. Just outside Newport on a

windy inlet of Clew Bay you can climb to the top of Car-
rigahowley Castle, once the home of Grania (or Grace)
O'Malley, Connacht's sixteenth-century seafaring Queen
of Clew Bay and Clare Island, for forty years the leader of
all rebellions in the West against the soldiers of Queen Elizabeth. Children who live in a nearby house will unlock the
keep and show you where she slept and guarded her fleet at
the same time. She tied one end of a rope to her big toe and
the other to her ships at anchor below in the harbor. Farther
west, the seascapes of the Corraun Peninsula and the dizzying cliffs around Achill Island have all the bold splendor of
the pirate queen whom Queen Elizabeth could not buy.
(When she tried to appease Grania with a title, Grania
haughtily replied that no matter what status Elizabeth
offered, the Queen of Connacht already possessed it.)

Swinging sharply north at Mallaranny, the road parallels
the wasted plain of Erris, but in the distance looms the Nephin Beg mountain range, haunt of the lovers in "The Brow
of Nephin," a poem of the oral tradition collected by Douglas Hyde in *The Love Songs of Connacht*:

> Did I stand on the bald top of Nephin
> And my hundred-times loved one with me,
> We should nestle together as safe in
> Its shade as the birds on a tree.
>
> How well for the birds in all weather,
> They rise up on high in the air
> And then sleep upon one bough together
> Without sorrow or trouble or care;
> But so it is not in this world

> For myself and my thousand-times fair,
> For away, far apart from each other,
> Each day rises barren and bare.

Synge knew *The Love Songs* by heart, and it is perhaps with this poem in mind that he makes Nephin the setting for Christy Mahon's most romantic fantasy:

Christy: Yourself and me should be pacing Neifin in the dews of night, the times sweet smells do be rising, and you'd see a little shiny new moon, maybe, sinking on the hills.

Pegeen: And it's that kind of a poacher's love you'd make, Christy Mahon, on the sides of Neifin, when the night is down?

Christy: It's little you'll think if my love's a poacher's, or an earl's itself, when you'll feel my two hands stretched around you, and I squeezing kisses on your puckered lips, till I'd feel a kind of pity for the Lord God is all ages sitting lonesome in his golden chair.

But the "fools of Mayo" will have none of the passionate, rebellious Kerryman, and their poverty of spirit is reflected in this mean landscape. Our guess is that the cottage where Pegeen Mike lives and loses her "only Playboy of the Western World" would have been situated on Tristia Hill, to the right off the Bangor-Gweesalia road. From "the scruff of the hill" you can see the sides of Nephin to the south and to the west Doolough Strand, where Christy, "grand lepper," would have won the "mule race on the sands below." Starting from this strand, until recently the setting of horse races at low tide, you can follow the route of Old Mahon and the men who in the play walked to Kate Cassidy's wake over the sands by Blacksod Bay to Belmullet (where to a question about which hotel Shaw stayed in on his Irish journey they answer, "You're now in the most *gargeous* part of Ireland, Missus, *bar none*").

Gorgeous is hardly the word for the landscape between Belmullet and Portacloy. But it is possibly the most primitive and—in a cold rain—sinister part of the country you'll find. The road east from Belmullet (T. 58) passes Glen Castle, perhaps the place Pegeen has in mind when she asks Christy if he has come from the tinkers "camped beyond in the glen." Just beyond Rathmorgan the road north to Barnatra passes along the western shore of Carrowmore Lake, surely Ireland's most desolate body of water, where Christy imagines himself sheltered from harm by "the angel's lamp" of Pegeen's loving heart, "and I abroad in the darkness, spearing salmons in the Owen, or the Carrowmore." On both sides of the Glenamoy-Carrowteige-Portacloy road stretches a vast bog, an image from *Playboy* country of the moldy submissiveness Christy Mahon escapes by his liberating act of psychic parricide. No spiritual bogtrotter, he breaks free from his father's constraining spell. For Synge, the movement towards manhood is in part a movement out of the quagmire of the Irish family.

Carrowteige, six miles northwest of Glenamoy, we recommend heartily, but only to the hardy. Mr. Garvin runs here a hotel of a kind, though without the Tourist Board's approval. A dank, two-storey building, unposted and hidden behind a few other ramshackle houses, it is a home of the richest Irish idiom, with all the lustre that has been tarnished somewhat in more accessible Gaeltachts. Cut off as it is by the great bog, Carrowteige has continued to shelter the Philly Cullens, Jimmy Farrells, and Michael James Flahertys of this world. On the right evening the hearth in the hotel is graced by a few regulars, who will translate their metaphorical Irish into a kind of English that has not been heard since Synge wrote. The only food may be a "fry" of bacon and eggs, the room you sleep in will be damp and cold as winter rain, and the rough ways and strange thoughts of Carrowteige's inhabitants may make the hair stand up on your head. But here is the unbroken spell of the mythic past, haunted imagination as vigorous as the waves of the sea that smash against the great cliffs of Portacloy two miles to the north.

THE SCENERY MELLOWS as, turning east, you leave behind the wild west coast of all the passionate and tragic riders to the sea. The Mayo-Sligo coast road (L. 133) passes Killala Bay, where in 1798 French troops under General Humbert landed to assist the Irish in a rebellion that had been in the works since the storming of the Bastille. They were joined by unarmed peasants, marched inland, and were surrounded. Yeats's play *Cathleen ni Houlihan*, set in a peasant cottage in the hilly grazing lands overlooking the bay, commemorates the French landing. For the character of Cathleen ni Houlihan, Yeats drew on the image of Ireland as the divine woman, based on the belief of the early Gaels in the mystical union of man with nature. He touched such depths

of emotion in his audience that he had to ask himself afterwards:

> Did that play of mine send out
> Certain men the English shot?

A symbol fashioned by Stone Age men helped fire a revolution in 1916.

Old Aran Man with Donkey. Irish Tourist Board

6.

THE MEN OF
THE WEST

◇◇◇

Counties Mayo, Roscommon, and Leitrim

While we honour in song and in story
The names of the patriot men
Whose valour has covered with glory
Full many a mountain and glen,
Forget not the boys of the heather,
Who marshalled their bravest and best
When Ireland lay broken and bleeding.
Hurrah for the men of the West!

The hilltops with glory were glowing,
'Twas the eve of a bright harvest day,
When the ships we'd been wearily waiting-
Sailed into Killala's broad bay;
And over the hills went the slogan
To waken in every breast
The fire that has never been quenched, boys,
Among the true hearts of the West.
. . . .

Though all the bright dreamings we cherished

Went down in disaster and woe,
The spirit of old is still with us
That never would bend to the foe;
And Connacht is ready whenever
The loud rolling tuck of the drum
Rings out to awaken the echoes
And tell us the morning has come.

TRADITIONAL SONG

GENERAL HUMBERT and Cathleen ni Houlihan's cavaliers, after several victories along the Killala-Ballina-Castlebar route, fell to the British Lord Cornwallis (of Yorktown fame) at Ballinamuck in 1798. County Mayo's version of the French Revolution was quelled and the Act of Union was read through the land, screaming "colony" for all it was worth. But despite the hardships of life in the back-o-beyonds of Mayo, Roscommon, and Leitrim—a topographical montage of a thousand years of pillage, famine, and brave endurance—the rebel spirit never died among the people of the heather. During his Great Crusade of 1649–52, Oliver Cromwell had routed the Gaels from their fertile lands in Leinster and Munster with the battle cry, "To hell or to Connacht." The region he thought held no material or human possibilities turned out to be as rich as the plains of Leinster in the stories of people who survived and in writers who have bodied forth stirring images of their courage.

When someone asked who was the blind man playing the fiddle, Anthony Raftery, the blind folk poet of Mayo, described himself in words that could also be read as a short folk history of Ireland:

> I am Raftery the poet,
>   Full of hope and love,
> With sightless eyes
>   And undistracted calm.
>
> Going west on my journey
>   By the light of my heart,
> Weak and tired
>   To the end of my road.
>
> Look at me now!
>   My face to the wall,
> Playing music
>   To empty pockets.

Driving southeast from Castlebar through the barony of Gallen, Balla, Claremorris, and the Plains of Mayo, you pass through the calm, undaunted country of his poem "County Mayo." In Kiltimagh, where he was born in 1780, people quote his most popular poems as well as the bawdy ones that Douglas Hyde and Lady Gregory never got wind of. In the Raftery Room of Jerry Walsh's hotel, where "four hundred and fifty people a night" come to summertime sing-songs, they have put up a painting of the famous faery fort and hearthstone, the only surviving landmarks of his birthplace. The actual site is well worth searching for. Tourists rarely catch this lovely expression of the hidden Ireland known to the folk.

About a mile and a quarter out of Kiltimagh on the road to Bohola (L. 140), an unmarked, narrow road turns to the right and leads to the village of Killeadan, praised by Raftery as "the village where everything pleases / Of berries and all sorts of fruit there's no lack." You can walk through the woods to Killeadan House, once the home of Raftery's patron, the landlord Frank Taafe. This local big shot's concern for his property unwittingly banished blind Raftery to the roads and finally to an obscure grave in Killeenan (a townland of Craughwell, County Galway). One night when the wine had run short, the blind poet took off on Taafe's best horse to find more. The horse broke its neck galloping down the long driveway, and Raftery, hearing later of Taafe's anger, ran away. No one ever knew whether the faeries, many of whom were of an evil disposition especially towards humans who met them late at night, had anything to do with the accident, nor has anything ever turned up about landlord Taafe's relationship with his resident faeries that might have landed a curse on his animals.

The Little People were believed to live nearby in "the place of the high fort," which you can see by asking permission of the McDonoughs of Killeadan to walk across their cow pasture and over a stone fence to the field where the hearthstone of Raftery's house still lies. Like a choir loft of trees, rustling forth the music of the wind, the fort rises circle-shaped over the fields bright with green and dark shadows. Here the faeries had celebrated their festivals, singing, dancing, and sometimes accompanied by human musicians who had been trained by them. As young Raftery passed the mound one evening, years before his self-banishment, the faeries asked him to serve as musician, theirs having failed to show up. He played his fiddle through the night and in the morning was offered the gift of song or music. Having both, he asked for the gift of poetry. Belief in the faery kingdom has eroded in Ireland, but stopping in these fields on a soft day one feels the magic of the place: luminous and astir, it could well have conferred on the blind fiddler the sweet dark grace of poetry.

JUST NORTHWEST OF Castlerea is an eccentric and little known Victorian mansion, set in the small demesne of Clonalis—all that remains of the ancestral lands of O'Conor Don, the oldest royal or noble title in Europe. ("Your Majesty" and "Your Highness" were unknown among the Irish lords. The head of the clan was addressed by his family name, as "O'Neill" or "MacCarthy Mor," simple titles of great pride indicating that the man addressed was the embodiment of his tribe.) The family of O'Conor Don is far more ancient than the Irish alphabet; and when the first written records lift the prehistoric veil, the O'Conors are here, long established as hereditary kings of Connacht. They gave Ireland its last two high kings; and as the other great Gaelic dynasties gradually sank beneath waves of invasion and conquest, the O'Conors somehow hung on, pushed back against the boglands, but passing the title from generation to generation. Subject to almost arbitrary confiscations of their land and living at times in a hovel, they came close enough to extinction. But even when famine stalked Connacht, the people of Castlerea brought cattle and grain to O'Conor Don, for he was "the Prince of a people involved in one common ruin."

Clonalis (open Tuesday–Sunday 2–6 P.M.) houses an odd collection of portraits and papers, including a lively image of a Countess O'Rourke who was maid of honor to the exiled Stuarts; a painting of Charles O'Conor, a nineteenth-century emigrant of the Clonalis clan, who became a New York lawyer and the first Catholic nominated for the U.S. presidency (he declined the nomination); and the Book of O'Conor Don, a priceless seventeenth-century manuscript collection of Gaelic poetry. Blind Turlough O'Carolan, "last of the Irish bards," was an honored guest of the O'Conors, and his skeletal harp is still with them. Should you be in luck, Miss Josephine O'Conor, who administers Clonalis for her brother, the present O'Conor Don, may give the tour. She is a worthy descendant, idiosyncratic as the house, noble as the name, fond of recalling a bit of traditional family wisdom: "Never be afraid of poverty, and then you'll never become guilty to avoid it." When she stands in the entrance hall beneath a likeness of Phelim O'Conor, fourteenth-century warrior-king of Connacht, the profiles are almost identical.

The plain of Rathcroghan, which stretches from Castlerea to Elphin, divulges the incredible antiquity of the O'Conors' story, as well as Ireland's most ancient literary associations. All around Rathcroghan Crossroads between Bellanagare and Tulsk, lies the evidence of occupation by prehistoric people over whom progenitors of the O'Conors held sway. To the right of the road southeast of the cross is the mound of Rathcroghan, inauguration place of the Connacht kings. Here Maeve was queen; and whoever wished to be king in Ireland had first to sleep with Maeve, who outdid all her sisters "in grace and giving and battle and warlike combat." She is really another manifestation of the earth goddess. Her name, a cognate in many languages for intoxication, alludes to the beer banquet in which a newly inaugurated and divinely intoxicated king was bedded down with the land.

In their fortress on Rathcroghan, Maeve and her then husband, Ailill, had their "Pillow Talk," which is the first episode in *Tain Bo Cuailnge* (*The Cattle Raid of Cooley*), the Irish Iliad and the oldest vernacular epic in Western literature. Ailill and Maeve compare their riches as they lie in bed one night. They are equal in all things, save one: Ailill has a magnificent, supernatural bull for which Maeve has no counterpart. This is insupportable to Maeve. Learning that there is another such bull—on the Cooley Peninsula in Louth—she resolves to have it. To Daire, the owner, she promises all manner of beneficence if he will part with the bull, "and my own friendly thighs on top of that"—no mean gift. When diplomatic negotiation fails, the armies of Connacht set out to capture the bull. The epic, in its many fabulous turnings, is a shimmering mirror of Ireland's heroic age. In the mystical final sequence the great bulls circle the whole of Ireland in mortal combat through the night. When morning comes, the Brown Bull of Cooley appears on the plain of Rathcroghan, the mangled remains of the White-Horned Bull of Connacht hanging from his horns. As he turns back across the breadth of Ireland to die in Cooley, he leaves a part of the White-Horned Bull's carcass in each place he passes, thus giving each place a name.

Among the many prehistoric landmarks, which the farmers of the plain will direct you to, is Knockannagorp, "Hill of the Corpses," surmounted by a seven-foot standing stone and believed to mark the grave of Dathi, Ireland's last pagan king. Not far from this is Oweynagat, "Cave of the Cats" or "Cave of Rathcroghan," a limestone fissure whose lintels bear Ogham scribings. This is the entrance to the Other-world. Well . . . go ahead.

ELEVEN AND A HALF MILES northwest of Tulsk on T. 77 lies the village of Frenchpark. In the Protestant churchyard, a mile and a half west of the village crossroad, is the grave of the man who cleared the way for Yeats, Synge, and Lady Gregory in the West of Ireland. Douglas Hyde, founder of the Gaelic League and first President of Ireland, was born in the nearby rectory in 1862. His home, Ratra House, lay a mile farther west on T. 77, but the house was pulled down in recent years and the place turned into a sheep pasture. That obscurity surrounds his name and land-scape makes a certain kind of sense: his most important work was to roam the remote hills west of the Shannon and write down in Irish and English the anonymous ancient poetry he heard spoken there. The treasures he uncovered were published in several volumes as *The Songs of Connacht*. Bursting with the passionate spirit of the Gaelic West, these collections awakened in many breasts the intense racial consciousness that made pos-sible the Literary Revival. His journeys revealed to him that "it is our Gaelic past which . . . is really at the bottom of the Irish heart."

Only when you see Carrick-on-Shannon do you realize

how funny is the passage in *Ulysses* where Bloom muses over his run-in with the Citizen:

The most vulnerable point too of tender Achilles, your God was a jew, because mostly they appeared to imagine he came from Carrick-on-Shannon or somewhere about in the county Sligo.

Off-season in the rain it can seem the most godforsaken place in the West. But for readers of the young Roscommon novelist John McGahern, there is the topographical excitement that springs from recognizing in the Roscommon and Leitrim landscapes the sources of his fine novels *The Barracks* (1963) and *The Dark* (1965) and the short stories in *Nightlines* (1970). He went to school at Presentation College, Main Street, Carrick, County Leitrim, Connacht, where his graduation picture hangs on a classroom wall and the hospitable Brothers remember him and some of the events he re-creates in *The Dark*, a rural version of *A Portrait of the Artist as a Young Man* and banned until recently.

McGahern grew up in Cootehall (midway between Carrick and Boyle, turn east off T. 3) in a police barracks that gave him the title and setting for his first novel. It stands to the left of the bridge as you enter the village. The people in the post office and shops chat freely about the real life counterparts of his characters and will direct you to Knockvicar, a lonely hamlet on the Shannon backwaters, where you can see "the three arches of Knockvicar Bridge with the scum from the creamery sewer along the sally bushes, names bedded for ever in my life, as eternal." These deserted regions bear the scars of poverty and poverty's sad offspring—jobless young people whose only future is to emigrate. Yet beneath the meanness of McGahern's environment, one senses the inexhaustible energy of the land and its dependents. At the end of *The Dark* he exalts the strength of the West embodied in his father, a man the world would call hideous: "You are marvellous, my father."

A signposted road twists through the Shannon backwater country northeast of Cootehall to Keadue and Alderford House where the eighteenth-century bard Turlough O'Carolan died with a Celtic flourish described by Oliver Goldsmith:

His death was not more remarkable than his life. Homer was never more fond of a glass than he; he would drink whole pints of usquebaugh, and, as he used to think, without any ill consequence. His intemperance, however, in this respect, at length brought on an incurable disorder; and when just at the point of death, he called for a cup of his beloved liquor. Those who were standing round him, surprised at the demand, endeavoured to persuade him to the contrary; but he persisted, and, when the bowl was brought him, attempted to drink, but could not; wherefore, giving away the bowl, he observed, with a smile, that it would be hard if two such friends as he and the cup should part at least without kissing, and then expired.

The blind bard is buried nearby in the cemetery of Kilronan Abbey close to the shores of Lough Meelagh. His stone stands perpendicular to the family tomb of the MacDermot Roes, its inscription revealing the poet's role in the drama of the Irish people's survival:

TURLOUGH O'CAROLAN

HARPER COMPOSER POET SINGER

OUR GREAT SOLACE IN OUR GREAT NEED

1670–1738

162_ /

Except for a few miles through County Sligo, the Boyle road from Ballyfarnan winds southwest through County Roscommon, passing the Rock of Doone, a wonderfully scenic overlook from which to view the storied waters of Lough Key. As the map shows, the route you have followed from Carrick-on-Shannon to Boyle could not have been more roundabout. As usual, the long way round is the most revealing way to go: meandering takes you straight to the heart of the heart of the country, wayward, circuitous, anarchic.

In Boyle you can explore the ruins of Boyle Abbey, Connacht's most important medieval abbey, and make arrangements at Tourist Information for hiring a boat to explore Lough Key. Navigating the island-spotted lake, extremely beautiful but occasionally treacherous, requires the skill of an experienced boatman. In the southwest corner of the lake is an island called the Rock, on which stands a Norman-style castle, once the seat of the MacDermot family. Yeats, who fished in Lough Key with Douglas Hyde, thought the Rock the ideal location for his "Castle of Heroes"—an unfulfilled dream Yeats nurtured of creating a bastion of Irish culture. He confided his dream to his beloved Maud Gonne. "Willy is so silly," said Maud.

Lough Key is full of broken dreams. The shore is dominated by the burnt-out remains of Rockingham House; and hidden in the woods between the shore and the main avenue of the estate is the ruin of an older mansion, the home of Edward King, Milton's "Lycidas." King was a young poet and alumnus with Milton of Christ's College, Cambridge. He was drowned in the Irish Sea in August, 1637:

For Lycidas is dead, dead ere his prime,
Young Lycidas, and hath not left his peer.
Who would not sing for Lycidas? He knew
Himself to sing, and build the lofty rime.
He must not float upon his watery bier
Unwept, and welter to the parching wind,
Without the meed of some melodious tear.

In the abbey of the lake's Trinity Island, monks compiled *The Annals of Loch Cé* (proper Irish spelling), a local medieval history. In the shadow of the long-abandoned abbey are the graves of Tomas Costello and Una MacDermot, an Irish Romeo and Juliet. Costello's poem to his dead love, "Una Bhan" ("Fair Una"), was one of the people's best-loved songs, collected by Hyde in *The Love Songs of Connacht*. In its plangent simplicity one discovers images that Yeats and Synge would later elaborate:

O fair Una, like a rose in a garden you,
And like a candlestick of gold you were on
    the table of a queen,
Melodious and musical you were going this road
    before me,
And it is my sorrowful morning-spoil that
    you were not married to your dark love
. . . .

O Una, O maiden, O friend, and O golden tooth,
O little mouth of honey that never uttered injustice,
I had rather be beside her on a couch, ever kissing her,
Than be sitting in heaven in the chair of the Trinity.

From their graves grew a lovers' knot of ash and laurel. Only recently the knot was cut down by ignorant volunteers engaged in tidying up the graceful, dove-haunted abbey. This was a shuddering blow to the old boatman whose life-long delight had been in pointing out to visitors the glories of the lake. He died soon after but, like the other romantic dead of Lough Key, he too has been remembered by a poem, Kathleen Raine's "Words for the Boatman of Lough Key":

> . . . On a lake of many isles
> Across whose surface pass
> Lovers' reflected dreams,
> Prayer and heroic deed
> Leave their unfading trace. . . .
>
> Though in the Abbey's nave
> The effacing ivy scrawls
> The Annals of Lough Ce
> No word or thought is lost
> Of love or song or prayer
> That once was uttered there.

Glencar Waterfall, Co. Sligo. Irish Tourist Board.

7.

THE LAND OF HEART'S DESIRE

◇◇

County Sligo

YEATS SPENT HIS boyhood summers in County Sligo, and returned here again and again throughout his life—not in person but in his poetry. Sligo, indeed, is a dense web of Yeatsian associations that resists being presented in any neat, orderly fashion. It will not obey the laws of prosaic logic, nor can it be confined to the limitations of a physical map. For Yeats's Sligo is not only a dramatic landscape but a thick mesh of imagery, controlled by the unfathomable laws of a great poet's imagination.

We divide the itinerary into eight small geographical areas, and for the sake of space—and pace—keep interpretation to a minimum. When you go to these places with *The Collected Poems* in hand, the vision comes clear in a way that our words would only cloud. At times you will be assaulted by conflicts of tone and perception when the young Yeats and the old Yeats seem to be speaking—in very different voices—in the same place. At other times you will come upon a place that seems to sum up a whole period of the poet's life. The river that runs underground between Thoor Ballylee and Coole Park is an image of Yeats's middle years. Lough Gill, we shall see, is the image of his youthful years, and Sligo Bay off Rosses Point the image of his age. Yeats's poetry is like these three waters: the earliest is soft and unreal; the middle period, as we have seen, draws on the hidden currents of friendship, tradition, and archetype; old age is a mad and raging sea.

The Ox Mountains

On T. 3, the road north from Boyle to Sligo, you pass the village of Collooney. The road west from Collooney leads to the Ox Mountains, which loom up like their name, dark-brown humps streaked with glimmering gneiss. About four miles beyond Collooney, just before the crossroads, you come to Gilligan's farm on the right. Behind the farm is the steep Hill of Tullaghan, at the top of which a brackish holy well sometimes rises. Though the impious are certain to find nothing more than weeds, the hill is an invigorating climb, and from its summit you can see the naked precipice of the Hawk's Rock, directly north, where small hawks whirl from their nests. This is the desolate setting of Yeats's play *At the Hawk's Well*:

> I call to the eye of the mind
> A Well long choked up and dry

And boughs long stripped by the wind,
And I call to the mind's eye
Pallor of an ivory face,
Its lofty dissolute air,
A man climbing up to a place
The salt sea has swept bare.

The twisted irregular lumps of the Ox Mountains bow north, beyond Hawk's Rock, towards the cairn of Queen Maeve on Knocknarea. A stiff wind sweeps over everything—ferns, grasses, and stripped trees—bending all in Maeve's direction.

At the crossroads turn left; then take the first right, which will lead you into the Ox Mountains and over a pass called Ladies Brae that runs under Knockalongy and Knockachree, the highest peaks in the range. Close by the road, but hidden in the lap of Knockachree, is Lough Achree, or Heart Lake. Not far from Hart's farm, the reedy marsh of its shore is surely the place Yeats had in mind in "The Host of the Air":

O'Driscoll drove with a song
The wild duck and the drake
From the tall and the tufted reeds
Of the drear Hart Lake.

And he saw how the reeds grew dark
At the coming of night-tide,
And dreamed of the long dim hair
Of Bridget his bride.

The high shrill winds from the mountainside are the sound of the faery host who steal away O'Driscoll's bride:

And never was piping so sad,
And never was piping so gay.

The dream world of Beltra Strand on the southwest shore of Ballysadare Bay—an inlet of Sligo Bay—could well be "The Valley of the Black Pig." The strand was the scene of legendary battles; and the Black Pig is a Celtic sign of apocalyptic carnage. Though a cromlech, once visible on the shore, is now covered entirely by sand, Maeve's cairn still reigns from Knocknarea:

> The dews drop slowly and dreams gather: unknown
>   spears
> Suddenly hurtle before my dream-awakened eyes,
> And then the clash of fallen horsemen and the cries
> Of unknown perishing armies beat about my ears.
> We who still labour by the cromlech on the shore,
> The grey cairn on the hill, when day sinks drowned
>   in dew,
> Being weary of the world's empires, bow down to
>   you,
> Master of the still stars and of the flaming door.

"The flaming door" is no doubt the Sligo Bay sunset.

Knocknarea

From Ballysadare (on T. 40 between Beltra and Sligo Town), where Yeats's Pollexfen cousins owned the flour mills, keep left on L. 132 and follow the signs for the access to Knocknarea. Scattered across the fields to the right of the road are the buildings of Stone Age men—forts, standing stones, and "the Firbolgs' burial-mounds" of Carrowmore, Ireland's largest megalithic cemetery. At Primrose Grange on the eastern shoulder of the mountain, a footpath leads by easy grades to the broad summit of Knocknarea where, once again, the strong clean wind whistles like faery song. The great cairn is a mound of stones, thirty-five feet high and two hundred feet in diameter, surrounded by satellite tombs. Within the cairn lies Maeve, Queen Mab in English folklore, warrior-queen of Connacht in the ancient sagas, and a manifestation of the Irish fertility goddess. From here the monstrous queen looks out over Lough Gill to the east and, just south of it, Slieve Daeane and tiny Lough Ia, the lake-grave of Clooth-na-Bare (the Hag of Beare—another personification of Ireland). To the north she surveys Sligo Town, Rosses Point, Drumcliff Bay, and Ben Bulben, and farther north the mountains of Donegal. As she dominates all of Sligo, she dominated the imagination of the boy Yeats and haunted the man.

The poet designated the foot of Knocknarea as the meeting place of Oisin and Saint Patrick in "The Wanderings of Oisin," his retelling of an ancient legend. Oisin, son of Finn MacCool, returns from the Land of Perpetual Youth to find Ireland Christian. Puzzled and disappointed, the old warrior meets Saint Patrick and tries to make him understand the value of the pagan adventure that the saint has destroyed:

> Sad to remember, sick with years,
> The swift innumerable spears,
> The horsemen with their floating hair,
> And bowls of barley, honey, and wine,

Those merry couples dancing in tune,
And the white body that lay by mine. . . .

Caoilte, and Conan, and Finn were there,
When we followed a deer with our baying hounds,
With Bran, Sceolan, and Lomair,
And passing the Firbolgs' burial-mounds,
Came to the cairn-heaped grassy hill
Where passionate Maeve is stony-still. . . .

At the end of the poem Oisin rejects Saint Patrick's ordered Christian society in favor of the old pagan lustiness. But whereas the original legend is the nostalgic backward glance of Gaelic society to the time of its green unchristian youth, Yeats's poem is a sustained lament for his own Sligo childhood, when he could celebrate each summer day unaware of the burden of mortality and "the fluttering sadness of earth." The poem is full of disguised images of this countryside, from the "pearl-pale" air to the "dove-grey edge of the sea."

Yeats in his rage against time and death returns many times to Knocknarea, abode of Maeve, Queen of the immortal *sidhe* (the faeries, pronounced "shee"). In his play *The Land of Heart's Desire*, a faery child lures away a young bride to timeless revelries under Knocknarea. In "The Hosting of the Sidhe," Niamh, the "pearl-pale" lady who brought Oisin to the Land of Perpetual Youth, beckons the reader:

The host is riding from Knocknarea
And over the grave of Clooth-na-Bare;
Caoilte tossing his burning hair,

And Niamh calling *Away, come away:*
Empty your heart of its mortal dream.
The winds awaken, the leaves whirl round,
Our cheeks are pale, our hair is unbound,
Our breasts are heaving, our eyes are agleam. . . .

From Primrose Grange take the road west and stop on the incline just before the road dips down to the coast. On the left you will find a small gate partially obscured by bushes. This is the entrance to Knocknarea Glen (or Alt), one of the world's most beautiful hidden places. Walk straight ahead after passing through the gate, and in about five minutes you will find yourself in a great hall of nature, walled by the cleft rock of the mountainside and decorated fantastically with druidic trees, creepers, and wild flowers. The chasm's lofty walls shut out all sound, and the moss-covered trees admit only the most delicate green light. Even Adam and Eve would have found it special. To this secret place of stone Yeats returns in "The Man and The Echo," as a guilt-filled old man seeking illumination:

In a cleft that's christened Alt
Under broken stone I halt
At the bottom of a pit
That broad noon has never lit,
And shout a secret to the stone.

Now at the end of his life's work, he finds himself in this setting of original innocence. But the place of childhood has become the dimly lit pit of age, where the poet must try to tie together all the loose ends of his life and fashion a final unity before death:

> O Rocky Voice,
> Shall we in that great night rejoice?

But the echo is silent.

The coast road north around Knocknarea passes near Strandhill, where the wind stirs up the foamy white "horses of the sea," and then near Cummen Strand of "Red Hanrahan's Song About Ireland":

> The old brown thorn-trees break in two
>   high over Cummen Strand,
> Under a bitter black wind that blows from
>   the left hand;
> Our courage breaks like an old tree in a
>   black wind and dies,
> But we have hidden in our hearts the flame
>   out of the eyes
> Of Cathleen, the daughter of Houlihan.

Sligo Town

Sligo is a thriving merchant town, unique in the West of Ireland. Its relatively healthy economy has encouraged modest traditions of civility and pluralism—religious, political, and cultural—and an esteem for the written word. Keohane's Book Store in Castle Street is a gold mine of Irish literature, and the Keohanes will ably field your questions. In the impossibly crowded back room of McLynn's pub in Old Market Street you may find yourself next to a young Maoist or an apprentice I.R.A. gunrunner bent in earnest dialogue with a well-dressed physician. But earnestness is soon dis-

pelled by the singing McLynns, who mix red-blooded traditional songs with thoroughly enjoyable contemporary material created for them by Alan Zesserson, an American
student at Trinity College, Dublin. At the Sligo quays the
Yeats family, who lived mostly in London, would disembark
from one of grandfather Pollexfen's steamships for their
summer holidays. Pollexfen's home, Merville, where they
stayed, looks out towards Ben Bulben and is today a part of
Nazareth House, an institution for the orphaned and the
aged along the southwest road on the outskirts of the town.

The Yeats International Summer School, held each August in Sligo, is organized to service a wide range of students. The amateur Yeatsian will take much delight in the
excellent lectures, both popular and scholarly, and in the
well-planned schedule of field trips, theatre, and film. The
serious student will find some of the top scholars in the field,
at their leisure and quite available. In the evening drinking
hours, the summer school carries on the tradition of the old
Gaelic Courts of Poetry, and any participant so inclined
will find the most congenial audience he could wish to encourage him on to verse or song. (For particulars, write to
The Secretary, The Yeats Society, Sligo.)

When Sir Frederick Hamilton sacked the town in 1641,
his troops burned Sligo Abbey, but the flames could not de-
stroy the walls or the wonderful little figures carved in
stone. In the story "The Curse of the Fires and the Shadows," Yeats recreates the event with his own emphasis:

Before them were burning houses. Behind them shone the
Abbey windows filled with saints and martyrs, awakened, as from

/   *175*

a sacred trance, into an angry and animated life. The eyes of the troopers were dazzled, and for a while could see nothing but the flaming faces of saints and martyrs.

This image of holy figures from another world staring through flames at corruptible mankind occurs also in one of Yeats's later poems, "Sailing to Byzantium."

Lough Gill

Much earlier in his poetic career Yeats used the softer images of the Celtic twilight to convey his desire to escape this world. In these early poems the beings beckoning him to another world are not stern ascetics but half-real girls and faeries. The setting for these romantic lyrics is often Lough Gill. The summit of Cairns Hill (or Belvoir), two miles southeast of Sligo Town, offers a fine panoramic view of the lake, which should be explored by boat if the weather is fair.

Along Lough Gill's south shore, not far from Cairns Hill, on wooded Dooney Rock the merry "Fiddler of Dooney" played and "folk dance[d] like a wave of the sea." Farther east is Slish Wood (which Yeats in "The Stolen Child" calls Sleuth Wood), with its hushed path of pine needles bordering the lake:

> Where dips the rocky highland
> Of Sleuth Wood in the lake,
> There lies a leafy island
> Where flapping herons wake
> The drowsy water-rats;
> There we've hid our faery vats,

Full of berries
And of the reddest stolen cherries.
Come away, O human child!
To the waters and the wild
With a faery, hand in hand,
For the world's more full of weeping than you can
    understand.

"The Stolen Child" abounds in Sligo references. The "leafy island" where the faeries hide their vats is tiny Innisfree, which lies in the lake opposite Slish Wood. (A man with a rowboat lives in a little house just east of Slish Wood; or you can swim out.) When Yeats wrote "The Lake Isle of Innisfree," his best-known poem, he was looking at the grey pavements of London and dreaming of the peace he would have if he could live alone in the island's "bee-loud glade" with the "evening full of linnet's wings" and "lake water lapping in low sounds by the shore." In another lyric, however, "To an Isle in the Water," he imagines he would like some company:

She carries in the dishes,
And lays them in a row.
To an isle in the water
With her would I go.

Southwest of Lough Gill in the village of Dromahair (County Leitrim), "The Man Who Dreamed of Faeryland" "stood among a crowd" with "his heart hung all upon a silken dress." Dromahair, seat of the O'Rourkes, Princes of Breffni, bears traces of their lordship including a friary with curious Franciscan carvings and, on the left bank of the

/ *177*

Bonet, the scant remains of their banqueting hall. A hereditary poet of the O'Rourkes composed for his patron the
usual poetic flattery, which Swift rendered mockingly into
English:

> O'Rourke's noble fare
>   Will ne'er be forgot
> By those who were there
>   Or those who were not.
>
> His revels to keep,
>   We up and we dine
> On seven score sheep
>   Fat bullocks, and swine. . . .

The family's famous hospitality did little for Tiernan
O'Rourke whose houseguest, Dermot MacMurrough, spir-
ited away O'Rourke's wife, Dervorgilla, from Dromahair.
(See Corcomroe, Clonmacnois, and Christchurch for the
rest of the story.)

In Yeats's day the scarlet berries of the rare arbutus flourished along the Hazelwood peninsula in the northwest corner of Lough Gill:

> I went out to the hazel wood,
> Because a fire was in my head,
> And cut and peeled a hazel wand,
> And hooked a berry to a thread. . . .

In "The Song of Wandering Aengus," perhaps the most
moving of Yeats's early lyrics, Aengus, the Celtic god of
love, grown old, catches with his wand and berry one of the
"little silver trout" that swim by the Hazelwood shore.

When the fish becomes a "glimmering girl" who vanishes, the old fisherman resolves on an impossible quest: to set out after her. Yeats would later explore the absurdity of such romantic dreams; and a nylon factory has today destroyed much of Hazelwood's beauty.

Rosses Point

The peninsula of Rosses Point northeast of Sligo Town has been altered since Yeats's day by a golf course and a hotel, arrogantly named The Yeats Country Ryan. Still, there is a great deal to see. The quaint old houses of "Memory Harbor" cluster along the southern shore as they do in Jack Yeats's painting of the same name. Beyond the nets and lobster boxes heaped among the houses, a statue, called the Metal Man, stands in the channel on its pedestal and points to where the water is deep enough for ships. Rosses Point was, even in Yeats's childhood, a hide-out for smugglers, and the boy would listen to sailors' stories till "the world seemed full of monsters and marvels." Yeats's cousins, the Middletons, owned all of Rosses Point and lived at Elsinore by the wharf:

> My name is Henry Middleton,
> I have a small demesne,
> A small forgotten house that is set
> On a storm-bitten green.

The Middletons, whose ancestors were smugglers, believed that Elsinore was haunted and would listen for three taps on the window pane. Today the house is owned by the Bruens,

/   179

whose name figures in pirate tales and who keep a salty old pub overlooking the harbor. A few pints, or some of their homemade apple tart and tea, will brace you against the chill winds of the Rosses.

A small road running east on the northern side of the hotel brings you to a Catholic church, where a left turn takes you to the pathless Green Lands, full of little hills and seven miniature lakes. To this enchanted stretch the poet brought his faery-obsessed friend, Æ. Rinn Point, the northernmost end of the Rosses, is "the little promontory of sand and rock and grass, the mournful haunted place" of *The Celtic Twilight* stories. Like the landscape of Yeats's poem "Into the Twilight," the Green Lands are an ideal world, rough and splendid, where nothing is seemy or craven or dull.

But if we find here, as at Lough Gill, the soft images of the young Yeats, the self-consciously world-weary romantic, Rosses Point also yields up the harrowing visions of the aging poet. The road from Sligo Town ends at Deadman's Point. Here is no "lake water lapping in low sounds by the shore," but the rough waves of the Atlantic, which conjure up the language of Yeats's later work: the two Byzantium poems, "Alternative Song for the Severed Head," "Three Songs to the One Burden," and "The Black Tower."

This is "Rosses' crawling tide," teeming with sea-life and furious with "all the complexities of mire or blood," where the buoy sounds *a low note and an iron bell* or, lashed by storm, creates "that gong-tormented sea." In this tempestuous twilight zone between two worlds, one might long to

turn away from "that sensual music" of "those dying generations" and sail "the mackerel-crowded seas" to "the holy
city of Byzantium" there to be purged of mortality.

To the right is Ben Bulben; to the left, Knocknarea. According to legend, the Fianna—the divine warriors of pre-
Christian Ireland—ride out at night from one mountain to
the other. Yeats imagines these great "tragic characters"
riding past the Rosses and disdaining "all that man is, / All
mere complexities, / The fury and the mire of human
veins." The Rosses with its teeming life—"whatever is be-
gotten, born, and dies"—is beneath them. Their place is on
the mountainside: *From mountain to mountain ride the fierce
horsemen.*"

Five days before he died, Yeats wrote his last poem, "The
Black Tower," an almost impenetrable, spell-like incantation. "The Black Tower" may be the lighthouse that stands
in the water on Black Rock off Deadman's Point. The
poem's "oath-bound men" may be the bands of oath-bound
smugglers that were plentiful in Rosses Point. From Deadman's Point one can look across to the side of Knocknarea
on which an ancient warrior, Eogan Bel, is supposed to be
buried upright, and hear Yeats's refrain for "The Black
Tower":

> *There in the tomb stand the dead upright,*
> *But winds come up from the shore:*
> *They shake when the winds roar,*
> *Old bones upon the mountain shake.*

/   181

Glencar and Ben Bulben

The road northeast of Sligo Town passes under the sheep-filled slopes of Lugnagall at the entrance to the Glencar valley, where "The Man Who Dreamed of Faeryland" found no comfort in the grave. From the south side of the Glencar valley when the winds are favorable you can see across the lake a waterfall that blows upwards to the sky. This is the cataract that "smokes upon the mountainside" in "The Mountain Tomb." If you round the lake, you will come to Siberry's thatched cottage, where Yeats once stayed, and another waterfall, which appears in "Towards Break of Day":

> "There is a waterfall
> Upon Ben Bulben side
> That all my childhood counted dear;
> Were I to travel far and wide
> I could not find a thing so dear."

This is the same waterfall that "gushes from the hills" in "The Stolen Child."

From Glencar lake, wind around the King's Mountain and take the little roads heading north into the west face of Ben Bulben. When the road ends, a footpath continues on through a wooded parkland of great beauty under Ben Bulben's head, which rises starkly like a high altar to the god of the world receiving the valley's fealty. According to Yeats, there is a white door in the limestone head: "In the middle of the night it swings open and those wild unchristian riders rush forth upon the fields." These legendary warriors are the heroic Fianna, led by the giant, Finn MacCool. One of their number, Dermot of the Love Spot, eloped with Finn's betrothed, Grania, in a story that is one of the early sources for Tristan and Isolde. Pursued through Ireland by the outraged giant, the lovers sought refuge in the many places throughout the land still known as the Beds of Dermot and Grania. At last, Dermot was wounded fatally on this mountainside by the magical boar of Ben Bulben. Only Finn, who had the power of healing, could revive him. Twice Finn in his bitterness let the waters of healing slip through his fingers; and the third time Finn approached with cupped hands, Dermot was already dead.

The intrepid may wish to climb the prowlike west face to the mountain's flat top, but mists descend without warning and the limestone is easily chipped. The more cautious will favor a guide and a roundabout route. For this, continue northeast around Ben Bulben, past the crooked hat of Ben Weskin, and into the surreal horseshoe valley of Gleniff. Cut out of the mountainside high above an abandoned school in the southwest corner of the valley is a natural cavern, the last Bed of Dermot and Grania. Nearby, at the head of the valley, the Miner's Path gives easy access to the mountain plateau. Local farmers are usually happy to act as guides.

Northwest of Gleniff at Creevykeel Crossroads is one of the country's best court cairns (chamber tombs with a semicircular courtyard), a structure dating from the third millennium B.C.

Lissadell

"That old Georgian mansion" of Lissadell stands near the northern shore of Drumcliff Bay west of Ben Bulben. The nostalgic picture of this house as it once was in summer opens, andante, the poem "In Memory of Eva Gore-Booth and Con Markiewicz,":

> The light of evening, Lissadell,
> Great windows open to the south,
> Two girls in silk kimonos, both
> Beautiful, one a gazelle.

Yeats's first visit here was his first reception at an Irish great house; and its order and ceremony made a deep impression on the young middle-class poet. Gore-Booths, in much reduced circumstances, still occupy Lissadell and have opened it to the public. Despite the minimal upkeep, the house—a crazy, cobwebbed museum of paintings, china, and unfinished needlepoint—has salvaged enough dignity to hint at its former riches. Among the great spaces and the creaking boards are oils by Æ, manuscripts of Eva's poetry, and the great table eternally set for dinner: "That table and the talk of youth. . . ."

Constance, who married a Polish count, exchanged her kimono for an I.R.A. uniform and consumed her days in the revolutionary landscape of jail, street corner, and guerrilla warfare. Eva, a poet of frail but real ability, went on to organize factory girls in England. To Yeats the process of their radicalization was like a graph on which he saw plotted the plummeting to destruction of the Anglo-Irish order. He would much rather have seen them continue unchanged at an unchanged Lissadell, performing the ceremonies of innocence. Since the Gore-Booth sisters were quite alive when Yeats wrote of Lissadell, this is a memorial poem not to them but to Yeats's memories of youth. Youth, beauty, innocence, and the aristocratic elegance he came to cherish have all departed the scene.

In our day, these attitudes of Yeats toward aristocracy and the place of women have provoked charges of fascism and male chauvinism; and Lissadell presents itself, not as a scene out of Yeats, but as one out of Somerville and Ross—humorous, pathetic.

Drumcliff

Yeats died in the south of France in 1939, leaving behind detailed instructions for his burial. These are contained in "Under Ben Bulben," the poem he placed last in his *Collected Poems* as his final statement. After World War II, his instructions were carried out; and he now lies in the churchyard at Drumcliff between Knocknarea and Ben Bulben, from which the heroic figures descend in pledge of apocalypse and a new order for the world:

> Swear by those horsemen, by those women
> Complexion and form prove superhuman,
> That pale, long-visaged company
> That air in immortality
> Completeness of their passions won;
> Now they ride the wintry dawn
> Where Ben Bulben sets the scene.

/ 185

He goes on to leave his legacy—his own poetry—as a model for future Irish poets. Scorn base subjects, he warns, and sing of the peasantry and the nobility

> That we in coming days may be
> Still the indomitable Irishry.

Finally, he describes precisely the scene the visitor sees as he enters the cemetery today, proceeding from the largest elements to the smallest detail:

> Under bare Ben Bulben's head
> In Drumcliff churchyard Yeats is laid.
> An ancestor was rector there
> Long years ago, a church stands near,
> By the road an ancient cross.
> No marble, no conventional phrase;
> On limestone quarried near the spot
> By his command these words are cut:
>> *Cast a cold eye*
>> *On life, on death.*
>> *Horseman, pass by!*

The words are there, enigmatic as a druid's rune, to be seen by mortal traveller or immortal horseman. As Yeats would wish, there is no one's feeble commentary or explanation. The great circle of his art is completed here where it began—in the place he loved, among his own.*

---

* For some of the information in this chapter, we are indebted to Sheelah Kirby, whose small book, *The Yeats Country*, we recommend to anyone interested in a more extensive treatment of Yeats's Sligo.

Muireadach's Cross, Monasterboice, Co. Louth. Irish Tourist Board

8.
WILD, UNCHRISTIAN WARRIORS

◇◇◇◇◇◇◇◇◇◇◇◇◇◇◇◇◇◇◇◇◇◇◇◇◇◇◇◇◇◇◇◇◇◇◇◇

The Province of Ulster and Counties Louth and Meath

THE SCENERY OF the Province of Ulster often rivals the South and West. County Tyrone is the soft, nostalgic landscape of William Carleton, the nineteenth-century novelist who lived in the Clogher Valley, and of his modern compatriots, the short story writer Benedict Kiely and the poet John Montague. Along the coast of Donegal, which is spectacular, you will find the outpost village of Glencolumbkille. Here Michael Hillier, a master gold- and silversmith, will rise to the challenge of creating for you an original piece of jewelry for as little as a few pounds. He works in obscurity, creating fierce images that seem to have risen like barbaric horsemen out of the bleak hills. In these parts, imagination is still of the earth.

Myth is woven like rough thread through the northern landscape. On the north coast, between Portrush and the green Glens of Antrim, is the marvellous Giant's Causeway, basaltic rock split into numberless hexagonal shafts by the primeval cooling of lava. The giant Finn MacCool was thought to have built the causeway to enable his comrade-in-arms to come over from Scotland, which masses against the horizon like an enchanted apparition. The low sky, here at the top of the world, almost touches the prim, white steeples that rise from the coastal settlements, looking more like images from Ingmar Bergman than Irish villages. In such a chaste, cold place, the poet Louis MacNeice was born; in the rectory at Carrickfergus, where his father was minister, he spent his frightened childhood.

Northern Ireland—the six counties of Ulster that are under the British crown—is twice as populous as the Republic and composed of threads of such clashing colors that the fabric seems always ready to rip asunder. Soldiers stand at every corner, rifles at the ready, in the industrial smog of Belfast, the busy, loveless city where Judith Hearne went mad in Brian Moore's novel, *The Lonely Passion of Judith Hearne*. The old hatreds seethe; human life and growth are disregarded amidst the claims and counterclaims of threadbare privilege and ancient grievance. Those who draw the battle lines ignore the misery they cause. The tribes are hosting still.

In the days when the sagas were first told, Louth (the coastal county just south of Northern Ireland) was a part of Ulster. The Brown Bull, the pride of Ulster and object of Queen Maeve's quest in the *Tain*, roamed the Cooley Peninsula. Carlingford on the peninsula's northern shore is an excellent vantage point: its medieval buildings overlook

Carlingford Lough, where the Mountains of Mourne come down to the sea, and at its back rise the brown, jagged heights of Cooley. When the armies of Connacht set out for Cooley to capture the great bull, the men of Ulster were stricken with the pangs of women in labor and could not rise to the challenge. The great boy-hero of Ulster, Cuchulainn, with all the gigantism of Irish mythology, withstood alone the armies of Connacht. Throughout the plain of Louth, called Muirthemne in heroic times, Cuchulainn has left his mark. His birthplace is Dun Dealgan, a tumulus near the Castleblayney road just west of present-day Dundalk (a horrible town). The Bronze Age hill-fort is topped by Castlefolly, built in 1780 and burned to a shell in this century. The raven, the bird that signalled Cuchulainn's death, flies around the battlements. Cuchulainn, when he had been mortally wounded, would not lie down, but strapped himself to a standing stone and held his sword in hand. His enemies, so fearing the strength of the dying man, dared not approach to administer the final blow, but waited till a circling raven alighted on his shoulder. Only then could they be sure he was dead. Cuchulainn's death is commemorated by a statue in Dublin's General Post Office; but far more evocative is the field where the real stone stands, surrounded by young bulls, about a mile before Knockbridge on the left of the road that leads from Dundalk to the village of Louth. Closer to Dublin, at Ardee, is the ford where Cuchulainn fought his best friend Ferdia by day and secretly bathed his opponent's wounds by night, till at last he killed him. These stories, more than two thousand years old, tell as much about Ireland as any twentieth-century novel.

PATRICK KAVANAGH GREW UP southwest of Dundalk in Inniskeen, County Monaghan, a shy piece of poet's country, overshadowed by the mountains of Armagh to the north and often hiding from the eyes of the road behind blank-faced hedges. In McNello's pub they will tell you the stories that "Paddy" told them. His sisters, who live nearby in the same house where Paddy did his dreaming, reminisce about the "thousands" at his funeral. From their parlor windows they will show you the hills of Shancoduff and from the front yard the valley he called Drumnay in his novel *Tarry Flynn*. Mr. Deery, the postmaster, will tell you about the monument he plans for Paddy and point out his grave, marked with steppingstones from his favorite stream and in spring with violets and daffodils. The cross says: "And pray for him who walked apart on the hills, loving life's miracles." But no one talks about the sexual famine Paddy described in his long poem, *The Great Hunger*. Nor do they talk much about his poems, those ordinary celebrations of everyday:

> Yet sometimes when the sun comes through a gap
> These men know God the Father in a tree:
> The Holy Spirit is the rising sap,
> And Christ will be the green leaves that will come
> At Easter from the sealed and guarded tomb.

The Irish mind is a great labyrinth of myth. Kavanagh identifies springtime with the regenerative Christ and worships God in a tree, as did the druids. The Boyne Valley, south of Inniskeen and north of Dublin, shelters other symbols from the labyrinth. Muireadach's Cross in the churchyard at Monasterboice is the best-preserved example of high cross art. Like medieval stained glass, its biblical tableaux are teaching devices, illustrating to the wayfarer the turning points in the history of salvation. On the lowest panel of the west face, Eve, the first woman, presents Adam with the forbidden fruit and thus brings evil on mankind. Between them the snake, the shameful phallic reality, is wound around the tree. Beside them are their children, Cain bludgeoning Abel's skull.

The Boyne Valley is a network of Stone Age tombs. It is monuments such as these that the country people of a later day believed to be the dwelling places of the faeries. From the size of the tombs you can see that "little people" is only an appeasing euphemism for the gigantic banished gods. The most impressive monument, near Slane, is Newgrange, perhaps the finest passage-grave in western Europe. The great mound, thirty-six feet high and three hundred feet in diameter, is decorated without and within with mysterious scribings. The boulders around its base, the passageway, and the chambers of the dead, all bear carved symbols to which we have lost the key: spirals, concentric semicircles, triangular series of zigzags, and diamond shapes. Though these signs can no longer be deciphered with any authority, they exercise an elemental power over the viewer. Their geometry, which could not be more basic, can be considered as two overall patterns of movement: straight lines, which rise to points, and circular, inward-turning curves. Perhaps what we have here is a bold primordial expression of fundamental images found in all primitive cultures, of reality grasped as male-female. The mound itself was originally a hemisphere, and as late as the end of the seventeenth century its summit was crowned by an upright pillar of stone.

Such a stone still stands on the Hill of Tara, southeast of Navan. Popularly known as Bod Fhearghuis, "Fergus' Penis," its formal name is Lia Fail, "Stone of Destiny," and it was believed to shriek out when a true king stood on it. Tara was once the seat of the high kings and center of a warrior aristocracy, but its wooden enclosures and banqueting halls have long since gone. All that remains of them are the earthworks that cover the hill. On the Hill of Slane to the north Saint Patrick kindled the first Paschal Fire in defiance of the pagan king's decree, and was brought to Tara for trial. Today an ugly statue of the saint has been erected on Tara, meant perhaps to neutralize the Lia Fail. The Christian missionaries tried to replace the tales of savage Cuchulainn with the warning-image of Cain and Abel. For fertility rites they substituted the story of Adam and Eve. They fought the pagan fires of Maytime with the fire of Easter.

In the labyrinth of the Irish mind, many myths, seemingly in conflict, have settled down to live side by side. In a country that remembers with pride the sounds of battle and the deeds of warriors, a woman—like Eve on the cross at Monasterboice—tends to be underrated. Mary Lavin, the best Irish short-story writer since Joyce, is a name you seldom hear in the male-dominated enclaves of Dublin's literary pubs. Her village, Bective, west of Tara, is tiny, scarcely signposted, rarely visited. In "A Likely Story" from *Tales from Bective Bridge*, she writes about the mysterious sweet presence of her neighborhood:

Do you know Bective? Like a bird in the nest, it presses close to the soft green mound of the river bank, its handful of houses no more significant by day than the sheep that dot the far fields. But at night, when all its little lamps are lit, house by house, it is marked out on the hillside as clearly as the Great Bear is marked out in the sky. And on a still night it throws its shape in glitter on the water.

Just beyond the triple-arched bridge which crosses the River Boyne is the gate to the ruins of Bective Abbey, a fifteenth-century Cistercian foundation. The best of all possible places to experience the craft and power of the stories in *Happiness* and *In The Middle of the Fields* is here in the shelter of the old stone walls on the edge of the fertile fields her stories imitate: "Drenched with light under the midsummer moon, the fields were as large as the fields of the sky." In touch with the quiet vitality of this Meath landscape, some of her characters embody deep human sympathies; others are as crabbed and tedious as the stunted thorns along the riverbank. She never goes far afield, but finds in the gardens of Bective the age-old cycle of growing things, of fatigue and energy. Like the circles of Newgrange, she turns inward, and has said that writing stories is simply "looking closer than normal into the human heart."

Celbridge Abbey, Co. Kildare. Thomas Cahill

9.

LOVE AMONG
THE HOUYHNHNMS

◇◇◇◇◇◇◇◇◇◇◇◇◇◇◇◇◇◇◇◇◇◇◇◇◇◇◇◇◇◇◇◇◇◇

County Kildare

ABOUT A DOZEN MILES from Dublin and four
miles off the Galway road lies the somnolent
village of Celbridge. It has but one street, where a dog
might safely doze in the sun, and one pub that serves lunch.
As in many small Irish communities, time seems nearly to
have stopped—or never started. But Celbridge, threatened
today by Dublin's suburban boom, has never really been
quiet. If we are to believe the legends, the village has its
abundant share of restless shades, who re-enact the turbu-
lent encounters in which they were participants more than
two hundred years ago. Both ends of the wide and leisurely
street lead to demesnes, each commanded by its historic
house, where fabulous personalities once lived and visited.

To the south stands Celbridge Abbey, home of Esther
Van Homrigh, the tragic woman Jonathan Swift called

Vanessa. The Abbey is full of secrets we shall never know; and a visitor must feel this instinctively, though he may know nothing of the house's history. There is a gloom about the place which could never be entirely dispelled even by systematic repairs and a fresh coat of paint. The house was built by Vanessa's father, Bartholomew, a Dutch immigrant to Dublin who made his fortune in ships in the latter decades of the seventeenth century. In those cutthroat times fortunes could be made or lost in a day, and foreigners amassed great wealth while the old aristocracy, often with a price on their heads, gradually departed the scene. Bartholomew Van Homrigh had his own moments of political insecurity, but his position in the new Protestant society was rather firmly fixed when in 1697 he was elected Lord Mayor of Dublin. The most enduring symbol of this *arriviste*'s good luck is his chain of office, made of linked, golden S's and still worn by Dublin's mayors. The chain was presented to him by his fellow countryman, William of Orange, who had received Bartholemew's active support during his Glorious Revolution and who now reigned as king of Great Britain and Ireland. Bartholemew had backed the right man.

Today his house, one of the oldest inhabited within the Pale, is the residence of the Hospitaller Brothers of St. John of God, who run St. Raphael's School for retarded boys, a cluster of buildings across the road from the Abbey. You may obtain permission there to visit the Van Homrigh mansion. The brothers, who have a vow of hospitality, are happy to admit interested visitors. The oldest of the school buildings was once the home of Dr. Arthur Price, a rejected suitor of Vanessa's, who plays his small part in her story.

It is difficult to assess the size of Van Homrigh's brown mansion from without, for it is not designed—as are the great houses that were built soon afterwards during Ireland's classical period—to overwhelm the observer with the simple sweep of massive grandeur. Rather, it is full of freakish turns, irregular masses and angles, and jutting parapets. Inside the architectural scheme is no more apparent, and one could easily get lost amid the odd-sized rooms and unexpected corridors. The woodwork is an elaboration of Gothic arches, some of the furniture a bad dream of twisted decorations and imaginary beasts. The vaulted cellars are particularly eerie, and it is here that ghosts have most often been reported. Workmen, staying in the basement for the night, have steadfastly refused to sleep there again. Some of the decoration is Gothic, the alterations of a subsequent owner, Colonel Marley, who in his attempt to change the ambiance succeeded merely in underscoring the tragedy that hangs in the air. Though the windows are large and plentiful, there are corners that the sun never reaches. It is a strange house —even for Ireland—a setting for actions never meant to bear the light of day.

On a day in late spring in the year 1723 Jonathan Swift, Dean of St. Patrick's Cathedral, Dublin, rode hard from the city till he reached the doors of Celbridge Abbey. Vanessa, who lived here alone with her servants (for all her family had died), saw him approach along the formal avenue. She was thirty-four, and if her face still held the girlish beauty that had first attracted Swift, it had begun to show the wear of chronic sadness, sickness, and drink. She was no longer the happy woman to whom Swift had written four years earlier (in French, to escape the attention of any curious interceptor): "Believe me, if anything in the world is believable . . . that all your desires will always be obeyed as commandments that would be impossible to violate." Their correspondence had been long and intimate. "I was born with violent passions," she had written to him in 1720, "which terminate all in one—that inexpressible passion I have for you." Now he dismounted and entered the front room as she came to meet him. The Dean said nothing, but his face pulsated with that terrible anger she could not bear. From his pocket he drew a letter, flung it down before her and left as quickly and as stonily silent as he had come. They were never to meet again. A month later Vanessa was dead.

Swift's prodigious shadow darkened the lives of two women, Vanessa and Esther Johnson, whom Swift called Stella. His evident closeness to Stella encouraged Dublin gossip of a secret marriage between them, a marriage that could not be revealed either because of the Dean's clerical reticence or some darker reason. Evidence, recently turned up, suggests strongly that Swift and Stella may both have been bastards of the powerful Temple family. If this should be so, the incestuous relationship of uncle to niece would have been reason dark enough for keeping private this union or, what is more likely, for the marriage never having taken place.

Vanessa was the other woman. The lady of Celbridge Abbey waned away in her shadowy existence, living for the occasional secret advents of her inconstant lover. If Swift's abiding friendship with Stella—a pillar of her church and widely admired by "persons of probity"—was almost certainly chaste, his relationship with Vanessa was probably carnal. The cryptic references to coffee drinking in the correspondence can only be allusions to making love: "I drank no coffee since I left you, nor intend to till I see you again. There is none worth drinking but yours, if myself be the judge"; "I wish I were to walk with you fifty times about your garden and then—drink your coffee."

Vanessa's pleasure grounds, arched with cherry trees, are maintained today by the brothers. You can see the couple strolling the shaded walks along the River Liffey, which rushes through the demesne, and whispering to one another in the private language of lovers. To Vanessa Swift was Cadenus:

> Yet why should I thy presence hail?
> To me no more the breathing gale
> Comes fraught with sweets, no more the rose
> With such translucent beauty blows
> As when Cadenus blest the scene
> And shared with me those joys serene
> When, unperceived, the lambent fire
> Of Friendship, kindled new desire . . .

To please him, she ordered life-size statues from the continent and had them placed along the Abbey walls. These cloaked nobles, like figures stolen from a medieval cathedral, still survey the patio behind the house, their colors faded by the Irish rain. On a minuscule island in the branching Liffey Vanessa built a lovers' bower, massed with roses, jessamine, and honeysuckle, and sheltered from all intrusion by yews, boxtrees, and solemn cypresses. (The bower has disappeared; the seat pointed out is inauthentic.) For each of Swift's visits she is said to have planted a laurel; but the laurels of Celbridge can give us no accurate count of his comings and goings, for today they are numberless.

Vanessa was mostly alone at Celbridge and longed for Swift's comforting arms. A solitary figure, she stands at one of the Abbey windows and stares at the violent storm: "We have had a vast deal of thunder and lightning. Where do you think I wished to be then? And do you think that was the only time I wished so since I saw you?" In the absence of a normal life, she requires more and more reassurance from him. "Rest assured," he writes her in July of 1721, "that you are the only person on earth who has ever been loved, honoured, esteemed, adored by your friend."

But his love begins to calcify with the deadly cynicism that affected his later years. He tries to arrange a marriage for Vanessa. One of the suitors was Arthur Price, who lived at Oakley Park across from the Abbey in the spare, sober Georgian block that is now a part of St. Raphael's. Perhaps Dr. Price was as cold and well ordered as his house, for Vanessa despised him. She was admirably obstinate and insistent on her own identity—even in the face of the demanding, overbearing Dean. In everything she was a contrast to Stella, who was a model of cheerfulness and good sense. Vanessa once wrote to her priest-lover:

I firmly believe, could I know your thoughts (which no human creature is capable of guessing at, because never anyone living thought like you), I should find that you have often, in a rage, wished me religious, hoping then I should pay my devotions to Heaven. But that would not spare you, for was I an enthusiast, still you'd be the deity I should worship.

Her wry obstinacy and iconoclastic bravery held out till the end. Her deathbed words were a last sally at God and her detested neighbor: "No Price; no prayers." Her intuition about Price was right on the mark: he rose higher in the Church than Swift ever did and, as Archbishop of Cashel, unroofed the cathedral on Cashel Rock, and left unprotected the most extraordinary collection of medieval architecture in Ireland.

But how could Swift, a man to whom words were so important, have deserted his "only person on earth"? What was there in the letter he flung at her that afternoon at Celbridge that could make him abandon the woman he had known for sixteen years? Tradition has it that the letter was Vanessa's own to Stella, demanding to know whether there was any truth to the Dublin gossip about her marriage to Swift.

Some of the critics would have us believe that the disordered Vanessa threw herself at the unwilling cleric, who merely tolerated her charitably till she encroached upon his private affairs. But even Swift's surviving letters to Vanessa hardly bear this out; and we may wonder what the entire correspondence would have included had it survived uncensored. The Freudian interpreters tell us that Swift was a very sick man who toyed with two women without being able to commit himself sexually to either. The scatology and depraved descriptions of bodily functions contained in poems like "The Lady's Dressing Room" and "A Beautiful Young Nymph Going to Bed" are seen as manifestations of his crippling obsessions. But these are the work of later years written by a lonely, unlucky man long after both women were dead. When he was younger, he had every hope of rising in the Church and looked forward to a bishopric in England. He never expected to end his days in the Dublin Deanery. Perhaps he simply could not marry Vanessa in Dublin, where he was already presumed to be married, without ruining the reputation of his other beloved, whom he could never marry. Perhaps the passion that Vanessa wakened in him turned to bitter rage in the impossible confines of Dublin's small city, which he came gradually to realize would be his final home. "I ever feared the tattle of this nasty town," he once complained. Perhaps marriage was unthinkable to Swift, who feared his own eventual madness and believed with Dryden that "great wits are sure to madness near allied." Perhaps—but we shall never be sure.

AT THE NORTHERN END of the village of Celbridge an immense demesne stretches out along the plain of Kildare. It is planned with an eye towards monumental drama, a perfect imposition of human artifice on natural topography. Here large lawns ebb towards the horizon and alternate with groves and forests, a lake, and the River Liffey. The park holds the best Palladian architecture in Ireland, and it is a delight in fine weather to spend a day exploring the demesne. This is Castletown, begun in 1722 as the seat of the Right Honourable William Conolly, speaker of the venal, unrepresentative Irish House of Commons.

The eighteenth-century visitor, permitted entrance to this formal Eden, was suitably impressed as he rode the approach in his carriage. For seldom in Ireland is this Georgian trick—the calculated impression of the approach—so well implemented. Expressionless stone sphinxes observe each other from the gate piers which lead to a seemingly endless avenue of perfect limes. Though the terrain is quite flat, no house can be seen against the sky. The visitor's mind travels from what he sees to what he cannot see and begins to form a suspicion of the enormity of these holdings. If the estate is so grand, what will the house be? Will the avenue never end? The avenue turns sharply to the left and the house is partially revealed. But only when the visitor is squarely before it and practically within its shadow does the building unfold suddenly and make its impact.

The massive balustraded central block is set back and flanked by the exquisite arcs of two identical colonnades of Ionic capitals, which extend out towards the visitor like gigantic cold, white arms. These flow into symmetrical pavilions, much smaller than the central block though in themselves quite grand. The unpolished stone of the central mass is very nearly white, the pavilions, a pattern of contrasting greys. Some eighty windows face the visitor, many pedimented and more than the height of two men. The house, which has two hundred and twenty-nine windows in all, was imagined to have three hundred and sixty-five, an eye for each day of the year. The line of the central balustrade is restated at a lower level atop the colonnades but complicated by the addition of surmounting urns at regular intervals. The urn motif continues along the top of the pavilions, where the stone bannisters solidify into unbroken parapets. The simple delicacy of the balustrade arrangement is but one thread in the graceful majesty of the whole. The architect, Alessandro Galilei, who also designed the façade of St. John Lateran in Rome, possessed that rare talent: an understanding of the disposition of great masses in such a way that they will delight, and even overwhelm, but never oppress the observer. Castletown, the first, largest, and most beautiful of all Irish Palladian houses, was to have many imitators during the eighteenth century. Its monumentality, especially, was copied. But none would have such complete success as Galilei in realizing a perfect harmony of formal regularity and subtle contrast, of massive grandeur and a feeling of light.

The visitor in his carriage, planning perhaps a house of his own, must have marvelled at the sight before him. The avenue and now the façade have had their intended effect: they have left him in proper awe of the people who live within. The rooms of the house are exhaustingly numerous; and, though their glory is in tatters, it is quite possible to form a picture of the life that was lived here.

In the dining room Tom Conolly, William's grand-nephew, is reputed to have held converse with the Devil. The local priest, summoned to perform exorcism, threw his missal at the Devil, thus accounting for the cracked mirror. His Satanic Majesty, exiting in a puff of smoke, damaged the hearthstone. Tom Conolly belonged to the Hell-Fire

Club, a group of upper-class rakes who met in the back
rooms of Dublin's eighteenth-century taverns to celebrate
black masses, engage in all manner of dark practices, and
give themselves over to "pure evil"—whatever that may
have meant by the standards of the time. In the streets of the
city, swaggering gentlemen of the Hell-Fire variety—the
Bucks, as they were called—would search out a man
unarmed and alone and "pink" him (that is, pierce him
many times with the points of their rapiers). All in a night's
sport.

In contrast, Tom's wife, the much esteemed Lady Louisa,
spent her days in the innocent task of interior decoration.
The winter of 1783 she gave over to creating the Print
Room. She decorated the room with reproductions of various shapes and sizes surrounded by garlanded swags. The
pictures of contemporary and heroic scenes, all sweetly idealized, form unintentionally a small museum of eighteenth-
century pop art. The Coke bottle, by comparison, represents an advance in popular taste. Like other ladies of fortune of the same period, she tirelessly invokes one adjective
throughout her correspondence: "I have just finished my
dressing room and its very pretty, its very plain, but very
neat, its hung with green paper and pictures, a quantity of
tables, pretty green and white linnen for my chairs, a book
case and china, does it not sound comfortable. . . . I have
furnished a delightful pretty room up in the attick story.
. . . Our gallery is finished—I think it is really pretty. . . .
The pond will be tollerably pretty as a river. . . . Mr. Riely
goes on swimmingly in the Gallery but I am doing much
more than I intended, that pretty grey, white and gold look

/   207

that I admired in the ends of the room, did look a little naked by the painted compartment when finished and upon asking Mr. Conolly's opinion about it, he meekly told me he had always thought it would be much prettier to have painting but thought I would know best, did you ever hear anything so humble upon which Mr. Riely has made some pretty slight sketches that end at the heads of the busts and are an addition but they make the stucco panels look so very bad that they are going to be knocked off smack smooth which"—and on and on. Like her taste, Louisa's pretty head is merely decorative. Her mind runs on, as do her muddled, never-ending sentences, in search of objects to fill the void.

In the Cartoon Room hangs a portrait of that handsome man, Lord Edward FitzGerald: dark, flushed complexion, black, bright eyes, full black hair. He played his romantic part as commander of the United Irishmen in the short-lived Rising of Ninety-Eight and died in prison of wounds inflicted by his captors. FitzGerald, whose gallantry was not matched by military acumen, was a favorite of his aunt, Lady Louisa. In marked contrast to the dignity of the portrait are the cartoons in the room, satirical drawings of the "mere Irish." The natives are portrayed as savages, drunks, incompetents, obsequious and dangerous by turns, with the simpering grins and blank eyes of idiots. But the hovels they inhabit and their tattered clothes give a hint of the cause for their condition: their poverty and dispossession. The attitude of the cartoonists towards their subjects is the usual one of victors towards the vanquished. The members of the established order are able to withhold mercy and assuage their guilt by assuming that the vanquished are not really human.

The staircase with its brass rails, which set another fashion for Irish great houses, leads to the Long Gallery above. On the east wall of the staircase you pass some elaborate rococo plasterwork, which incorporates medallion busts of Conollys as well as the requisite cupids. They placidly surround a scene of violence, an oil painting called *The Boar Hunt*, depicting the moment at which the dogs attack their prey. Hunting men were always made welcome at Castletown.

In the Long Gallery Louisa's abhorrence of the vacuum finds its most outlandish expression. The walls, covered thoroughly with intricate, colored designs "in the Pompeian manner," are further adorned with the busts of ancient philosophers. The red, pink, gold, and blue of the elaborately molded ceiling clash with the gaudy Venetian chandeliers, which sprout flowering pinwheels of every hue. From the windows may be seen between the woods the Folly, which Katherine Conolly, the Speaker's widow, had erected in 1740 "to answer a vistow at the bake of Castletown" and to provide a little local employment during a bitter winter. It is a one-hundred-forty-foot fantasy of arches, birds, balls, and pineapples, crowned by an obelisk. The grounds are adorned by other architectural whimsies, most notably the Wonderful Barn, a conical oddity with triangular windows.

Cromwell had ended his Irish campaign only seventy years before Castletown was built, and the memory of his righteous savagery was still vivid. His soldiers had opened great wounds in the landscape—plundered castles and abandoned towers, desecrated friaries and roofless churches, and the countless graves of the massacred. Time and weather

/   *209*

had not yet given these memorials the misty charm they would have for a later age. The countryside's need for cosmetic furbishing must have been felt most keenly by the new landlords of the forfeited estates, among whom the children of Cromwell's soldiery formed a sizable part. These burgher lords would instinctively have realized the importance of disassociating themselves from scenes of ruin and usurpation and of creating throughout the land a new look of order and grandeur with which they could identify themselves. If their taste, like Lady Louisa's, was sometimes uncertain, or their manners, like Tom Conolly's companions', occasionally brutish, their ideal was the utter composure and simple magnificence embodied in the façade of Castletown. Like *The Boar Hunt* on the stairway, scenes of brutality were to be made invisible in settings of calm, decency, whiteness.

Though it cannot be proved beyond all doubt that Swift was a guest of the Conollys, it is a likely presumption, given the circle he travelled in. At all events, he knew to its darkest corners the sensibility that built this house and the other great houses that followed it. Castletown's façade is the face the planters wished to show to the world: great order, elegant simplicity, precise formality, a model of eighteenth-century rationalism. It is just this ideal that animates Swift's noble, horsey race, the Houyhnhnms, those unruffled, superior beings of Book IV of *Gulliver's Travels* who live in accordance with Nature, as informed by Reason. One can imagine the graceful, stoical Houyhnhnms striding Castletown's halls and the ample lawns, where nature and human invention blend in harmony. The Houyhnhnms' systematic industriousness, which shields them from the base temptations of idleness, finds its historical expression in Anglo-Irish busy-ness, in the steady expansion of building activity throughout the eighteenth century.

But if the Houyhnhnms are the Anglo-Irish, the Yahoos, those vile beasts in human form, are the native Irish. The blank, cruel faces in the Cartoon Room belong to Irish Yahoos. "The poorer sort of our natives," writes Swift in a letter, "live in the utmost ignorance, barbarity and poverty, giving themselves wholly up to idleness, nastiness and thievery." They are "uncultivated people . . . savage, beastly, [with] filthy cabins, miserable half-starved creatures, *scarce in human shape.*" Beyond the trees of Castletown, which could screen its inhabitants from such unseemly sights, lived these half-starved creatures in their windowless hovels, the price paid for Castletown's magnificence.

Swift is never able to shape the Houyhnhnms, for all their stoical grace, into anything more than cold, affectionless beings who never rage at anything—not even death. Gulliver, despite his horror, finally realizes he is a Yahoo, not a Houyhnhnm. Though he was always to remain very much a member of his own class, Swift somewhere in his depths finds the rationalist ideal wanting and, thus too, his own society and its great personages, who had often been chillingly formal to the clever young parson of questionable origins. He throws in his lot with the vile mass of Yahoos—humanity itself—and identifies himself with common men in a way that the lords and ladies of his acquaintance could never have done. This identification, exceedingly reluctant in *Gulliver's Travels*, was to become with passing years more sympathetic and complete. It was the beginning of a personal evolution that would make of Swift the first Irish nationalist and leave him mad, a broken crusader repeating over and over at the end of his days, "I am what I am."

The puzzle of Swift's life and personality can never be set together in a satisfactory whole. Some of the pieces lie ahead in the City of Dublin, the road to which follows closely the course of the River Liffey. In the last pitiful month of her life Vanessa must often have watched the course of the river, flowing through Celbridge and on through Dublin not far from the tower of St. Patrick's Cathedral, whose Dean had severed all connection with her.

St. Patrick's Cathedral, Dublin. Irish Tourist Board

10.
THE DEAN OF
ST. PATRICK'S

❖❖❖❖❖❖❖❖❖❖❖❖❖❖❖❖❖❖❖❖❖❖❖❖❖❖❖❖❖❖

Dublin City

DUBLIN SHOULD FIRST be visited by night. In early morning, when the air is heavy with white smog from thousands of chimney pots and the sky is overcast, Dubliners are silent, white-faced people, who greet the day begrudgingly and often belatedly. Towards evening the rhythm of the city quickens, the noise level rises, and faces flush. The genial hours hardly end with the official closing of the pubs. Among people who have never been scrupulous about the law's letter, the right knock at the right door opens up a fresh barrel of possibilities; and there is always singing somewhere in the streets till three. For those interested in the Dublin of centuries past, the gathering darkness obscures the façade of modernity and reveals the patterns of an ancient settlement.

As prelude to a night tour of old Dublin, a visit to the

crypts of St. Michan's in Church Street sets a properly macabre tone. The church (Monday–Friday 10–5, Saturday 10–1) occupies the site of the first parish church of Oxmanstown, the medieval Norse suburb. Though the present building dates from the seventeenth century, its Victorian restoration has left little of interest, save a battered organ in the vestibule that Handel is thought to have played, the font where Edmund Burke and Swift's sister, Jane, were christened, and the vaults beneath the church. Constructed of magnesium limestone, the vaults afford a kind of preservation to the corpses entombed within. The most famous occupants are the Sheares Brothers, revolutionary partisans executed for their part in the Rising of Ninety-Eight, whose bodies are decently encased in laurelled coffins. But reverence for the departed is not the impression one takes away from the crypts of St. Michan's. For in another vault five bodies, at least four or five hundred years old and wrinkled and brown as leather, lie on display. Among them are the Nun, "with her ear still cocked," as the verger says, "listening to everything that's going on," and the Crusader, in his day an eight-foot giant. The skin of his right hand is partially worn away, since generations of visitors have been offered the dubious pleasure of shaking his hand. Dubliners treat the exhibit with humorous nonchalance, thus pointing up the invisible bonds this city has with ancient patterns. Death, the unavoidable fact, is seldom masked in a city where funerals are terribly important events and otherworlds are often more real than the one of flesh and blood.

The other remain of Oxmanstown is a small chapter

house, which almost no one knows is there, the only relic of
St. Mary's Abbey. It is now the basement to a warehouse in
the blind alley of Meeting House Lane, which runs perpendicular to a small street called Mary's Abbey. The street
level has risen seven feet since the abbey was founded in
1139. In the Chapter House before the Council of Ireland,
Silken Thomas, another of the romantic line of FitzGerald,
Earls of Kildare and uncrowned kings of Ireland, flung
down the Sword of State, which he held as Henry VIII's
Lord Deputy, and declared himself enemy of the English
king. This gesture, for which Silken Thomas was to pay
with his life at Tyburn, set Henry to smother the line of
FitzGerald in its own blood as an example to any who
might think to champion Irish independence against the
power of the Crown. The clanging of the sword in the
ribbed stone vault of the Chapter House sums up much of
Irish history, and Thomas is a model of its aristocratic rebels—dressed dramatically in silk, untactical, outraged by rivals, sensitive only to his own ancestral prerogative, moved
to symbolic defiance by the insistent chanting of his family
bard.

The Dublin of Swift's birth, and of his college days and
first appointments, was still medieval in character. None of
the buildings that now grace Trinity College were known
to Swift when he was a student there. Only in his last years
as Dean, in fact, did the city begin to assume its Palladian
grandeur. What remains of the Dublin of Swift's earliest
years is quickly itemized and can be seen in an evening's
walk: a bit of medieval wall and gate, two cathedrals, both

/   217

altered, the layout and names of a dozen streets, and a pub. From these fragments, shrouded by night, imagination can resurrect the rest.

As you cross the Father Matthew Bridge, leading to Winetavern Street, Christchurch with its squat friendly tower is outlined against the sky on a ridge in the distance. On this ridge, less than a half mile in extent, the medieval walled "city" was built. Christchurch was founded by Strongbow, leader of the Norman invasion of Ireland, who in 1172 handed Dublin over to Henry II and thus introduced English power to this island. The black knight in the nave is believed to be an effigy of the invader. The oldest part of the building is the crypt, the only one of its period in Ireland or England to stretch the length of the church. Though "restored" by Gothic-revival enthusiasts, the building, in outline, has all the warmth and simplicity one expects from the best Romanesque. (Dublin has made Christchurch the locus of its New Year's Eve tradition. As the church's fine peal, which can be heard throughout the city, greets the new year, celebrants dance in giddy circles round the church under the windowed archway that spans St. Michael's Hill, and out as far as O'Connell Bridge. It is a custom Swift must have known.)

As you mount the hill towards the cathedral, the first right takes you into Cook Street, quiet as a grave, and along a section of the medieval wall. (Cook Street leads west to Mullinahack, a corruption of the Irish Muileann a Chaca and best rendered into English, as it is in a medieval rent roll, as Schyte Mill. Mullinahack, in its turn, wound off towards Dunghill Lane. Dubliners should take heart, since the conditions of their streets, however deplorable to them, have obviously improved.) St. Audeon's, the wall's only surviving gate, is nearly as forbidding in our modern night as it would have been hundreds of years ago, if you squint through the gloom for the armed shades who stalk the parapet, guarding the gate from attack and treachery. The thick, irregular wall and its large blackened archway had no decorative, only functional, purposes. Beyond the archway a fragile light shimmers on vague forms as a wide stairway climbs in a curve around the shell of the Norman chancel of St. Audeon's, the tower of which was erected shortly after Swift was born.

On gaining "The High Street," one may embark on a circuit of back alleys dating from earliest times. A few have been widened, the names of others respectably altered, and none is bordered by truly ancient buildings. Yet many are still crooked and twisting, enclosed like caverns by surrounding structures, and narrow as threads. Sadly, the number of interesting streets dwindles yearly before the bulldozer.

Back Lane, which forks south from High Street, is a recent casualty, though its Tailors' Hall survives, built in the opening days of the eighteenth century, one of the few buildings left from Queen Anne's reign, and the single remaining guild hall of the many that flourished in this part of the city. For here in the southwest lived Swift's workingmen—the weavers, the tailors, and other craftsmen—whose rights he defended so vigorously when their trade was being wiped out by England's one-way mercantilist policy. "Burn everything from England but her coal," was the retaliation he advised in his first Irish pamphlet, *A Proposal for the Universal Use of Irish Manufacture*. His most successful incitement to boycott (long before the word had been invented) was over a simpler issue, Wood's Half-Pence. An English ironmonger, Mr. Wood, by bribing the King's mistress, had succeeded in obtaining a royal patent to manufacture copper money for Ireland. Assuming the disguise of a shopkeeper, Swift published *The Drapier's Letters*, their irony thinly veiled by plodding middle-class reasonability, and turned back a threat that would once more have reduced the purses of the Irish public to fatten a private English pocket. The *Letters* were a brilliant political tactic. The people rallied together and refused to accept the coins. When the author was accused of sedition and a price offered for his name, not a Dubliner came forward, nor would any jury convict the printer. Posters of Swift's likeness were hung everywhere in the city, and till his death the Drapier-Dean was a popular hero. "I walk the streets in peace," he wrote, "without being jostled, nor ever without a 1,000 blessings from my friends the vulgar." Whenever he returned after an absence, bells of celebration were rung and bonfires lit in the narrow streets. Though the vulgar leave few memorials, there is none more dignified than the red-brick parapeted Tailors' Hall with its thick pedimented gate.

If you cross St. Nicholas Street and continue east you come to Ship Street Little, which runs along the outside of the medieval wall and brings you to the Ship Street Gate of Dublin Castle. A plaque proclaims that Jonathan Swift was born here at No. 7 Hoey's Court, now demolished.

Whether this was indeed his birthplace is, like much of his subsequent biography, a matter of some dispute. The contradictions may have their origin in Swift's intention of hiding his illegitimacy by confusing the record. Swift's friend, Dr. Delany, best known for his wife's diary, was rector of nearby St. Werburgh's. Castle Street, which runs by St. Werburgh's, brings you before the Castle Yard, once known as the Devil's Half-Acre. Over the gate the bronze figure of Justice holds her scales. In former times rain caused these to unbalance, which was more symbolism than the Castle authorities could bear. They had holes drilled to drain the water. The Castle, open to the public, was splendidly redecorated without and within in the late eighteenth and early nineteenth centuries. Bram Stoker, a nineteenth-century Dubliner and the author of *Dracula*, worked here for ten drear years as a clerk. Only the Record Tower, dating from 1205, retains some of the ominousness this pile once had, though even it has been altered. By the Chapel Royal's north door a carved head of Jonathan Swift, who once was chaplain here, surveys the modifications that fashion and politics have wrought.

Heading north across Lord Edward Street, you come to Exchange Street Upper and then Exchange Street Lower, once the Blind Quay, which crooks sharply to the left around the bottom of the ancient ridge and brings you to the foot of Fishamble Street. Here on April 13, 1742, in the Musick Hall (of which only the doorway remains, now the entrance to Kennan's Ironworks) the *Messiah* was first performed, George Frederick Handel conducting from the harpsichord. The Lord Lieutenant of Ireland had invited the composer to Dublin, a city of happy memories for Handel, and here he decided to unveil his masterpiece. It was one of Dublin's few hours of unalloyed greatness. The choirs of both cathedrals, Christchurch and Swift's St. Patrick's, took part. Ladies were asked to leave their hoops at home and gentlemen their swords to accommodate the crowds. But the Dean of St. Patrick's was not present; he was already under the care of guardians.

The wanderer may now feel it is time to head in the direction of Dublin's oldest drinking establishment, the Brazen Head. On the west side of Bridge Street, a low archway, undistinguished from its surroundings and easily overlooked, leads to a tunnel and then to a small courtyard of broken flagstones which has resounded with arrivals and departures of Viking horsemen, Strongbow's Norman adventurers, Swift's fellow students, and Robert Emmet's gentlemen-revolutionaries. The Brazen Head Hotel was formally chartered in 1688, but an establishment for refreshing the weary wayfarer has existed on this spot probably since the twelfth century. The present building has stood since the time of the charter and gives evidence of its antiquity by the uneven planes of its floors and walls. No signs point the way to the bar, but if one keeps to the right along the dark, narrow corridor, he will reach the heart of the hotel—a close, low-ceilinged room, uncertainly lit and filled with patrons in quietly talkative circles. Only beers of the bottled variety are served, for the Brazen Head has never had a tap installed. At the bar an ancient device with a cumbersome screw-curl dates back to the days when all bottles were stopped with cork. The huddled forms, seen through the veils of smoke, could almost be United Irishmen whispering their nightly intrigues. In the 1790's Wolfe Tone, Lord Edward FitzGerald, and their followers made this their meeting place. Robert Emmet lodged in a room above, and his writing desk is kept by the bar. Another of Ireland's revolutionary idealists, he was hanged for leading the hopeless Insurrection of 1803, the final afterburst of Ninety-Eight. He is best remembered for his "Speech from the Dock," and especially its moving peroration: "Let no man write my epitaph . . ." Towards closing you might find someone who'll give a chorus of "Bold Robert Emmet," the old patriotic ballad, or even recite Emmet's famous last words.

OF THE BUILDINGS neighboring St. Patrick's Cathedral Marsh's Library is the oldest. Sober but thoroughly charming, it was founded as Dublin's first public library in 1702 by the scholarly, circumspect Narcissus Marsh, then Archbishop of Dublin. Even Marsh did not escape Swift's barbs. Earlier, when he had been Provost of Trinity while Swift was a student there, the teen-age satirist had written that Marsh "has the reputation of the most profound and universal learning; this is the general opinion, neither can it be easily disproved. An old rusty iron chest in a banker's shop, strongly locked and wonderfully heavy, is full of gold; this is the general opinion, neither can it be disproved, provided the key be lost." But students were, it seems, a vile lot in those days and, whenever they came to read a book in Marsh's Library, had to be locked up in the cages still on view, lest all the books in the library disappear. Swift himself, during his student years, was "remarkable for nothing else but making a good fire," and received his degree only by special dispensation. As to whether this state of affairs was more a reflection on the student or the college, Swift had no doubt: at Trinity he had received "the education of a dog." (In the *Autobiographical Fragment* on display in Trinity Library he also blames his poor performance on "the ill treatment of his nearest Relations.") Swift, capable of a thousand contradictions and reversals, left instructions in his will that he be buried in St. Patrick's Cathedral next to the Provost-Archbishop. It is hard to know which might unsettle Marsh more: the body that lies near him or the things that are housed in his library. Within you will find Swift's personal collection of books, their margins filled with his deft, cutting pen, and the dark oak, crescented table at which the Dean of St. Patrick's wrote the drafts of *Gulliver's Travels*.

The bite of Swift's prose arrested his career in the Church. *A Tale of a Tub* so outraged Queen Anne's piety that she would never acquiesce to his appointment as bishop; and the image of Gulliver urinating on the private apartments of the Lilliputian queen was a calculated dishonor to Her Majesty's memory. Swift's genius could not submit to the humiliations necessary to bring about further preferment. "Would you rise in the *church*," he questioned,

> Be stupid and dull;
> Be empty of learning, of insolence full;
> Though lewd and immoral, be formal and grave,
> In flattery an *artist*, in fawning a *slave*. . . .

The satiric artist rose no higher than the Deanery of St. Patrick's. The present building, which faces Upper Kevin Street, was built in 1781 on the site of Swift's residence. Behind the house he planted his walled garden; and in the courtyard between the Deanery and St. Patrick's School a mysterious boy would play in the evenings after the other boys had been shooed away. So much did the boy resemble the Dean that the servants believed he was Swift's son by Stella. Others speculate that he was Vanessa's child. And so we are brought back to the maze of those three tangled lives.

St. Patrick's Cathedral, the largest church in Ireland, was given cathedral status by a medieval archbishop who had fallen out with the Dean of Christchurch. At the Reformation the cathedral, like all churches under English administration, became part of the Church of Ireland. Though the granite spire was added soon after Swift died and the medieval fabric has undergone some Victorian restoration, no corner of Dublin belongs more to Swift than St. Patrick's. For those who are fond of sitting awhile amid arches and hymns, Sunday matins (the 11:15 A.M. service) is a glorious treat. In their blue cassocks and billowing surplices, the boys' choir and the vicars-choral, whom Swift took such care to improve, still soar impressively in a manner that would satisfy even the Dean. A display in the north transept includes his enormous black leather chair, no Georgian lady's parlor piece but a fitting seat for the broad, healthy cleric, and the plain, wooden pulpit from which he preached "good, plain stuff" to his flock.

You can almost see him on the cathedral steps as he warmly greets two deformed old creatures half hidden in their tattered shawls. They have names like Stumpa-Nympha, Cancerina, Pullagowna. He buys some apples from one, from the other a trinket, and insisting they have undercharged him presses on them some extra coins, coins that keep them from starvation. As they take their leave with many an old saying, Swift is approached by a weaver from the nearby Coombe, who badly needs a loan to open a small business. He lays his plans before the Dean. For tradesmen like the weaver, Swift has set up a private bank to provide loans at a simple interest rate of .02 per cent. (The profit was used only to increase the bank's lending power.) To each he fiercely encourages diligence and frugality, the Houyhnhnm virtues, but his compassion is broad.

On a lonely afternoon he paces the aisles of his cathedral, a man never at rest, the best walker in Dublin, a powerful figure plotting the tactics and phrases that will help his powerless charges: "In reason all government without the consent of the governed is the very definition of slavery." The sentence was to do its revolutionary work in the American colonies, travel to France, and then back to the land where it was written to make of its author the Irish protopatriot. But the constructive target of political change recedes before the chilling ironies of *A Modest Proposal* and gives way at last to a powerless rage against the gigantic forces of injustice and greed. He ends his days "a slobberer and a show," kept from self-destruction by his servants, running up and down the Deanery stairs for the exercise he always craved.

In the south aisle of the cathedral, opposite the second freestanding pillar, two bronze plaques mark the graves of

Swift and Stella. Subsequent deans have moved Stella's body next to Swift's or away from it, depending on whether they believed in the marriage theory. Even in the tomb propriety must be observed. By the vesting-room door is the world's most famous epitaph, composed by Swift for himself. Yeats translated it from the Latin:

> Swift has sailed into his rest;
> Savage indignation there
> Cannot lacerate his breast.
> Imitate him if you dare,
> World-besotted traveller; he
> Served human liberty.

The "world-besotted traveller" (the phrase is Yeats's touch, not Swift's) should now visit the place Swift wished to be his memorial, St. Patrick's Hospital in Bow Lane West near Heuston Station. The man who died mad left his entire legacy for this foundation, the first modern mental institution in Ireland. He would have approved of the building: dignified, pleasing but plain, of grey stone, designed according to Swift's utterly functional specification that it be constructed in such a way as to allow almost indefinite additions to its rear. The Board Room, which may be visited on application to the secretary, is filled with Swiftiana. In "Verses on the Death of Dr. Swift," the Dean imagined the Dublin gossip his legacy would occasion:

> "O, may we all for Death prepare!
> What has he left? And who's his Heir?"
> "I know no more than what the News is,
> 'Tis all bequeath'd to publick Uses."

/   227

"To publick Use! A perfect Whim!
What had the Publick done for him?"
"Meer Envy, Avarice, and Pride!
He gave it all:—But first he dy'd."
"And had the Dean, in all the Nation,
No worthy Friend, no poor Relation?
So ready to do Strangers good,
Forgetting his own Flesh and Blood?"
. . . .

"He gave the little Wealth he had,
To build a House for Fools and Mad:
And shew'd by one satyric touch,
No Nation wanted it so much. . . ."

The satyric touch cannot hide the compassion of the giver whose hospital was meant to accept all applicants without charge, though its charter has sadly been altered in this respect.

Swift's "friends," the members of his own class, hardly needed his legacy. As he withered, they were beginning to build a new city, an Augustan Dublin whose elegance would rival that of any in Europe. The splendor was built on the backs of the Publick, a dazzling curtain that hid the squalor of ordinary life. Throughout the century the Dublin death rate was nearly three times that of English cities. In 1800 the architectural flowering came to an abrupt halt when the Irish Parliament, "a set of venal prostitutes," as Swift had called them, agreed to dissolve itself and formally unite the Kingdom of Ireland with Britain. Thus, for money and preferments, they destroyed the last vestiges of Irish political freedom. With the Act of Union, Dublin became once again a provincial city, and the Parliament became a bank. But the Palladian buildings have remained—Trinity College, the Parliament-Bank, Leinster House, the Rotunda, the Casino at Marino, the perfect rows of Georgian townhouses—reminders of the time when the outermost wave of the Renaissance at last reached Irish shores and the medieval fortress of Dublin opened up in its Georgian glory with all the proportioned majesty of Handel's *Messiah*.

National Library, Kildare Street, Dublin. Irish Tourist Board.

11.

PORTRAIT OF
JAMES JOYCE
AS A YOUNG MAN

◇◇◇◇◇◇◇◇◇◇◇◇◇◇◇◇◇◇◇◇◇◇◇◇◇◇◇◇◇◇◇◇◇◇◇◇

*Counties Wicklow and
Kildare and Dublin City*

JAMES JOYCE'S BIRTHDAY, February 2, 1882, was to
him a sign of vocation. The feast of Light and Pur-
ification in the Catholic Church, it reminds us today of his
fidelity as an artist to the date's liturgical significance. For
his books are festivals of illumination in which he is the cele-
brant of light and dark. There is no record that he saw the
place of his birth, 41 Brighton Square West, Rathgar, as
particularly significant, though the name of the square and
its triangular shape must have delighted his taste for finding
coincidence and paradox in the ordinary details of life. To
get to the house from Dublin, take the Rathgar bus (No. 15)
from O'Connell Bridge to Brighton Road, then walk along
to the "Square" through a conventional neighborhood that
could just as well be a suburb of Columbus, Ohio. Around
on the left side is the plain two-storey brick house marked

with a plaque commemorating the birthplace of "James Joyce, Poet-Novelist." On the afternoon of our visit the street lamp in front of No. 41 was still lit from the night before. Oddly, this beacon of someone's happily neglected duty seemed a perfect piece of Joycean street furniture, relieving the monotony of the quiet residential pocket. The golden crocuses blooming in the tiny front garden made us think of a little boy who may have knelt up at the bay window in 1884 to look out at his garden, singing the lines of the song remembered on the first page of *A Portrait of the Artist as a Young Man: "O, the wild rose blossoms/On the little green place.* He sang that song. That was his song."

When Joyce was five years old the family moved to Bray, a seaside town thirteen miles south of Dublin. For John Joyce the purpose of the move was to get away from his wife's relatives. The father of the artist would never bow before the shrine to the sacred Irish family, not his wife's or his own. His irreverence towards the keepers of the other national altars—to the Church and the Union—sparked his oldest son's imagination as powerfully as the sound of the waves which in winter raged over the sea wall, flooding the walk in front of the house at No. 1 Martello Terrace. All the childhood memories of home in Book I of *A Portrait of the Artist* focus on this house next to the Baths and the sea, at the bottom of the Esplanade leading towards Bray Head. From the Dublin-Wicklow road which runs through Bray the place is easily found by turning at the sign that points to the seafront beside the Royal Starlight Hotel and following the road straight, under the railroad arch, past the Harbour

Inn, to the first row of seven houses perpendicular to the Irish Sea.

At times the beloved home at Bray was wilder than the sea beside it. In the famous Christmas dinner scene, Joyce re-creates his experience of the political and religious quarrel over Parnell that actually took place in December, 1891, two months after the death of "The Chief." The assembled anticlericals, nationalists, Parnellites, and loyal Catholics argued with such volume that they were heard by the Vances three doors down at No. 4 Martello Terrace. How confused the Protestant family of Eileen of the "long thin cool white hands" must have been to have heard the scream of "God and religion before the world!" answered by roars of "No God for Ireland!" and "Away with God!" echoing down the sidewalk from this Catholic household bursting with babies and exploding over Parnellism. The place may have a tired look to today's visitor, but in 1891 it figured in a psychic explosion within a little boy that ultimately contributed to his breaking up the establishment of modern English prose.

The violent political arguments about Kitty O'Shea and Charles Stewart Parnell, stories told by a dramatic father, the music around the piano, with James's younger brother Stanislaus singing "Finnegan's Wake," the children's plays based on Bible tales directed by James, who acted the part of Satan—such experiences did little to prepare a boy for the atmosphere of Clongowes Wood College in County Kildare, the Jesuit boarding school in which Joyce was enrolled in the fall of 1888. The beautiful drive from Bray to Clongowes crosses Synge's Wicklow Mountains and descends into the sleepy countryside around Sallins and Clane. (Route: Bray to Enniskerry; west from Enniskerry to L.94; south on L.94 to Sally Gap; northwest on 161 to T.42; south to Blessington; northwest on 181 to Naas; north on 25 to Clane.) A mile and a half beyond Clane the high, unmarked gates of Clongowes open upon a long tree-lined avenue leading to the main building, a medieval castle restored in the eighteenth century. Clongowes Wood is a place set apart from the workaday world. If the comfortable look of the house at Bray suggested an easy, somewhat sloppy life style, essentially Irish and suited to children, the appearance of the well-kept demesne at Clongowes Wood bespeaks a way of life combining a gentleman's code of order and self-sufficiency with a monastic discipline of obedience and loneliness. Visitors are welcome to see the various places mentioned in *A Portrait of the Artist*. A phone call in advance of arrival helps insure that someone will be available to point them out (telephone: 045-68202).

The castle itself, destroyed by British troops in 1641, purchased by the Jesuits in 1813, has a historical background that would have stirred the mind of a young boy already obsessed with the Parnell story and its theme of the heroic patriot destroyed by the mob. In 1794, the patriot Hamilton Rowan escaped to the castle, having been convicted of sedition. On his trail were British soldiers who shot at him through the front doors. Rowan threw his hat out the window of what is now a long reception room onto the narrow moat to make his pursuers think he had fled across the fields. His decoy successful, he was able to hide in the tower and later escape to France. As Stephen Dedalus walks across the landing above the entrance hall on his way to the Rector's Office, he remembers this story; and years later Joyce was to give the main character in his play *Exiles* the name Richard Rowan. But more significant is Joyce's adoption of the hero's style into his own works and life. Rowan's display of cunning in the face of bullies and his devotion in service to a revolutionary ideal become a theme played with variations in *Ulysses* and the stance of Joyce's later life. Pursued by debts, blindness, and family sorrow, he went resourcefully and faithfully about the artist's business.

It is important to realize that *A Portrait of the Artist* is a fictional autobiography and that Stephen Dedalus is a fictional character whose experiences and personality differ in many respects from those of his creator. Joyce adjusted well to Clongowes, but he makes Stephen unhappy here. He changes the details of his own experiences to suit his purpose, which is to render the quality of an extremely imaginative child's sensibility. The story of Stephen's artistic unfolding is in every part the story of his sense of place.

In the playroom, which Joyce would have known, now equipped with pool tables on the ground floor of a wing connected to the castle, Stephen sits "in a corner of the playroom pretending to watch a game of dominos" and listening for the "song of the gas," his words for the noise made by the burning gaslamps out in the corridor.

The college chapel distracts him from the words of the prescribed prayers led by the prefect and inspires his intense contemplation of images of earthly beauty, the process most basic to the artistic experience. Today the distractions have been removed or changed. The marbles that were for him "the colour the sea was at night" are now the color of pine. The students attend a new chapel built in 1907 and filled with brilliant stained-glass windows by Evie Hone and Michael Healy. The chapel used in Joyce's day is still open to parishioners from Clane and Sallins, though they would not like to be called peasants, however holy, having moved since then from thatched cottages to stuccoed bungalows.

One look around the dormitory on the third floor, and it is no wonder that a small boy would curl himself into a haunted sleep. No wonder, either, that the prayers offered up from his hammock-shaped mattress acknowledged the dormitory as the dominion of demons and death. The institutional rigor of the rows of beds brings to mind the texture of punishment and the ordeal of inmates. Stephen dreams of "ghosts of murderers" serving an eternal sentence along the dark corridor outside his curtained cell. Undoubtedly, one of the stories from Clongowes' past with which he was familiar helped to stir his terror. He had heard that the ghost of Marshal Browne, whose family had sold the castle to the Jesuits, was said to have been seen on the landing above the entrance hall the same night that he had been killed at the Battle of Prague in 1757, and that the former owner still haunted the premises, believing, even in death, that a man's castle is his home. This association, coupled with the friendlessness of the surroundings and his own wide-awake imagination, induces an encounter with the dark that both terrifies and thrills him. "O how cold and strange it was to think of that!" This scrutiny of what is strange links his penetration of the dark in the dormitory with his preceding meditation on smell in the chapel. Both experiences show the child artist going about the pleasure and the terror of the artist's business in the properly suggestive places of his masters' house.

Similarly, the next morning, on the way to the infirmary, he passes the swimming bath, the oldest indoor heated pool in Ireland, still in use. Ignoring the voice of the martinet cracking, "Quick march! Hayfoot! Strawfoot!" he attends secretly to the sensations of place: "As he passed the door he remembered with a vague fear the warm turfcoloured bog-water, the warm moist air, the noise of plunges, the smell of the towels." Today the infirmary, the oldest part of the school, is still as gloomy as the fantasy of death with which Stephen responds to its atmosphere.

Cruelty is natural behavior for the man in league with monotony, and the classroom, often enough, the stage for his works and pomps. Father Dolan, the prefect of studies who beats Stephen for having broken his glasses, is the first of Joyce's one-eyed strong men, a clerical Cyclops, personifying monotony. Practically all the classrooms used in Joyce's time have been pulled down to make way for newer buildings. The one exception is the present junior boys' playroom, which was formerly divided by a folding partition and used as classrooms for first and second year students. The partition was folded back each morning and evening when the whole area was used as a study hall for the small boys.

The refectory where Stephen sits worrying over how to save his skin and pride from the prefect's might on the morrow has been converted, appropriately, into a theatre. To save himself, he decides to play a heroic role like the great men of history whose courage had brought them to immortality in the pages of Peter Parley's *Tales About Greece and Rome.* Ulysses was one of the heroes whose adventures are told in this old Clongowes textbook. Leaving the refectory, he goes up the stairs to the right and enters the Serpentine Gallery, the "low dark narrow corridor that led to the castle," its walls hung with framed faces from the Jesuit past. At the end of the corridor—in the eyes of the adult-sized visitor, a wide, pastel-colored passageway—"he came out on the landing above the entrance hall" and walked to the door at the far end which still conceals the Rector's Office, but is barred to the casual visitor.

After the interview Stephen runs outside to the playing fields, vast and green, with the same paths and tracks arcing through them, though the sound of bouncing basketballs has been added to that of cricket bats. The small moat, or ha-ha, on which Hamilton Rowan threw his hat is still there. Through a gate at the side of the castle and down the end of a path are the woods with the same little stone altar where Stephen acts as boatbearer in this "strange and holy place." The Corpus Christi procession through the woods to the tiny pedestal of an altar is enacted yet. This sanctuary of birds and sunbeams on green shade and winding paths arched high with trees holds an atmosphere at once holy and sensuous that suggests the attraction which the Catholic experience held for both Stephen and Joyce. For here, love of the physical world and love of God could be compatible.

John Joyce withdrew his son from Clongowes Wood sometime during the fall semester of 1891 as the cost of making him a gentleman was too high for the boozing father of a growing brood of children. To this day the last tuition bill has never been paid. He sold the house in Bray and moved his family to "Leoville," No. 23 Carysfort Avenue, Blackrock, nine miles closer to Dublin. (Take the No. 5, 6, 7, or 8 bus from the city center.)

The house in which Stephen pores over *The Count of Monte Cristo* in the first part of Book II and where Joyce, according to Stanislaus, started his first novel in collaboration with the boy next door is privately owned, but the neighborhood Joyce played in for eighteen months is little changed, there for anyone to explore. Below Idrone Terrace, a seaside promenade and charming residential retreat, Stephen and his friends fought suburban gang wars on "the shaggy weedgrown rocks." Still lovely, too, is Blackrock Park, on the right side of Rock Road going towards the city. Here Stephen runs track and feels the first rushes of mistrust towards Uncle Charles, his old trainer. Blackrock, situated between Bray and Dublin, is the place where he suffers "so many slight shocks to his boyish conception of the world"; it occupies a similar place on the psychological map of Stephen's life as on the geographical map. Closer to the city of his adolescence and young manhood than to Bray, the resort of his childhood, it is, in fact, neither one place nor the other, a space in-between for a time in-between.

"THE SUDDEN FLIGHT from the comfort and revery of Blackrock, the passage through the gloomy foggy city," and the arrival at No. 14 Fitzgibbon Street, the first of the

Joyces' many Dublin addresses, now a vacant lot east of Mountjoy Square, bring Stephen to the subject and setting of all Joyce's books—Dublin City. For Joyce, the significant world and the modern artist's territory are both to be found in metropolis. Stephen's first experiences of the flesh coincide with his discovery of the city. But at the novel's end, though he has spent much time in exploration, he is an unhappy lover and an impotent artist because, unlike Joyce, he sees neither the sexual mystery nor the city's diverse and commonplace actuality with compassion. To follow his route by walking, the dominant form of action in *A Portrait of the Artist* and *Ulysses*, is to get a thorough slow-motion look at the world he did and did not see as an abstracted apprentice in the home of the Muse.

At first, Stephen strikes out hesitantly into the urban wilderness: "Dublin was a new and complex sensation. . . . In the beginning he contented himself with circling timidly round the neighbouring square or, at most, going half way down one of the side streets." The neighboring square is Mountjoy Square, designed for Luke Gardiner, Lord Mountjoy, banker, landlord, and leader of the Crown's soldiers against the rebels of 1798. It is now undergoing a slow restoration, but along its south and west sides can still be seen the tenement world that Joyce saw and that Sean O'Casey, who lived in No. 35, described as "Hilljoy Square" in *The Shadow of a Gunman*.

Following Gardiner Street South, one of Stephen's regular routes—"When he had made a skeleton map of the city in his mind he followed boldly one of its central lines until he reached the customhouse"—calls for an act of imaginative architectural restoration. Laid out in 1787, it was then, along with Henrietta, Dominick, North Great George's and Eccles streets, one of the most fashionable streets north of the Liffey, affording a downhill view of the Custom House. But after the Irish Parliament was dissolved by the Act of Union, the disestablished lords turned from politics to real estate, selling their northside mansions for quick cash or converting them into multiple dwellings and retiring to London as absentee slumlords. Most of the disease-ridden tenements they milked for a century in Gardiner Street have been replaced with low-income public housing.

Port cities the world over have the knack of making men out of little boys. In front of the Custom House, focus of Dublin's foreign commerce, Stephen begins to sense the narrowness of his horizons and a world beyond Ireland:

He passed unchallenged among the docks and along the quays. . . . The vastness and strangeness of the life suggested to him by the bales of merchandise stocked along the walls or swung aloft out of the holds of steamers wakened again in him the unrest which had sent him wandering in the evening from garden to garden in search of Mercedes. And amid this new bustling life . . . a vague dissatisfaction grew up within him as he looked on the quays and on the river. . . .

Today there is little bustle. The anchored ladies *Grania, Gwendolyn,* and *Patricia*—the boats that transport Guinness stout—sometimes grace the quiet quays, tokens of Dublin's halfhearted trade with the rest of the world. The strong character of the Custom House can best be appreciated from the south quay across Butt Bridge. "Commerce," the statue atop its dome, has never looked so sensual. Designed by James Gandon in 1781 as the headquarters of key departments of British rule, seized and burned by the I.R.A. in 1921 as its way of crippling that rule, the building is one of Dublin's grandest, its history telling the twin stories of the power of the empire and the retaliation of the colonized.

From the North Wall, a long walk the length of Sheriff Street, through O'Casey's dockside territory, leads via Buckingham Street, Summerhill Parade, and North Circular Road to North Richmond Street, home of some minor *Ulysses* characters and setting for several *Dubliners* stories. "Araby" begins in a tone that matches what the visitor feels on every street of Dublin Northeast:

North Richmond Street, being blind, was a quiet street except at the hour when the Christian Brothers' School set the boys free. An uninhabited house of two storeys stood at the blind end, detached from its neighbours in a square ground. The other houses of the street, conscious of decent lives within them, gazed at one another with brown imperturbable faces.

The old Christian Brothers' School, which Joyce attended for a short time, has been replaced by a new building, and No. 17, the former home of the twelve Joyces during part of the time Joyce attended Belvedere College, has recently had its dead-brown face emboldened by a few coats of fire-engine red, but the street still suggests the same "scrupulous meanness" that Joyce defined as the appropriate style for his stories about the city's paralyzed soul.

One and a half blocks west of Mountjoy Square at No. 6 Great Denmark Street is Belvedere College, where the traditional Jesuit education that Joyce received from 1893 to 1898 winds on, unaffected by changes in the school's physical facilities. Old Boys continue to register their middle- and upper-class sons at birth, anxious to deliver them from National Schools and the Christian Brothers, nicknamed the "Paddy Stinks and Mickey Muds" of Irish education by Simon Dedalus. The new boys, however, will never know the gymnasium-theatre where Stephen acts in the Whitsuntide play, it having been demolished in 1971; and the chapel where he cowers before the hell-fires of the Retreat sermons has been converted into the science department. Gone, too, are the days when the Fathers recoiled at the mention of their most famous Old Boy. On holidays and during after-school hours, they receive his readers graciously, softened perhaps by his reputation as the greatest novelist of the century and by his public praise of their educational methods. "From them," Joyce said, "I have learnt to arrange things in such a way that they become easy to survey and to judge." He acknowledged, though they for a long time would not admit, the profound effect of his fourteen years among the Jesuits: "You allude to me as a Catholic . . . now you ought to allude to me, for the sake of precision and to get the correct contour on me, you ought to allude to me as a Jesuit."

The mansion, built in 1775 as a rural retreat from the central city, boasts one of the finest interiors of all the Georgian houses left in Dublin. Ascending the grand staircase, the visitor passes exquisite plasterwork along its walls and ceilings. On the floor above are Belvedere's three most beautiful rooms, their elaborate ceilings decorated in plaster by Michael Stapleton and named for Venus, Diana, and

Apollo. Today the community rooms of the Jesuit staff, in Joyce's time they were used as classrooms, the settings in which he studied Charles Lamb's *Adventures of Ulysses*, submitted a composition about Ulysses entitled "My Favourite Hero," and became so fascinated by Belvedere's associations with carnal love that he planned to write a book about them. Mary, Countess of Belvedere, wife of Robert, first Earl of Rochfort, was convicted of having committed adultery with her husband's brother and imprisoned for thirty years on the cuckolded husband's farm in Westmeath, where she never ceased protesting her innocence. Here, in the late afternoon dusk, Stephen savors the Latin words of the Little Office of the Blessed Virgin, wondering how the same person can find the Marian liturgy so alluring and relish his trips to the brothels north of the Custom House. Surely a boy so responsive to the female body, who "chronicled with patience" everything he saw, would have noticed and wondered that on the ceiling of the Venus Room Venus had been hidden beneath a floral design while on the other two ceilings Diana and Apollo remained on view in bold painted relief.

What the Jesuits had desecrated and destroyed, the artist would adore and re-create with all the resources of his jesuitical imagination. The seagirl in *A Portrait of the Artist*, Gretta Conroy in "The Dead," Molly Bloom in *Ulysses*, and Anna Livia Plurabelle in *Finnegans Wake* are the mythical figures he uses to restore the goddess of love to the center of things. In *Ulysses*, when Father Conmee muses about Belvedere and its sexual associations, "he smiled at smiling noble faces in a beeswaxed drawingroom, ceiled with full fruit clusters." The priest's recollection of one of Stapleton's ceilings in the context of his secret revery about *ejaculatio seminis inter vas naturale mulieris* suggests a relationship between the concealed Venus and Joyce's fictional women. A collection of neopagan goddesses who cluster on the elaborate ceiling of his imagination, they have been fashioned as if from a great jesuitical distance with mystical awe and dazzling word magic, the products of his Irish-Catholic experience and his own sexual fantasies. Like Belvedere's first priestly owners who tampered with the image of Venus out of idealistic celibacy, Joyce distorts real women in the process of worshipping and projecting idealized images of the passionate goddess veiled from him in youth.

In Upper Gardiner Street, a block and a half east of Belvedere and north of Mountjoy Square, is the Jesuit Church of St. Francis Xavier where the Joyces were parishioners and where the lights still fall, as they do in the *Dubliners* story "Grace," "on dark mottled pillars of green marble and on lugubrious canvases." Stanislaus remembers that his brother and mother often went together to morning Mass here; James would stay on to pray after the service, and his mother would whisper to him that breakfast was ready at home. A few years later he acknowledged the Catholic Mass as a rich metaphor of his art, remarking to Stanislaus:

Don't you think there is a certain resemblance between the mystery of the Mass and what I am trying to do? I mean that I am trying . . . to give people some kind of intellectual pleasure or spiritual enjoyment by converting the bread of everyday life into something that has a permanent artistic life of its own . . . for

/ 245

their mental, moral, and spiritual uplift. . . . It is my idea of the significance of trivial things that I want to give the two or three unfortunate wretches who may eventually read me.

A few changes have been made in the Mass since the days of Joyce's liturgical passion, but Gregorian Chant can still be heard at High Mass from the Palestrina Choir of the Pro-Cathedral in Marlborough Street, the church of the brow-beating Mrs. Mooney in the *Dubliners* story, "A Boarding House."

The residence of the Jesuit Provincial stands next door to the Church of St. Francis Xavier. Passing it on his way home to Drumcondra, Stephen realizes "he would never swing the thurible before the tabernacle as priest." Farther north on Lower Drumcondra Road, past Clonliffe Road where he had been beaten up by schoolmates for preferring Byron to Tennyson, the future artificer of earthy Celtic goddesses tries to free his soul from the mystical spell of his beloved Virgin:

He crossed the bridge over the stream of the Tolka and turned his eyes coldly for an instant towards the faded blue shrine of the Blessed Virgin which stood fowlwise on a pole in the middle of a hamshaped encampment of poor cottages.

A new stone statue has replaced the one Joyce knew when he lived a block away in one of the poor cottages of Mill Lane.

Bull Island or the North Bull on Dublin Bay is the setting for Book IV's apocalyptic climax, Stephen's vision of the seagirl. (Take the No. 30 bus from Marlborough Street in the city center to Clontarf Road and Dollymount.) The island is unique as a lonely bird sanctuary within the city limits where in the course of an afternoon you can spot widgeon, teal, pintail, geese, shoveler, shelduck, oyster catcher, black-tailed godwit, plover, dunlin, and knot. The wooden bridge to the Bull, on which Stephen passes a squad of Christian Brothers, is now open to automobile traffic, but the rest of the island remains almost exactly as he describes it.

Beyond the bridge is the Bull Wall, the northern breakwater of Dublin harbor, "the spine of rocks that pointed against the river's mouth" from where one can look back towards "the dim fabric of the city . . . prone in haze." Ships still follow "the course of the slowflowing Liffey," past the two lighthouses and northwards to Howth, shaped like a recumbent man sprawled across the water. From the waves on the shore and the ships in the distance and the thousands of birds swooping out of the drifting clouds, landing and feeding on the sand and water, come sensations of unceasing motion and spiralling flight and descent, which, in the novel, culminate in Stephen's "ecstasy of flight." Walking at low tide over the wet strand, experiencing the moods of the place—its austerity and loneliness and sudden radiances—you can understand its perfect harmony with the artistic vocation Stephen accepts here. It is significant that he beholds the seagirl, the image of that vocation, alone, on an island, his back to the city: this setting contains the seeds both of his failure as a young artist and of his potential growth. Joyce knew the artist's need for isolation, but he knew, too, how essential it is for a man who would extend the frontiers of art and his own humanity to come down out of the clouds and make his way back into the city and the lives of ordinary men.

To walk the routes taken by Stephen in Book V is to cover several miles through contrasting sections of the city, which Joyce as a university student saw on his daily walks or tram rides from home on the run-down northside to the University in the fashionable southeast. Begin in the lane behind No. 8 Inverness Road, Fairview, called "Royal Terrace" when Joyce lived there, "Royal Terrors, Fearview" in *Finnegans Wake*, the starting point of Stephen's daily "morning walk across the city." Fairview's sewage system has not improved over the years, the lane's array of refuse slowing the visitor's steps as it once opposed the flight of Stephen's spirit. His need to rise above his dispirited environment becomes understandable as you approach the city center via North Strand Road, passing at the junction of Killarney, Seville, and Amiens streets the Five Lamps, an elaborate Victorian street light where O'Casey used to meet his friends in the evening.

In the city south of the Liffey, Stephen feels like an outsider at the world's feast. Indeed, Southsiders regarded Joyce as a "man of another town," and today the river, a smelly class barrier at low tide, still separates the middle class of the southside suburbs from the northside workingmen. Last cleaned for the Eucharistic Congress in 1932, the Liffey is expected to be cleaned again for the Second Coming.

At the top of Grafton Street Stephen passes under the triumphal arch and enters the place he calls "my Green" in

Stephen Hero. In *A Portrait of the Artist* it reminds him of the buried past of "the gallant venal city":

. . . the trees in Stephen's Green were fragrant of rain and the rainsodden earth gave forth its mortal odour. . . .

A common since the twelfth century, the Green has been used variously as a grazing place for the Lord Mayor's cattle and sheep, a military exercise ground, a source of firewood for Dubliners, the place of public executions. Because Dubliners relax here at all hours and in most seasons, Stephen's Green vibrates with the city's perpetual holiday rhythm. Children, beggars, students, lady shoppers stroll past neat lawns, feed the swans, and sit on benches along paths winding over bridges and through secluded corridors of willows. They also seek out the privacy of the platform bearing the Yeats memorial sculpted by Henry Moore. On the first sunny spring day, offices empty their pale-faced captives onto the Green; shirt-sleeved businessmen sprawl beside star-shaped flower beds, thumbing their noses at the wintry gods of profit and duty. Lovers relax, as Samuel Beckett describes them in *Eh, Joe,* "in the early days of our idyll. When we sat watching the ducks . . . holding hands, exchanging vows."

Along Stephen's Green South visitors are welcome to explore the buildings of University College, which John Henry Newman founded as the Catholic University in 1853. Nos. 85 and 86 are used today as the Student Union. (Consult its bulletin boards for news of concerts and plays often not listed in *The Evening Press* and *The Evening Herald.*) In Clanwilliam House (No. 85) you can see the physics theatre where Stephen discusses the nature of beauty with Father Darlington and Joyce read "Drama and Life," a paper in defense of Ibsen, before the Literary and Historical Society founded by Newman and still in existence today. Here, too, are the same corridors and wide staircases where Stephen and his fellow students gather to argue about women's rights and universal peace. No. 86 was built for "Burn Chapel" Whaley, a notorious priest-hunter during penal times and father of the rake "Buck" Whaley of the Hell-Fire Club after whom Oliver St. John Gogarty is named "Buck" Mulligan in *Ulysses*. Cardinal Newman, who often preached in the church next door, envisioned intellectual excellence as the only standard for an institution of higher education, but his idealism did not prevail. By the time Joyce was an undergraduate, a young writer aspiring to the quality of the first rector's "silver-veined prose," the university was little more than a degree factory.

Leaving Newman House, Stephen and Lynch follow a straight line from Stephen's Green South along Lower Leeson Street to the Grand Canal. Their walk through the southeast section covers a few miles of the finest Georgian townscapes, a fitting route for the last part of Book V, a discourse on the qualities of universal beauty.

Detours from Stephen's route are also worth your time. Turn left off Lower Leeson Street, for instance, into Upper Pembroke Street and walk down to Fitzwilliam Square, the jewel of Georgian Dublin. (You will pass the Focus Theatre at No. 6 Pembroke Place, one of Dublin's repertory and experimental companies.) As you return along Fitzwilliam Square East to Leeson Street, you walk towards the vista of the Dublin mountains which closes the southern end of the street. Fitzwilliam Street, stretching north to Merrion Square and south to Leeson Street, was once the longest Georgian street in Dublin before the government's Electricity Supply Board demolished the mansions between Baggot and Upper Mount streets in 1965. If you are in this area on weekends, you can enjoy the open-air "Dandelion Market."

The eighteenth-century Grand Canal flows west to the River Shannon, carrying tourists on British cruising craft as it once moved goods and travellers across the midland bogs. The original pattern of canal lined with towpaths, trees, and Georgian mansions on either side has been altered somewhat by the construction of a few modern office buildings, but the trees continue in their traditional role of sheltering lovers: "The trees along the canal are more sinned against then sinning."

High up on his ladder of abstraction, Stephen regards the neighborhood below as a distraction:

They had reached the canal bridge and, turning from their course, went on by the trees. A crude grey light, mirrored in the sluggish water, and a smell of wet branches over their heads seemed to war against the course of Stephen's thought.

Other literary characters, fictional and real, older and less anxious for definitions than Stephen, have sought peace beside these sluggish waters. Belacqua Shuah, hero of Beckett's only short-story collection, *More Pricks Than Kicks* (his *Dubliners*, once banned from Dublin bookstores), finds rest at Leeson Street Bridge across the street from the fictional Red Swan Hotel of Flann O'Brien's *At Swim-Two-Birds* where Mr. Dermot Trellis lives and creates John Furriskey "by the banks of the Grand Canal." Walking east of the bridge, you can imagine any one of the houses along the canal as the place in Beckett's *Krapp's Last Tape* where Mr. Krapp's mother lay dying as he sat on a canal bench watching and waiting for the blinds to fall for the last time. Near the canal locks at Baggot Street Bridge where Patrick Kavanagh often sat, a stone bench has been erected by his friends in accordance with the request he made in his poem "Lines Written On A Seat On The Grand Canal, Dublin":

> O commemorate me where there is water,
> Canal water preferably, so stilly
> Greeny at the heart of summer.
> O commemorate me with no hero-courageous
> Tomb—just a canal-bank seat for the passer-by.

Zealots who have crossed all the seedy and lovely paths of Stephen Dedalus and the young Joyce should now cross Baggot Street Bridge into Ballsbridge, formerly called Pembroke township, and walk along Pembroke Road where Stephen and Cranly amble and hear the servant girl singing "Rosie O'Grady" in the kitchen of one of the mansions, as they argue about the conflicting demands of truth and love:

They had walked on towards the township of Pembroke and now, as they went on slowly along the avenues, the trees and the scattered lights in the villas soothed their minds. The air of wealth and repose diffused about them seemed to comfort their neediness.

University students now rent many of the flats in this area, but the air of repose remains, especially just past the American Embassy in the meticulously landscaped Herbert Park, better loved than Stephen's Green by many Dubliners.

For a more interesting route than the one Stephen and Lynch follow—Lower Mount Street to Merrion Square and the National Library—return to the canal walk, and one block east of Baggot Street Bridge turn left at Huband Bridge, passing Stephen's Church and approaching Merrion Square from Upper Mount Street. At the corner where the street crosses Fitzwilliam Street, stop to take in the vistas of Mount Street closed at the end by the little church so similar to St. George's near Eccles Street, and of Merrion Square bordered on four sides by beautifully preserved Georgian houses. The width of Upper Mount Street is related to the height of its buildings, and the church at the top of it is sited purposely to form part of the view. The crescented fanlights over the doors and the wrought-iron balconies at the ground floor windows help create the street's unity. Merrion Square and environs show why, of the "three beautiful sisters of eighteenth-century architecture in these islands," in the words of Frank O'Connor, Dublin is usually preferred to Edinburgh and Bath. Within this formal system of architecture and street planning can be seen the dominant qualities of tasteful elegance and the symmetrical arrangement of space and line which express so clearly the philosophical tone of the Age of Reason.

The content of Stephen's aesthetic philosophy and the cold formal style in which he discourses to Lynch harmonize perfectly with the neighborhoods they walk through. But he is so wrapped up in his pedantic monologue that he does not point out along Merrion Square East and South the

/ 253

obvious exemplifications of Saint Thomas's three qualities of universal beauty: wholeness, harmony, and radiance. Joyce, at Stephen's age, would have been familiar with the names of some of the past, present, and future residents of Merrion Square South: in No. 58 lived Daniel O'Connell, to whom Joyce was said to be related on his paternal grandfather's side; Joseph Sheridan Le Fanu, author of horror stories, died in No. 70 of a nightmare; as of 1922, William Butler Yeats occupied No. 82; in No. 84, Plunkett House, George Russell (Æ) worked as editor of the *Irish Homestead*, encouraging and publishing young unknown writers including Joyce and later Frank O'Connor.

Merrion Square, now a public square, was once owned by the Catholic Archbishop and closed to the public, a situation often protested by Protestants and Catholics in the delightful letters' column of the *Irish Times*. The site was bought by a predecessor for the hideous purpose of building a cathedral there, which would certainly make visible the hand-and-glove relationship of Christ and Caesar referred to in Joyce's poem "Gas From A Burner." For across the street on the far side of Merrion Square West is Leinster House, the seat of the Irish government. Built in 1745 for the Duke of Leinster, the first of the great eighteenth-century houses to be built in the then unfashionable southern part of the city, it has two formal fronts and is said to be the model for the White House in Washington, D.C. There is a public tour on Fridays and the visitors' gallery is open at 3 P.M. during sometimes circuslike sessions of the Dail (the Irish Parliament). Ask to be admitted at the Kildare Street entrance.

Next to Leinster House is the National Gallery, where Mrs. "Dante" Hearn Conway, young Joyce's governess, used to take him to see an apocalyptic picture entitled *The Last Day*. While growing up in Dublin, George Bernard Shaw, whose statue stands outside the gallery, spent a good number of his school days playing hookey here, planning to become a painter. Schoolboys still wander through, stopping to hear the attendants' rare accounts of the people in the paintings and the stories connected with them. Their version of Ireland's literary and political history, along with the comments of the school children, yields a rich dose of oral history, giving a sense of how modern Dubliners relate to their inherited mythologies. Most of the gods are here in oil or water color: Yeats, Synge, O'Casey, James Stephens, Lady Gregory, George Russell, Edward Martyn, George Moore, Douglas Hyde, Countess Markievicz, Maud Gonne, Tom Moore, William Allingham, William Carleton, Edmund Burke, Daniel O'Connell, Parnell, and James Joyce. An attractive restaurant-with-bar is open when the gallery is: Monday–Wednesday 10–6, Thursday 10–9, Friday–Saturday 10–6, Sunday 2–5.

A few steps down the block and across the street from the National Gallery is No. 1 Merrion Square North, former home of the Wildes of Dublin: Sir William Wilde, surgeon and writer, Lady Wilde, who wrote patriotic protest poetry for *The Nation* under the name of "Speranza," and their son, Oscar, born in 1854 around the corner in No. 21 Westland Row and raised in this corner house, a citadel of radical chic in Victorian Dublin.

While Joyce was at the University, the literary elite gathered one and a half blocks south in the home of George Moore at No. 4 Ely Place. It is worth backtracking on the way to the National Library to see the orderly mansions in this cul-de-sac and those of Hume Street, which links Ely Place with the trees of Stephen's Green. In *Hail And Farewell*, Moore describes the personalities of the Literary Revival who soireed in Ely Place. One of them was Oliver St. John Gogarty, then a student at Trinity College; his flicking tongue tickled the literati and won him invitations to their parties. But his rude unkempt friend Joyce, from the seedy northside, never became a cult among the swanks. "Why, he's nothing but a beggar," said Moore.

At the National Library (Monday–Friday 10–10, Saturday 10–1) in Kildare Street, Stephen and Lynch wind up their walk around southeast Dublin, joining some students "sheltering under the arcade of the library." The Library and the National Museum across the quadrangle are matching buildings (1885–90) by Thomas Deane. Ascending the library's graceful marble staircase past the stained glass windows depicting Michelangelo and Da Vinci, Joycean pilgrims may recognize the name of the man commemorated on the bronze plaque at the top of the stairs, Thomas Lyster, who presided over the Reading Room during Joyce's student years and was immortalized in the Scylla and Charybdis episode of *Ulysses* as the urbane, purring, Quaker librarian. Joyce used the Reading Room regularly from 1894 to 1904, sitting up front on the right-hand side near the entrance, writing verse on call slips, going through Skeats' *Etymological Dictionary* and works of continental literature, especially Dante and Ibsen. In the streets and houses of

Dublin he found the material for all his books; in the library he studied the language with which he would change the bread of the living city into the living body of art. In his own life with Nora Barnacle and among ordinary men and women he would experience the compassion of which Stephen Dedalus at the end of *A Portrait of the Artist* knows so little:

26 *April*: Mother is putting my new secondhand clothes in order. She prays now, she says, that I may learn in my own life and away from home and friends what the heart is and what it feels.

A good way to end your walk around the Dublin of Dedalus and the young Joyce is to spend some time in this Reading Room, an extremely comfortable and friendly place with its warm mahogany woodwork. You obtain a reader's ticket by showing your passport. A look at the columns of the *Irish Times* for June 14, 15, and 16, 1954, describing Dublin's first slap-happy celebration of Bloomsday, "the major literary feast day of the twentieth century," provides a comic introduction to the itinerary of the next chapter and to the spirit of the city that eludes Stephen and both depresses and delights the older James Joyce, Dubliner in exile.

River Liffey, Dublin. Irish Tourist Board

12.

THE WANDERINGS OF ULYSSES

◇◇◇

Dublin City

More than any other work of fiction, . . . *Ulysses* creates
the illusion of a living social organism. We see it only for
twenty hours, yet we know its past as well as its present.
We possess Dublin, seen, heard, smelt and felt, brooded
over, imagined, remembered.

EDMUND WILSON, AXEL'S CASTLE

E PISODE 1: Telemachus
8 A.M.

Originally one of fifteen towers built between Bray and
Dublin to ward off an invasion of the British colony during
the Napoleonic wars, the Martello Tower at Sandycove is
today Dublin's only official monument to the memory of
Ireland's most famous writer. (Take the No. 8 bus from
Eden Quay to Sandycove Avenue East.) Modelled on a de-
fensive fortress the British had first encountered in Mortella
Bay, Corsica, in 1794, it served as Joyce's sleeping quarters

/ 259

upon the invitation of its lessee, Oliver St. John Gogarty, for one week in September, 1904, a month before Joyce left Ireland for good. When he returns through the pages of *Ulysses* under the inspiration of the myth Homer told in *The Odyssey*, he begins his epic at the Tower and thus introduces the consonance of place and perception that he sustains throughout eighteen episodes. Nine miles south of Dublin, the Tower suits his theme of the young artist's estrangement from the city, paralleling Telemachus' separation from his patrimony in *The Odyssey*. A symbol of occupied Ireland, the Tower suits, too, the theme of Ireland's paralyzing experience of imperialism that embitters Stephen, paralleling Penelope's hospitality to the strangers in her house that so humiliates Telemachus he leaves home to search for his wandering father, Odysseus.

Visitors to the Tower are more likely to delight in its oceanic vistas than respond to the unhappy harmony of the episode's setting and themes. On the parapet, at the top of "the dark winding stair," Stephen Dedalus appears, casting his mind upon the Irish Sea, to him a "bowl of bitter waters." To the blasphemous Buck Mulligan—Gogarty's fictional counterpart—it is the "scrotumtightening" and "snotgreen sea." (A friend of F. Scott Fitzgerald once said he had eyes the color of the Irish Sea, meaning, of course, the throattightening, jadegreen sea perceived by foreigners.) Those who have seen the Joycean seascapes from Bray, Blackrock, and Bull Island will recognize here not only Stephen's restless seaside mood but also Howth Head to the north. Just beyond Sandycove Point is Dun Laoghaire (formerly Kingstown) Harbour; Scotsman Bay and Bullock

Harbour spread out calmly in front of the Tower; to the south, Dalkey and Muglin Islands lie in "warm sunshine merrying over the sea." But the allusion of Haines, the third resident of the Tower, to *Hamlet* makes even the most sea-struck visitor see the place as Joyce intended, in its bitter historical context: "this tower and these cliffs here remind me somehow of Elsinore. *That beetles o'er his base into the sea . . .*" On June 16, 1904, the day on which *Ulysses* takes place, Stephen feels many things are rotten in Ireland, most of all her artistic imagination. He calls Mulligan's broken shaving mirror "a symbol of Irish art. The cracked look-ingglass of a servant."

Stephen, resolving to leave the Tower for good, returns his key to Buck Mulligan, who is sporting below at the Fortyfoot, still a favorite with hardy and naked "Gentlemen Bathers." He then begins a one-day journey away from the nightmare of history towards the freedom of art, travelling away from the Tower and through the city to No. 7 Eccles Street, a far humbler dwelling than the proud cliff-top fortress. Sharing Stephen's contempt for the Tower's shameful and barren historical associations, Joyce finds in the modest Dublin home of Leopold and Molly Bloom a rich and illuminating metaphor. Yeats, on the other hand, despising the "filthy modern tide" of townlife and townspeople, found in his Galway tower a many-layered symbol of his art and vision. Joyce's rejection of the Irish Literary Revival, so important to Yeats of Thoor Ballylee, is embodied in this image of the young artist surrendering his Tower key indifferently and walking away "along the upward-curving path." Focused on the past, the Revival's eyes were Celtic, its soul ancestrally proud. Joyce writes of his preference for more continental fare in *Finnegans Wake*:

He even ran away with hunself and became a farsoonerite, saying he would far sooner muddle through the hash of lentils in Europe than meddle with Irrland's split little pea.

A city boy, he could never settle down behind the hedges or on the rock islands where Synge, Yeats, and Lady Gregory found their material. Still, this sophisticated cosmopolite never really made it out of Dublin.

Episode 2: Nestor
10 A.M.

Joyce taught for a few weeks in 1904 at Clifton School, and here Stephen conducts a class and talks with Mr. Deasy, the headmaster. Take the No. 8 bus from Sandycove to the last stop in Dalkey and walk up Dalkey Avenue to the "lions couchant on the pillars" of the gate marked "Summerfield." The gravel paths are patterned with "the checkerwork of leaves," and in old gardens, where "the sun flung spangles, dancing coins," you can squint through the heavy drooping boughs and catch a glimpse of the sea. The house, a private residence, is still used as a day school for small boys who shout and run in the same backyard playing field that Joyce knew.

Shouts rang shrill from the boys' playfield. . . .
Stephen jerked his thumb towards the window, saying:
—That is God.
Hooray! Ay! Whrrwhee!

262 /

—What? Mr. Deasy asked.

—A shout in the street, Stephen answered, shrugging his shoulders.

The neighborhood is a pleasure to explore. Turn your eyes in all directions while climbing Dalkey Hill and Killiney Hill cliff-walk with their vistas of Dublin City in the distance, suburban sprawl, Joyce's Tower, the port of Dun Laoghaire, Bray Head, the Big and Little Sugarloaf of the Wicklow Mountains, and Killiney Bay arcing widely around a white crescent of bathers' strand, a montage justifying instantly Dublin's pride in the beauty of its natural surroundings. Midway up Dalkey Hill on Torca Road is Torca Cottage or Shaw's Cottage, marked with a plaque and closed to the public. In *Sixteen Self Sketches* Shaw, admitting his lack of formal education, attributes his powers of imagination to his childhood exposure to famous paintings in the National Gallery, to great books, majestic music, and to having been removed "at the age of ten from the street in which I was born . . . to the heights of Dalkey Hill." (He was born in 1856 in No. 33 Synge Street, a dreary place marked with a plaque and privately owned. Take the No. 19 bus from O'Connell Street and get off at Synge St. and South Circular Road.) From Dalkey he could see what Shakespeare meant by "that majestical roof fretted with golden fire." As a child he could not believe that Shakespeare had written this description without himself having been to Dalkey Hill at sunset. From Torca Road descend the long flight of steps leading down the side of the mountain onto the Vico Road, named for the philosopher Giam-

/ 263

battista Vico, whose cyclical theory of history informs the design of *Finnegans Wake*. Follow the Vico Road around Sorrento Point, past Coliemore Harbor, and back to the Dalkey bus stop. The walk is long, but full of Mediterranean brightness, palm trees, flowers and their fragrances, villas wedged into roadside cliffs, and always below the sea glinting green and silvery.

EPISODE 3: Proteus
11 A.M.

To have gotten in a few minutes from Dalkey to Sandymount (where Yeats was born in No. 2, Georgeville, Sandymount Avenue), Dedalus must have taken the train. Today the bus runs more frequently. You can still walk along the mudflats of Sandymount Strand towards the city center, observing the movements of the tide and sand, seeing their correspondences with the protean disposition of Stephen's mind in this episode. Like Proteus, the god of the sea, who easily changes his appearances, Stephen's mind breeds a variety of words in response to life's unceasing flow of sensations, emotions, and thoughts.

Ineluctable modality of the visible: at least that if no more, thought through my eyes. Signatures of all things I am here to read, seaspawn and seawrack, the nearing tide, that rusty boot. Snotgreen, bluesilver, rust: coloured signs. . . . Am I walking into eternity along Sandymount strand?

Detouring towards the electricity works—its name, the Pigeon House, suggests the Holy Ghost—Stephen, who followed mortal beauty with his back to the city on Bull Island, now, as solipsistic and abstracted as ever, crosses the strand in the shadow of the Pigeon House towards the saving waters of Bloom's compassion and Dublin's rich and various actuality.

EPISODE 4: Calypso
8 A.M.

Today only a façade is left of No. 7 Eccles Street, house of Molly and Leopold Bloom, the most intimately known couple in twentieth-century fiction. In *Stephen Hero*, the Eccles Street houses are described as "the very incarnation of Irish paralysis," but more importantly, Joyce associated No. 7 with his own cataclysmic experience of Irish treachery and human friendship.

In the course of one of his return visits to Dublin, he ran into Cosgrave, an old drinking and whoring companion who made up a story that Nora Barnacle had two-timed Joyce with him before she and Joyce had left for Europe. Cosgrave's campaign to break his "friend's" spirit almost succeeded. Believing that Nora had been unfaithful during their courtship, Joyce went to pieces. The scene of one breakdown was No. 7 Eccles Street, then the home of his friend, J. F. Byrne, Cranly in *A Portrait of the Artist*. Byrne convinced Joyce that he and his faithful Nora were the victims of a malicious conspiracy to separate them. Joyce believed him, but he never forgot this vicarious experience of sexual betrayal. In *Ulysses*, Byrne's house becomes the home of Leopold Bloom, cuckold, who, like Ulysses, longing to go

/ 265

home to Penelope but trapped on the island of Calypso, wishes for the sexual happiness he had shared with Molly before the death of their infant son. But Bloom is trapped by memories of infant mortality and Molly's subsequent infidelities.

At 8:15 A.M. on June 16, Mr. Bloom goes around the corner to the butcher's in Upper Dorset Street, where some of the places he passes still stand, some renamed, all ripe with voices and faces from *Dubliners, Ulysses*, and the plays of Sean O'Casey. Larry O'Rourke's pub is now the modernized Whiskey House of publican James McGowan. Saint Joseph's National School still fills the sidewalks with sounds of "brats clamour" and the chant of "Ahbeesee defeegee." Dlugacz's, the porkbutcher where Bloom buys the last kidney, never existed. Joyce got the name from a shop in Trieste. On the sidewalk at the corner of Dorset and North Frederick streets, northwest Dublin still weighs in on the scale outside Murray's Chemist, as Mr. Bloom used to "by the graduated machine for periodical selfweighing in the premises of Francis Froedman, pharmaceutical chemist of 19 Frederick street, north." Just down North Frederick Street, Prescott's Cleaners has not advanced its drycleaning methods since the days when Mrs. Bloom took her gowns here. Cassidy's, the pub that served the bent hag Bloom sees "clutching a noggin bottle by the neck" now has two titles, The Dorset House and Sheary's Bar—but no customers before 9 A.M.

Returning to Eccles Street of the "blotchy brown brick houses" Mr. Bloom serves Molly her breakfast and uses the steeple bells of George's Church in Hardwicke Place to keep track of the time:

A creak and a dark whirr in the air high up. The bells of George's church. They tolled the hour: loud dark iron.
Heigho! Heigho!

Today the bells of George's Church toll only through the half hour before the Wednesday and Sunday services at 7 P.M., but then the streets ring with jubilation. At these times visitors may see the church's fine interior woodwork and hear the great organ once used by Edward Bunting, the first collector of Irish folk music. The building's grace from porch to spire, not unlike London's St. Martin-in-the-Fields, is the work of Francis Johnston, who has here designed Dublin's finest church, its clear iron music a celebration of the neighborhood's finest gentleman.

EPISODE 5: Lotus Eaters
10 A.M.

Joyce's Dublin is both dirty and dear, and native Dubliners, as the visitor who has trailed Stephen Dedalus knows, frequent both sides. Perhaps to steer clear of nosy acquaintances ubiquitous in such a small city—Dublin is often called "the world's largest village"—Bloom follows a roundabout route on his way to the Westland Row Post Office to call for his mail from his secret pen pal. He crosses the Liffey at Butt Bridge near the Custom House, walks east along dreary Sir John Rogerson's Quay, turns right into Lime Street of warehouses and coal yards, and sees a slum child smoking a chewed fagbutt outside Brady's cottages, replaced now with working-class flats, their sidewalks teeming with cocky Dublin "gurriers"—streetchildren, in local parlance. "Tell him if he smokes he won't grow," thinks Bloom.

At the corner of Townsend he crosses into Lombard Street East and passes Nichols' the undertaker's at No. 31, known today as "Nichol's Funeral Directors and Car Hire, Est. 1814." With a "tooraloom, tooraloom, tooraloom" he crosses Great Brunswick Street, renamed Pearse Street after Patrick Pearse, born in No. 27.

He goes about his seedy business in a fairly seedy part of town, though compared to the lonely horrors around public terminals in most cities the neighborhood of Westland Row Railroad Station is quite decent. Stopping under the railway bridge, a fine example of Victorian ironwork, Bloom reads the names of the tea blends through the window of The Belfast and Oriental Tea Company, now "The Arch," a tobacco and sweet shop, and then, sauntering across the road and posing as Henry Flower, Esq., calls for his mail in the post office next to the railroad station. Today the only landmark of his mail-order romance is a post box that stands outside the station's main door, about a hundred yards from where Bloom passes the time of day with M'Coy while enjoying the "silk flash rich stockings white" which waits across the road outside the Grosvenor Hotel, still in business on the same spot. He finally escapes, taking a right around the corner of Brunswick/Pearse Street, and, a block later, bearing right again, "he turned into Cumberland street and, going on some paces, halted in the lee of the station wall."

Meade's timber yard is gone, but the neighborhood where Bloom reads Martha Clifford's mawkish letter is still as impoverished as her prose. Raggedy children pick through the trash cans by the rear doors of St. Andrew's Church (which Joyce calls All Hallows). "The cold smell of sacred stone called him" and Bloom enters "by the rere." No church service has ever been as funny as the one which Joyce recreates here from the baffled point of view of the "non-Catholic." He leaves through the front porch where the "cold black marble" holy water font is still at low tide for "furtive hands."

Following Bloom "southward along Westland Row," you pass Oscar Wilde's birthplace at No. 21 and in No. 36 you may see the fine ceilings and wall plaques of the Royal Irish Academy of Music. Sweny's Chemist at No. 1 Lincoln Place, where Westland Row ends and Bloom buys Pears' lemon-scented soap for Molly, still dispenses drugs and cosmetics at the same address under the sign of "A. Flynn." Realizing there is not enough time to walk back to the public baths (still open in Tara Street) and get out to Dignam's funeral by 11 A.M., he heads for the closer baths at No. 15 Lincoln Place, now a warehouse. The design on top of the building could still "remind you of a mosque . . . the minarets." From his side of the street Bloom greets the gatekeeper at the Lincoln Place entrance to Trinity College Park where his successor still mans the same porter's lodge, preventing suspicious characters from invading College Park's crickety green acres.

EPISODE 6: Hades
11 A.M.

As *Dubliners* and *A Portrait of the Artist* provide the best preparation for the city and people of *Ulysses*, so the *Dubliners'* story "Grace" serves as the best preface to this episode. All its characters who palaver around the bedside of Tom Kernan now join Paddy Dignam's cortege to Glasnevin (officially titled Prospect) Cemetery. The exact mourners' route, which proceeds along a diagonal line starting in the southeast part of the city and ending in the northwest, can only be followed on foot and takes about two hours to walk leisurely.

Fittingly, the journey to Glasnevin traverses neighborhoods reeking with futility. Tritonville Road, which takes you through Irishtown and Ringsend, both enclaves of the ripest Dublinese, is hardly tourist country, but then *Ulysses*, as an unexpurgated walker's guide to a city, is really antitourist literature. "Mr. Bloom smiled joylessly on Ringsend road. Wallace Bros the bottleworks. Dodder Bridge." These have survived brokenly and joylessly, as have the gasworks on the other side of the Grand Canal Bridge. Were Bloom to follow Dignam's hearse today along Great Brunswick/Pearse Street, he would recognize only the mournful presences of St. Andrew's National School (No. 121-114) and the graveyard and church of "the bleak pulpit of Saint Mark's" (No. 40). The building next door (No. 42) is the former Antient Concert Rooms where Yeats's *The Countess Cathleen* was first performed in 1899 and Joyce during his brief singing career once shared the stage with the tenor John McCormack (later transmuting the events of one disastrous concert into the short story "A Mother"). This venerable old concert hall has changed its name: the Academy Cinema now features foreign films, a risky venture in a city bred from the pulpit to enjoy films suitable for General Family Entertainment. And, clearly, pulpits outnumber everything but pubs. Farther along the Sandymount-Glasnevin route, the Church of the Blessed Sacrament on D'Olier Street now molds souls where the Red Bank restaurant, named for an oyster bed in Galway Bay, once dispensed its famous seafood.

"This race did ever love great personages," someone once wrote of the Irish, and Dublin abounds with their statues. Reminded of his own failure as husband by the jaunty figure of Blazes Boylan, whom Joyce first presents to us in the doorway of the Red Bank, Bloom surveys dispiritedly the stone images of energetic manhood that line the mall up the center of O'Connell Street: Daniel O'Connell, the Liberator; William Smith O'Brien, Young Irelander; Sir John Gray, the great proprietor of the *Freeman's Journal*; and Lord Nelson atop his pillar. Three of these can still be seen, but Nelson's Pillar was blown up in 1966 to observe the 50th Anniversary of the Easter Rising.

Of the shops and other establishments he notices along this stretch, only Gill and Macmillan's bookshop (No. 50) and The Catholic Commercial Club (No. 42) have survived the transformation of the so-called widest street in Europe into a thoroughfare "resplendent with cinemas and ice-cream parlours" in the regretful words of one Dublin writer. Unlike the Dublin culturati, however, Joyce would have participated in the cinema cult of contemporary

O'Connell Street with as much fascination as he attended the early cinemas in Italy and Paris. Far from looking down his literary nose on the modern cinema and pop culture, he tried to open the first movie theatre in Dublin around the corner in Mary Street and used the cinematic method of montage in *Ulysses*, a style which he saw as correlative to the manner of the modern city and the mind of urban man.

Diagonally across the street from the Carleton Cinema, which once featured only horror films, is the Gresham Hotel where Gretta and Gabriel Conroy of "The Dead" stay the snowy night after the Christmas party on Usher's Island. Like Gabriel, residents of the Gresham may still look out the front windows at images of flight and freedom. The trees in O'Connell Street outside the Savoy Cinema have been an urban nature reserve since the late twenties. In winter before dusk, hundreds of pied Willy Wagtails and Jennies of the Road play in the branches, wound with colored Christmas lights.

A sense of life's futility descends on Bloom as he sees the incomplete Parnell monument at the top of O'Connell Street and an infant's coffin being drawn down Parnell Square East (then Rutland Square). Today, Parnell's image tops the obelisk, his right arm extended as if to point out the Rotunda Lying-in Hospital in Parnell (formerly Great Britain) Street. The exotic ceiling of the Rotunda's second floor chapel, the only baroque work in Ireland, has been praised and damned with vigor. Its gorgeous plasterwork, an excrescence of blooms, berries, and babies, shows forth the Irish mystique of motherhood. In the foyer are busts of the hospital's past masters, among them "R. Dancer Purefoy." It is no accident that Joyce used the name of this obstetrician for his exponent of maternity, Mrs. Purefoy, who lies in labor throughout June 16th in the Holles Street National Maternity Hospital. Next to the hospital is the Ambassador Cinema, formerly the Rotunda proper where in 1852 John Henry Newman, the first Rector of Dublin's Catholic University, gave the lectures that were later collected under the title "The Idea of a University." Bloom takes no notice, however, of the historic old building. Preoccupied with his companions' blather about suicide, his memory travels to his father, who killed himself in the Queens Hotel, Ennis, County Clare. For the rest of the way—along Parnell Square East, past Findlater's Church, through North Frederick and Blessington streets, into Berkeley Road past *Mater Misericordiae* (Mother of Mercy) Hospital in Eccles Street ("My house down there"), around Doyle's or Dunphy's Corner into Phibsborough Road, across the bridge at the Royal Canal, past the Brian Boroimhe (Boru) public house and into Finglas Road—it comes clear that Bloom is in mourning not only for Dignam but also for his own life. For as husband, father, and son, he feels himself a failure. The journey across the city ends as on the right

The high railings of Prospects rippled past their gaze. Dark poplars, rare white forms. Forms more frequent, white shapes thronged amid the trees, white forms and fragments streaming by mutely, sustaining vain gestures on the air.

The "O'Connell Circle," with its gargantuan cone over the crypt, where Simon Dedalus weeps self pityingly, faces the main gates. The mortuary chapel, to the left of the entrance, is not open to the public, but visitors may roam the paths bordered with great cypress trees. Their swaying motion and the dizzy play of birds mock the stasis over the "saddened angels, crosses, broken pillars, family vaults, stone hopes praying with upcast eyes" and the glum Sacred Heart statues observed by Mr. Bloom:

Heart on his sleeve. Ought to be sideways and red it should be painted like a real heart. Ireland was dedicated to it or whatever that. Seems anything but pleased.

The grave of Joyce's parents, Mary Jane Murray and John Stanislaus Joyce, is to the right of the path leading to Parnell's grave. Other famous ones buried here who "once walked around Dublin" are Arthur Griffith, Michael Collins, James Larkin, Brendan Behan, Frank Sheehy-Skeffington, Maura Laverty, and in the Republican Corner, James Stephens, John O'Leary, the Fenian leader of Yeats's poem, "September 1913"—"Romantic Ireland's dead and gone, / It's with O'Leary in the grave"—and Jeremiah O'Donovan Rossa at whose graveside Patrick Pearse gave the famous eulogy warning the British of the insurrectionary power dead Irish heroes hold over the living: "The fools, the fools, the fools!—They have left us our Fenian dead, and while Ireland holds these graves, Ireland unfree shall never be at peace." A man of real sorrows, Bloom cannot become for the hour convivially lugubrious, so like Ulysses who visits Hades, the land of the dead, and hears the prophecies of Tiresias, Bloom roams around Glasnevin, conversing with his own life-loving, death-debunking spirits:

Plenty to see and hear and feel yet. Feel live warm beings near you. Let them sleep in their maggoty beds. They are not going to get me this innings. Warm beds: warm fullblooded life.

EPISODE 7: Aeolus
Noon

The offices of the *Freeman's Journal* at Nos. 4–8 Prince's Street, where part of this episode takes place, have been converted into the headquarters of *The Irish Independent* and *Evening Herald*, and a concrete island outside the General Post Office now occupies the site of Nelson's Pillar, designated by Joyce as "The Heart of the Hibernian Metropolis." But noontime Dublin still blusters and tumbles, and you can feel its rhythms if you stand somewhere near the flag pole and flower stalls that inherited Nelson's old place and watch the flow of giggly shopgirls and baby-faced clerks, motorcycles and double-decker buses, womenchildren navigating prams swollen with babies and parcels—the city as a variety show—the perspective and style of *Ulysses*. Joyce said he wrote his epic "from eighteen different points of view and in as many styles."

Under the porch of the Post Office the shoeblacks of 1904 have been replaced by the hawkers of Dublin's indigenous drug trade, consisting of nothing stronger than pamphlets from the Legion of Mary and political broadsheets like "The United Irishman." Republicans peddle here to remind middle-class Dublin of the Easter rebels who in 1916 consecrated the G.P.O. by making it the altar where they sacrificed themselves. Inside, you can see their bronze memorial, a statue called the Death of Cuchulainn. In Samuel Beckett's novel *Murphy*, Neary tries to smash his head open against the buttocks of heroic Ireland's superhuman image.

You can still turn your face to the gales of rhetoric blowing through the city by reading the Letters to the Editors in

Dublin's five dailies or joining the crowd at the Abbey Street Mooney's where Stephen Dedalus and the gentlemen of the press wind up their chat with a midday jar. Here, too, Beckett's Neary "sat all day, moving slowly from one stool to another until he had completed the circuit of the counters, when he would start all over again in the reverse direction." The Abbey's Victorian ceiling, gaudy and determinedly ingenious, matches well the inflated voices and bulbous faces of this episode.

EPISODE 8: Lestrygonians
1 P.M.

In *The Odyssey* the Lestrygonians are cannibals who seize the ships of Ulysses and eat up his men. As Bloom walks from Prince Street to the National Library he observes various forms of cannibalism tearing away at the Irish colony of the Holy Roman and British empires. Though the lingering effects of colonialism may easily be overlooked, the visitor will have no trouble finding the places along Bloom's lunchtime route.

About to cross from Bachelor's Walk over to O'Connell Bridge, he spots one of Simon Dedalus' daughters outside Dillon's (now Sheeran's) auction rooms and thinks of Mrs. Dedalus, the recently dead mother of ten children:

Birth every year almost. That's in their theology or the priest won't give the poor woman the confession, the absolution. Increase and multiply. Did you ever hear such an idea? Eat you out of house and home. No families themselves to feed. Living on the fat of the land.

Children suffer, too, as their parents dutifully fill the earth:

Good Lord, that poor child's dress is in flitters. Underfed she looks too. Potatoes and marge, marge and potatoes. It's after they feel it.

His Grace, John Charles McQuaid, till recently Roman Catholic Archbishop of Dublin, proclaimed in his Lenten pastoral of 1971 that legislation to allow the sale of contraceptives in Ireland would be "a curse upon our country." Packs of pale children and worn-out women of thirty-five push through northside markets looking for second-hand clothes and cheap vegetables.

Crossing O'Connell Bridge, you see a big sign flashing "Guinness Is Good For You" from a building in Burgh Quay. Deeming this a dull slogan, Joyce wanted to replace it with "Guinness, the free, the froh, the frothey freshener." Underneath the flashing news of the national staple, which has a lot to do with Ireland's having the highest caloric intake in the world, is "the heart of the city." Joyce located it a few blocks north at Nelson's Pillar. But O'Connell Bridge at twilight, winter or summer, sends forth the city's strongest life beats. The riverrun below hung high with the skidding cloths of heaven, the view upriver of the Ha'-penny Bridge and the dome of Adam and Eve's, the sea gulls swooping low on Anna Liffey, and on land the surge of cars and people—here is the "joyicity" of *Finnegans Wake* and there goes Bloom feeding the birds and musing, "It's always flowing in a stream, never the same, which in the stream of life we trace. Because life is a stream."

Surely of all the earth's tyrants, time is the greediest cannibal, and along Westmoreland Street Bloom grieves for its victims, himself and Molly, Josie and Denis Breen, Mrs. Purefoy. Outside the building known as the Ballast Office, which used to have a timeball on the roof controlled from Dunsink Observatory to fall at 1 P.M., he checks the time and after crossing the street passes the offices of the *Irish Times*, today the country's best newspaper, which has outside its building the only outdoor clock in the city that always works. Opposite the old Irish House of Parliament, now the Bank of Ireland, Bloom sees more lackeys of colonial cannibalism, members of the Royal Irish Constabulary marching to and from their headquarters in College Street, still Dublin's main police station. Presently, "he crossed under Tommy Moore's roguish finger. They did right to put him up over a urinal: meeting of the waters."

At "Trinity's surly front" you might leave Bloom staring across the street at Parnell's brother and walk through the college's cobblestone quads, past its campanile and classic buildings, towards the old library where in the immense quiet of its great hall under a dramatic, dark wood vaulted dome you can pass a marvellous few hours perusing the manuscripts of Trinity's former students, Swift, Goldsmith, Burke, Berkeley, Congreve, Farquhar, Tone, Oscar Wilde, Synge, and Beckett. The most popular exhibit is the Book of Kells, which Joyce used as his model:

In all the places I have been to Rome, Zurich, Trieste, I have taken it about with me, and have pored over its workmanship for hours. It is the most purely Irish thing we have, and some of the big initial letters which swing right across a page have the essential quality of a chapter of *Ulysses*. Indeed, you can compare much of my work to the intricate illuminations.

Especially, one might add, the mind of Leopold Bloom.

Continue along the straight line of Grafton Street past the fine Georgian mansion of the Provost of Trinity College—"Wouldn't live in it if they paid me," thinks Bloom—across Nassau Street to the window of Yeates and Son, where he stops to price field glasses. He walks one block up Dublin's Fifth Avenue:

Grafton Street gay with housed awnings lured his senses. Muslin prints, silk, dames and dowagers. . . . He passed, dallying, the windows of Brown Thomas, silk mercers. Cascades of ribbons. Flimsy China silks. . . . High voices. Sunwarm silk. Jingling harnesses. All for a woman, home and houses, silk webs, silver, rich fruits, spicy from Jaffa.

Brown Thomas, the best department store in the city, is always aswarm with bedecked ladies.

Just beyond it, are the iron-lace shopfront of "Combridge's Corner" and the corner of Duke Street, both much as they were when Bloom rounded them on his way to the Burton restaurant. Now called The Bailey, it is a busy pub, where the door of No. 7 Eccles Street is enshrined. Bloom can't get away fast enough from its cannibalistic clientele:

Perched on high stools by the bar, hats shoved back, at the tables calling for more bread no charge, swilling, wolfing gobfuls of sloppy food, their eyes bulging, wiping wetted moustaches. . . . Out. I hate dirty eaters.

Chances are the kindhearted Mr. Bloom would have hated, too, the literary Bailey of a few decades later. "Out of the Bailey poured limericks, verses, epigrams, witty sayings.

/   279

. . . They would sacrifice their mother for a witty phrase," writes Gogarty's biographer.

Requiring a civilized pub lunch, he crosses the street to Davy Byrne's "moral pub," then a "nice quiet bar" where he could sit reminiscing, but now a slicked-up bar. After leaving Davy Byrne's, Bloom walks along Duke Street towards Dawson Street, singing a few lines from *Don Giovanni*, Joyce's favorite opera. (This area—Duke, Anne, Dawson, Molesworth, Nassau, and Grafton streets—has a variety of good shops and pubs and four bookstores: Browne & Nolan, Hodges Figgis, the Eblana, and Fred Hanna.) At the corner of Duke and Dawson streets, he helps a blind man across Dawson to the corner of South Frederick and Molesworth streets. Before he escaped to London in 1876, George Bernard Shaw worked four and a half miserable years as a solicitor's clerk in No. 15 Molesworth Street—"of all the damnable waste of human life that ever was invented, clerking is the very worst," he said. During the day he ran errands to the Custom House, and at night he took long walks around Dublin. On reading *Ulysses* he wrote, "to me it is all hideously real: I have walked those streets, and known those shops and heard and taken part in those conversations. . . . and forty years later [I] have learnt from the books of Mr. Joyce that Dublin is still what it was, and young men are still drivelling in slackjawed blackguardism just as they were in 1870."

The Molesworth Street approach to Leinster House in Kildare Street is one of the city's most attractive streetscapes. Dublin's visual beauty is not lost on Bloom. Catching sight of the National Museum, he thinks of the statues of

Venus—"Goddesses"—which in his day adorned its foyer. Inside you will find cases of amazing gold ornaments and jewelry worn by Celtic goddesses, but the Venuses, like their sister on the ceiling at Belvedere College, have been ousted, their places usurped by models of Celtic crosses.

This storehouse of the High Kings' splendid treasures calls to mind the controversial questions of the relationship between ancient Gaelic culture and contemporary Irish literature. Viewing such wonders as the Ardagh Chalice, the Tara Brooch, and the Cross of Cong brings to mind Yeats's words: "There alone is the stuff that dreams are made of to keep us busy a thousand years."

EPISODE 9: Scylla and Charybdis
2 P.M.

The National Library, the setting of final scenes in *A Portrait of the Artist*, belongs to the world of Stephen Dedalus. It is not Bloom's territory. Like Ulysses who had to steer his ship between Scylla, a monster on a rock, and Charybdis, a dangerous whirlpool, Bloom gets in and out quickly, passing between Stephen, in this episode a literary killjoy destroying *Hamlet*, and Buck Mulligan, as usual, a whirlpool of opinions and spite.

EPISODE 10: The Wandering Rocks
3 P.M.

Beckett wrote of Joyce, "Here, form is content, content is form, and you cannot separate the two." Thus the strategy of this episode, a series of nineteen long shots and close-ups. Its technique of montage and the labyrinthine prose are identical with its content: the texture of urban experience.

Tracing the routes presented in each fragment means covering ground already seen: Father Conmee walks through the northeast area branching out from Mountjoy Square; the one-legged sailor wanders through Eccles Street; the throwaway bearing the message "Elijah Is Coming" floats down the Liffey under the Loop Line Bridge between the Custom House and George's Quay; Blazes Boylan shops at No. 63 Grafton Street; Stephen and Artifoni chat in College Green near the statues of "Goldsmith's knobby poll" and "the stern stone hand of Grattan, bidding halt"; Lambert shows the groined ceiling of Mary's Abbey to the Reverend Love; Paddy Dignam's son shops for pork-steaks along Wicklow, Grafton, and Nassau streets; Lenehan and McCoy walk in the neighborhood of Dublin Castle on their way to the Ormond Hotel.

No idle drifter, Bloom spends this hour looking for a book for Molly outside Francis Fitzgerald's bookshop under the Merchant's Arch—"A darkbacked figure scanned books on the hawker's cart." A barrow of second-hand books crammed with Ian Flemings still stands outside the same bookstore. A wider choice of used books is available one block away at Charles Webb's in Aston Quay where Gabriel Conroy of "The Dead," Joyce, Synge, and O'Casey once bought and traded books; and at Green's Booksellers in Clare Street across from Wilde's corner in Merrion Square. Of the four, the bookstore where Bloom browses has the most private and picturesque location. The Merchant's Arch, one of the last arched passageways in the city, is named for the Guild of Merchant Tailors, founded in 1420. Through it you can see the charming Ha'penny or Metal Bridge, the Liffey's only foot bridge, so-called because pedestrians once had to pay a half-penny toll to cross it. Nowadays, Beckett's bums sometimes panhandle there, as miserable and gay on a rainy afternoon as Molloy or Malone or Mahood.

EPISODE 11: The Sirens
4 P.M.

The Ormond Hotel, which has been completely remodelled, still stands at No. 8 Upper Ormond Quay. In the lounge a television has replaced the piano Father Cowley played to accompany Simon Dedalus' song from *Martha*. But at four o'clock in the afternoon of our visit, the bar buzzed with the conversation of seven or eight Dubliners, making the place where Bloom gets the "best value in Dublin" seem part of local rather than tourist territory.

After leaving the Ormond, Bloom walks up the quays and looks in the window of Lionel Mark's antique shop at No. 16 Bachelor's Walk. Visitors interested in picking up some Bloomtime junk are in the right neighborhood. The quays have been the antique dealer's mecca since the early 1800's. Here is a list of shops, from the slightly touristy to the very cheap: Balfe's and Gately's at the end of Ormond Quay; Skelly's and Goyers in Wellington Quay; Slowey's near O'Connell Bridge in Bachelor's Walk; Pictures, Books and Curios and The Ha'penny Steps, both near Ha'penny Bridge.

Episode 12: The Cyclops
5 P.M.

Nothing is left of Barney Kiernan's pub at Nos. 8, 9, 10 Little Britain Street. But you can roam the drear neighborhood of the Cyclops episode and still find patriotic landmarks evoking the bitter history that had poisoned the bloodstream of the Citizen, the one-eyed monster who with his dog Garry Owen attacks Bloom viciously.

From the quays Bloom walks north on Capel Street. In the *Dubliners* story, "A Little Cloud," Little Chandler observes "the dull inelegance of Capel Street," and asserts what the young Joyce had felt: "There was no doubt about it: if you wanted to succeed you had to go away. You could do nothing in Dublin." In such a confining town, the Capel Street Public Library, just beyond the corner of Little Britain Street, was the staff of life to O'Casey and Stephens, and to Joyce while he was a student at Belvedere. Bloom remembers on the morning of June 16, "Must get that Capel street library book renewed or they'll write to Kearney, my guarantor." If at the top of the street you bear left and left again into Green Street, you approach Little Britain Street from the direction taken by the Narrator and Joe Hynes— two of the episode's main speakers—and you also pass the Central Criminal Court where the patriots Robert Emmet, the Brothers Sheare, William Smith O'Brien, and the Fenian leaders of 1867 stood trial. At the corner of Green and Little Britain streets is a park on the site of the old Newgate Gaol where Lord Edward Fitzgerald died and the Young Irelanders of 1848 were imprisoned. A neighborhood so marked by reminders of the unjust courts of British colonialism and the violent lore of Irish nationalism could not have been chosen accidentally as the setting in which the mythology of Sinn Fein bears its teeth.

EPISODE 13: Nausicaa
8 P.M.

There is small point in following Bloom to Dignam's house in Sandymount where he now pays a sympathy call to the widow. The routes of the "Proteus" and "Hades" episodes passed through this neighborhood nine hours earlier. Star of the Sea Church where Gabriel Conroy's brother is curate and the Presbyterian Church across Sandymount Road are still there, but the most important details of the episode's setting have changed. At the bottom of Leahy's Terrace, the rocks from which Bloom watched "those girls, those girls, those lovely seaside girls," have been replaced by a sea wall. It faces a dump and a fence inscribed more in the vigilant vein of the preceding chapter—"No E. E. C.," "Join the I. R. A."—than in "Nausicaa's" sad sleepytime mood. Young girls still babysit on the strand, but a likelier time and place to look for Gerty MacDowells is during lunch hour in Clery's Department Store in O'Connell Street where Gerty herself bought the trimming for her "little love of a hat."

EPISODE 14: Oxen of the Sun
10 P.M.

Visitors may walk the corridors of the National Maternity Hospital at Merrion Square and Holles Street and imagine any one of the ground floor waiting rooms as the place where the medical students roister, and Bloom keeps watch—"Woman's woe with wonder pondering"—while Mrs. Purefoy gives birth upstairs. The callow students' irreverence towards the miracle and pain of birth corresponds to the bestiality of Ulysses' crew who ate the holy cows in the Sun's pasture, though they had been told of their sacredness.

You can still follow the path these "overgrown children" take after Mrs. Purefoy's delivery. Fleeing the house where "teeming mothers are wont to bring forth bairns," they duck across Holles Street into Denzille Lane, an unmarked, raggedy alley, one vomiting, the others scurrying to fortify themselves for the whores of Nighttown. Which they do in the womb of "Burke's pub," today the refreshingly unmodern Mulligan's in Poolbeg Street. In the back room dockers and students put down their evening stout warmed by the light of gaslamps, a huge open fire, and each other. The press of bodies, rough, wild-bearded faces glistening through veils of smoke, the centrality of the fire all seem to transport Mulligan's back towards the time when small bands of men huddled together in camaraderie in wattle enclosures on dark hillsides.

EPISODE 15: Circe

Midnight

The area around Amiens Street Station (renamed Connolly Station) is no longer the city's brothel district, in Bloomtime a busier whoredom than any in Paris, Algiers, Bombay, or Cairo. An embarrassment to the new Irish Free State, it was purged in 1924 after a series of bloody murders, and it has not been resurrected. But Dubliners remember the old geography of the "dark slimy streets" where Stephen Dedalus, Sodalist, two-timed the Virgin in *A Portrait of the Artist*: today's Foley Street was Montgomery Street, source of the nickname "Monto" for the whole area; Corporation Street was Mabbot; Railway was Tyrone, and before 1887, Mecklenburg; and Sean MacDermott was Gloucester Street. Mabbot and Beaver lanes have kept their original names, though the latter is not signposted.

Coming from Talbot Street, where Bloom buys "pig's crubeen and sheep's trotter" at Olhousen's, Dublin's still-thriving porkbutcher's, Stephen and Lynch reel down Mabbot Street towards Bella Cohen's brothel at No. 82 Tyrone Street, near the corner of Mabbot (Corporation Street) and Mecklenburg/Tyrone (Railway Street). Later, Stephen runs up Mecklenburg Street and is knocked down by a British "tommy" at the corner of Beaver Lane where Bloom rescues him and sees a mirage of his dead son, Rudy. The tourist who traces their steps today sees the city's economic and social underworld, inhabited, as in Joyce's day, by "outcasts from life's feast." Respectable Dubliners do not recommend a midnight tour.

A right turn at the corner of Talbot and Marlborough streets leads to a landmark of deprivation out of Shaw's youth, which has not changed its name or its game. Across from the Pro-Cathedral in Marlborough Street you can walk through the prisonlike grounds of the Central Model Boys School where Shaw was sentenced in 1868 after he was thrown out of the now-defunct Wesleyan School in No. 79 Stephen's Green. A unit of the National Schools of Ireland, the school was open to all classes and denominations in theory, but in fact served the Catholic sons of the lower middle class. Shaw, the son of an Irish Protestant merchant and gentleman—also a drunkard like John Joyce—paid a high price for going to school with poor Catholic trash. He recollected the experience as "Shame and Wounded Snobbery" in *Sixteen Self Sketches*:

I now confess to an episode in my boyhood formerly so repugnant to me that for 80 years I never mentioned it to any mortal creature, not even to my wife. . . . I was sent to Marlborough Street, and at once lost caste outside it and became a boy with whom no Protestant young gentleman would speak or play.

Over the school's high iron gates, he said, there might as well have hung a sign bearing Dante's phrase, "All hope abandon, ye who enter here."

EPISODE 16: Eumaeus
1 A.M.

Bloom in "orthodox Samaritan fashion" steers Stephen out of Nighttown towards the cabman's shelter, "hardly a stonesthrow away near Butt Bridge. . . ." Today a similar "unpretentious wooden structure" stands near the Custom House on the same spot where the two drink awful coffee. Now a Guinness Canteen, it dispenses free stout to dockers from the brewery's boats and sometimes to Joyce pilgrims. Between Beaver Lane and Butt Bridge you can still identify as surviving structures of this episode's unpretentious streetscape: the North Star Hotel, Mullet's and the Signal House in Amiens Street, the railway station, the City Morgue, the C Division police station in Store Street, and the Loop Line Bridge, a monstrosity that blocks the down-river view of the Custom House from O'Connell Bridge. The neighborhood's transient flavor and down-at-the-heels look blend with the murky talk in the cabman's shelter to yield an almost unrelieved sensation of physical and human exhaustion.

But suddenly, at the end of the episode, Bloom and Stephen appear, making tracks, "arm-in-arm across Beresford place . . . stepping over a strand of mire," chatting about music, Bloom praising Meyerbeer and Mozart and Mrs. Bloom, and Stephen finally singing a ballad that dispels the neighborhood's gloom. These images embody the Joycean cure for a depressed environment and humanity: human sympathy arm-in-arm with the insurrectionary, transforming spirit of the artist. It is no accident that Joyce re-creates his comic messianic vision in seedy Lower Gardiner Street. A believing socialist and a master of paradox, he builds his "jocoserious" new Jerusalem north of the Liffey.

EPISODE 17: Ithaca

2 A.M.

If you have walked the Dublin of Stephen Dedalus and Leopold Bloom, you will, on following their tracks in this episode, have a sense of *déjà vu*. The way they go home is the same way Stephen leaves home in *A Portrait of the Artist* on his first journey into the strange, complex city. The only difference is that Stephen walks down Gardiner Street hill and they go up—towards Eccles Street and the strange and complex phenomenon of woman.

Joyce charts their course with the scientific precision that is the style of this episode:

Starting united both at normal walking pace from Beresford place they followed in the order named Lower and Middle Gardiner streets and Mountjoy square, west: then, at reduced pace, each bearing left, Gardiner's place by an inadvertance as far as the farther corner of Temple street, north: then at reduced pace with interruptions of halt, bearing right, Temple street, north, as far as Hardwicke place. Approaching, disparate, at relaxed walking pace they crossed . . . the circus before George's church diametrically. . . . At the housesteps of the 4th of the equidifferent uneven numbers, number 7 Eccles street, he inserted his hand mechanically into the back pocket of his trousers to obtain his latch-key.

Having forgotten his key to the kingdom, Bloom enters through the basement. Passionate for accurate detail, Joyce wrote from Paris to his aunt asking her to find out if it were possible for "an ordinary person to climb over the railings at Number 7 Eccles Street . . . lower himself from the lower part of the railings until his feet are within two feet of the ground, and drop unhurt." It was. Having sipped the Passover cocoa, Bloom and Stephen leave the house and come outside where at 2:30 A.M., on any clear summer night, the weary but faithful explorer may witness the same "spectacle" they behold together:

The heaventree of stars hung with humid nightblue fruit.

At the same hour the literary pilgrim will also observe a good many Dublin gentlemen addressing themselves to a great many Dublin walls, engaged like Bloom and Stephen in passing a nighttime of Guinness.

EPISODE 18: Penelope

Joyce once said that a film on astronomy, in particular some sequences dealing with the moon, gave him the idea for the rhythm of Molly Bloom's soliloquy, the half-asleep reverie that closes *Ulysses*. Howth demesne, in particular its romantic rhododendron gardens, can bring you close to the texture of her mindless sensuality. The gardens are open April 11–30: 2:30–6; May 1–June 30: 11–9; July 1–Sept. 15: 11–6. The No. 31 bus from Lower Abbey Street gets you there in half an hour; on Sunday afternoons it is full of couples and families, bound for Howth Harbor or Gardens or Summit, their chatter and gaiety giving the expedition a feeling of glad pilgrimage.

The woods behind Howth Castle are dense with two thousand species of rhododendron, flowertrees hung heavy with full fragrant circles of red and pink and yellow. The views from the flower-covered slopes become the more spectacular the higher you climb the narrow, steep paths. The view from the Species Slope is particularly grand. But at the summit, called the Top View, you will come upon the panorama of the sea, Dublin Bay, the far-off city, the green-growing fields and pastures of Howth demesne, and the radiance of flowers and ferns all down the mountainside. Molly's words bespeak a spirit in touch with this extravagant feast of unspoiled earth:

I love flowers Id love to have the whole place swimming in roses God of heaven theres nothing like nature the wild mountains then the sea and the waves rushing then the beautiful country with fields of oats and wheat and all kinds of things and all the fine cattle going about that would do your heart good to see rivers and lakes and flowers all sorts of shapes and smells and colours springing up even out of the ditches primroses and violets nature it is . . .

Even on a spring weekend when Dubliners roam the paths, it is easy to find a private spot on the cliff or in the forest where you can enter the tender heart of Joyce's world.

the sun shines for you he said the day we were lying among the rhododendrons on Howth head in the grey tweed suit and his straw hat the day I got him to propose to me yes first I gave him the bit of seedcake out of my mouth and it was leapyear like now yes 16 years ago my God after that long kiss I near lost my breath yes he said I was a flower of the mountain yes so we are flowers all a womans body yes that was one true thing he said in his life and the sun shines for you today yes that was why I liked him because I saw he understood or felt what a woman is . . .

On Howth Head, *Ulysses* ends and *Finnegans Wake* begins, Joyce's final celebration of the stream of life:

riverrun, past Eve and Adam's, from swerve of shore to bend of bay, brings us by a commodius vicus of recirculation back to Howth Castle and Environs.

The River Liffey, Anna Livia Plurabelle, another Molly, the eternal woman, flows past the Church of Adam and Eve on the south quays, washing at last the shore of Howth— Howth Castle and Environs, or H.C.E., or H.C. Earwicker, or Haveth Childers Everywhere, or Here Comes Everybody. But we must leave the exploration of this nightmaze to you who have the time for endless Plurabilities.

General Post Office, Dublin. Irish Tourist Board

13.

IF EVER YOU GO
TO DUBLIN TOWN

◆◆◆◆◆◆◆◆◆◆◆◆◆◆◆◆◆◆◆◆◆◆◆◆◆◆◆◆◆◆◆◆◆◆◆◆◆◆

If ever you go to Dublin town
In a hundred years or so
Inquire for me in Baggot Street
And what I was like to know.
O he was a queer one,
Fol dol the di do,
He was a queer one
I tell you.

> PATRICK KAVANAGH, "IF EVER YOU
> GO TO DUBLIN TOWN"

T HOUGH THE GUNMEN have gone underground, the
sauntering, eavesdropping visitor can still find
the world of Sean O'Casey who lived forty-eight of his
eighty-four years on the city's north side.

Veterans of the *Ulysses* tour will recognize the neighborhood around No. 85 Upper Dorset Street where O'Casey
spent the childhood he evokes so tenderly in *I Knock At The
Door*, the first volume of his autobiography. On the site of
his birthplace stands the Hibernian Bank, a mocking monu-

ment to the man who saw capitalism lurking in the shadows of every tragedy. Five-year-old "Johnny Casside," as O'Casey calls himself, began his miserable schooldays at St. Mary's National School, four blocks south in No. 20 Dominick Street, right around the corner from No. 12 Dorset Street, birthplace of the eighteenth-century dramatist Richard Brinsley Sheridan. Today, St. Saviour's Orphanage for Boys occupies the splendid Georgian mansion that O'Casey remembers as the place where he was sentenced to "the misery of sitting still and stiff and sleepy in the droning out of the song of the spelling and the sums." Visitors are permitted to ascend the wide, graceful front staircase, extravagantly decorated with ladies and birds in high relief, some of Dublin's best plasterwork. You may also see the chapel ceiling, a playground of chubby Cupids taking aim at the congregation below. Venus has fared better here than at Belvedere, and her room may be seen, depending on the disposition of your guide, one of the St. Saviour's boys. The craftsmanship of the mansion's flamboyant stuccodore, Robert West, which the Dominican Fathers have preserved well in the attempt to create a pleasant environment for the children, dispels for the visitor the usual institutional gloom that nonetheless tyrannized the young O'Casey's schooldays.

Continuing one block south along Dorset Street, you come to Henrietta Street where Little Chandler of Joyce's short story "A Little Cloud" walks from the Kings Inns (the Irish Inns of Court) at the top of the street and sees the grimy children playing "under the shadow of the gaunt spectral mansions in which the old nobility of Dublin had roystered." Once the most fashionable of all north Dublin's great eighteenth-century residential streets, it evokes today the ambiance of O'Casey's first three plays, *The Shadow of a Gunman*, *Juno and the Paycock*, and *The Plough and the Stars*, all set in "the unhealthiest city in the world," according to a conservative medical journal of 1880, the year O'Casey was born. The Sisters of Charity have preserved No. 9's past glory in the staircase hall and chapel, but the rest of the mansions have long been stripped of their staircases and marble fireplaces and packed with the tubercular poor.

The Mollsers and the Bessie Burgesses, indeed all the women of the slums who became the heroines of O'Casey's plays, have their descendants in today's women who cluster on the stoops and sidewalks outside the still proud façades, watching their children's street games and passing the time of day. A late afternoon visit to Henrietta Street on the right day, when even in bitterest winter the children lick orange ices and ply you with friendly questions, reveals the city's magic as no other place can:

Often in the evening when the stars were still pale in the sky, the boys would see the girls skipping at the other end of the street, as many as ten or fifteen of them jumping gracefully over a regularly turning rope. The boys would slink up nearer and nearer to the skipping girls; the girls would occasionally glance disdainfully at the boys, but in their hearts they wished them to come closer. With a defiant shout, weakened with the tone of a shy shame in it, a boy, bolder than the rest, would jump in merrily; the rest would follow him, and joyous faces of boys and girls would shine out of thin dusty clouds raised out of the road by the beating of the skippers' feet dancing in the way of peace. Tired of skipping, someone would suggest a ring; and boys and girls, their shyness gone, would join hands in a great ring. . . . with arms held high while a player would dart in and out of the ring under the upraised arms as the circle of boys and girls sang

> "Chase him all round Dublin, chase him all round
>   Dublin, chase him all round Dublin,
> As you have done before."

O'Casey was baptized and went to services at St. Mary's Protestant Church, on the corner of Mary and Jervis streets, a short walk from Henrietta Street. Today the Sunday morning pews are sparsely filled with a few old Dubliners, but one can imagine the bewhiskered Reverend T. R. S. Hunter up in the old mahogany pulpit "in his white surplus with a solemn puss on him" lording it over the children below whose antics O'Casey remembers in *I Knock At The Door*. St. Mary's, the first Dublin church with a gallery, was built in 1697 and became one of the city's wealthiest and most influential parishes, its pride the Harris organ, now an unplayed but exquisitely carved museum piece. When Stella and her companion, Rebecca Dingley, lodged in nearby Stafford Street, Swift warned Stella that St. Mary's was too expensive a church for her to belong to. In 1711 a seat in the mahogany box pews sold for sixty pounds. The church's reputation is also based on the famous babies who have been brought to its font: Theobald Wolfe Tone, Richard Brinsley Sheridan, O'Casey, and Archibald Hamilton Rowan, who later fled the British out the back window of Joyce's Clongowes Wood. If you talk to an old-timer after the service, he will give you fanciful capsules of their careers, show you their memorabilia in the vestry, tell you that your man Sean O'Casey became an agnostic the day his mother died, "he felt that bad," and then escort you to his baptismal certificate displayed beneath the font of Connemara marble. Next to it on the wall hangs a biblical line, "Ye must be born again," a spiritual law that O'Casey observed throughout his creative life and one that inspires the dramatic characters he most admires: Mary Boyle of *Juno and the Paycock*, Nora Clitheroe of *The Plough and the Stars*, and Ayamonn Breydon of *Red Roses For Me* struggle against the devil of a dispirited environment to re-create their lives in beauty. O'Casey attended Bible classes in this musty old church and memorized the Old Testament prophets so well he won a scroll "for proficiency in Holy Scripture." Like most Irish writers, Protestant or Catholic, he eventually left the Church, banging the doors of the pews behind him and shouting, "Will none of you ever guess that man can study man, or worship God, in dance and song and story!" But he took with him the rage and sympathy of the prophets met in childhood and installed them in his own dramatic pulpit.

The sounds of the O'Casey Country, loud and clear along Mary and Henry streets (north Dublin's Grafton Street), crescendo and explode at the motley carnival of the Moore Street market, one of the best places for hearing the accents of the Dublin usually hidden from tourists. In late afternoon, when the likelihood of unsold produce increases, so does the frenzied clatter of bargaining at the open-air stalls. The raggle-taggle women of Moore Street make wry asides to one another as customers pass by, shout jibes at competitive stalls, and hoarsely chant their wares: "Meush-ereu-ums! Berreussel Sperreou-uts! A shee-lin' a pow-end! T'anks, luv. Ta-ta." Long before Joyce began imitating these chants at parties and O'Casey gave the sounds to modern drama, Swift had loved these hawkers and written for them "Verses made for Women who cry Apples, &c.," which suit their spirit perfectly, as in this one for Asparagus:

> Ripe 'sparagrass
> Fit for a lad or lass,
> To make their water pass:
>   O, 'tis pretty picking
>   With a tender chicken!

Shoppers, including O'Casey's viragos, battered wives, and pretty young women, pour through the open market, hauling children, haggling prices, tossing coppers at sidewalk musicians, arguing, laughing, debunking all the way. Oliver St. John Gogarty selected one motif from this kaleidoscope of verbal energies:

> The plainer Dubliners amaze us
> By their so frequent use of "Jaysus!"
> Which makes me entertain the notion
> It is not always from devotion.

At the corner of Mooré Street and O'Rahilly Parade a streetlamp bears a poster of Yeats's poem "The O'Rahilly," commemorating the spot where the patriot O'Rahilly was shot down in heavy guerrilla fighting during the 1916 Rising. At the meeting of Moore and Parnell streets a poster marks the place where the rebels surrendered unconditionally.

One block east of this site, a few doors up the west side of Parnell Square, called Granby Row, is the present head-quarters of the Irish Transport and General Workers' Union founded by James Larkin and familiar to readers of one of Ireland's best-sellers, *Strumpet City* by James Plunk-ett. A Larkin devotee, O'Casey broke with him over the ad-mission of Countess Markievicz of Lissadell to the union's Citizen Army. As far as O'Casey was concerned, an aristo-crat doesn't change her spots. One block east on the north-east corner, you can sit down among Dubliners and flowers in the Garden of Remembrance, a memorial to the patriots of 1916–22. Their mystique of Christlike martyrdom, which helped finally to estrange the Protestant O'Casey from Catholic Republicanism, is expressed in the garden's shallow cruciform pool. Committed to the goals of the Labor Movement, O'Casey detected in the rhetoric of the Republican leaders, not political realism, but only the reli-gious obsessions of sacrificial suicide. In *The Plough and the Stars* he quoted from the speeches of Patrick Pearse:

it is a goodly thing to see arms in Irish hands. . . . We must ac-custom ourselves to the thought of arms, to the sight of arms, to the use of arms. We may make mistakes in the beginning and shoot the wrong people; but bloodshed is a cleansing and a sanc-tifying thing, and the nation which regards it as the final horror has lost its manhood. There are many things more horrible than bloodshed; and slavery is one of them.

The Covey, O'Casey's persona, responds: "Dope! Dope!"
Such politics he abandoned for art. You can follow in his direction either by walking half a block south and buying a

ticket at the recently restored Gate Theatre of Michael MacLiammoir and Hilton Edwards or by crossing over to the north side of Palace Row and the Municipal Gallery of Modern Art (closed Mondays; Tuesday – Saturday 10–6; Sunday 11–2; lecture Sunday noon). Its small but fine collection, assembled in the former house of Lord Charlemont, one of Dublin's grandest eighteenth-century mansions, includes Impressionist painting, contemporary Irish and European painting and sculpture, and the ingenious stained-glass "Geneva Window" which bears images from modern Irish literature. A northside place, it is off the official tourist trail. You can, usually, therefore, wander the galleries alone and find the space in which to view the large canvases of Jack B. Yeats—the poet's brother, an overlooked painter of astounding vitality—and, down the corridors of portraits, the silence in which to contemplate the words of W.B. in "The Municipal Gallery Revisited":

. . . Mancini's portrait of Augusta Gregory,
"Greatest since Rembrandt," according to John
   Synge;
A great ebullient portrait certainly;
But where is the brush that could show anything
Of all that pride and that humility? . . .

And here's John Synge himself, that rooted man,
"Forgetting human words," a grave deep face.
You that would judge me, do not judge alone
This book or that, come to this hallowed place
Where my friends' portraits hang and look thereon;
Ireland's history in their lineaments trace;

Think where man's glory most begins and ends,
And say my glory was I had such friends.

The faces of O'Casey's friends you will find in no gallery, but rather in the northside streets and pubs whose slumscapes he immortalized on the stage of the Abbey Theatre. The new Abbey, opened in 1966 to replace the one that burned down, is on the corner of Lower Abbey and Marlborough streets, one block east of O'Connell Street (box office: Monday–Saturday 10–6). The dull institutional exterior of the new building suggests that life inside has settled down since the hurly-burly of rioting prudes and patriots plagued the Abbey geniuses. Audiences now keep their seats except for the national anthem.

There were three great riots. In 1899 the Irish Literary Theatre—forerunner of the Abbey—brought to the boards Yeats's *The Countess Cathleen*, in which the main character sells her soul to the Devil to prevent her tenants from starving during the famine. Theological havoc broke loose. No Catholic would do such a thing! shouted the mob. In 1907 Synge's *The Playboy of the Western World* presented the passion of a peasant girl for a parricidal Kerryman and dared refer to a woman's undergarment by using that most indecorous word, "shift." Vegetables hurled toward the stage. In 1926 at O'Casey's *The Plough and the Stars* the mob was outraged by what they took to be the portrayal of Irish patriots and Irish women as cowards and prostitutes by a "guttersnipe of the slums," one critic's description of O'Casey. As shoes, chairs, and stink bombs winged forward, Yeats bellowed out: "You have disgraced yourselves again! Is this to be an ever-recurring celebration of the arrival of Irish

/ 303

genius? . . . The fame of O'Casey is born here tonight. This is his apotheosis."

The apotheosis was short-lived, however. Two months later O'Casey left for London and permanent exile. The plays that once unleashed such furor are today impressively mounted and played with great style in the ensemble manner for which the Abbey is so justly famous. But however much the productions may delight the tourist, there are no new Synges or O'Caseys to breathe through the Abbey its old rakish vigor. Samuel Beckett had the old theatre in mind when he drafted his will in *Murphy*:

With regard to the disposal of these my body, mind and soul, I desire that they be burnt and placed in a paper bag and brought to the Abbey Theatre, Lr. Abbey Street, Dublin, and without pause into what the great and good Lord Chesterfield calls the necessary house, where their happiest hours have been spent, on the right as one goes down into the pit, and I desire that the chain be there pulled upon them, if possible during the performance of a piece, the whole to be executed without ceremony or show of grief.

The new toilets are on the left.

O'Casey's vision of the human situation is hardly so ashen. Walk west along the quays, preferably at sunset, stand on Essex Bridge facing the Four Courts, and listen to his hymn from *Red Roses For Me*:

Take heart of grace from your city's hidden splendour. . . . There's th' great dome o' th' Four Courts lookin' like a golden rose in a great bronze bowl! An' th' river flowin' below it, a purple flood, marbled with ripples o' scarlet; watch th' seagulls glidin' over it—like restless white pearls astir on a royal breast. Our city's in th' grip o' God!

O'Casey, like his character, Fluther Good, "a Dublin man, born an' bred in th' city, see?" never stops celebrating "the kingdom of heaven in the nature of everyman."

YOU CAN TASTE and see the world of Brendan Behan all around Publin, but for a truly seminal introduction, begin at Guinness's Brewery (No. 21A bus to St. James's Gate; tours at the Visitors' Hall in Thomas Street, Monday–Saturday from 1). The brewery is a two-edged shrine. The guide will tell you in reverential tones of the fatherly goodness of the Guinness family towards their workers ("Never a strike in the history of the brewery; the Guinnesses have been very good to the people of Dublin"). At the tour's end a cheerful bartender serves you as much free goodness as you desire—Dublin's "black wine," the source of a fortune built on an accident. One day in 1759, a struggling young brewer named Arthur Guinness accidentally burned the wort and hops and gave away the resulting product gratis. The tipplers returned the following day for more of "that dark stuff," since when the people of Dublin have been very good to the Guinnesses. Flann O'Brien sums up the Dubliner's credo in "The Workman's Friend," a poem included in his brilliant novel-within-a-novel-within-a-novel, *At Swim-Two-Birds*:

> When things go wrong and will not come right,
> Though you do the best you can,
> When life looks black as the hour of night—
> A PINT OF PLAIN IS YOUR ONLY MAN . . .

With his grandmother's benisons, Behan took to the Workman's Friend when he was eight years old. His childhood was further nourished with the leavening of revolutionary politics. As an infant he had been introduced to his father through the bars of Kilmainham Gaol where Stephen Behan was defending his faith in the I.R.A. Years later his rebel son wound up in Mountjoy prison (not open to the public) on the Royal Canal, the setting for *The Quare Fellow*. But it was filmed in Kilmainham, now a restored memorial to Irish Republicanism, like Guinness, an acquired taste, depending, in this case, on your stomach for blood sacrifice. (Take No. 78 bus to Kilmainham, open Sunday 3–5.)

The "Kilmainham Devils" or the five demons of crime restrained by the chain of Law and Justice are carved in weird stone relief over the gaol's entrance, an ironic preface to the macabre place where political prisoners were often held illegally and turnkeys had a price for everything. "Too great a sacrifice makes a stone of the heart," said Yeats, and too much injustice masquerading as Law and Order can breed a fathomless cynicism. The dark side of the rebellious Dublin poor has never been better expressed than in "The Night Before Larry Was Stretched," an anonymous poem of the early nineteenth century in the old Dublin dialect, referring to the times when the city's gaols were the scenes of every imaginable outrage. On the night before a man was to be hanged he could buy beer for himself and his mates from the money he'd got by selling his body in advance to the surgeons. Using his coffin as a card table, they would pass the night in their accustomed rough sport and wisecracks, with the widow-to-be in attendance.

> The night before Larry was stretched,
>   The boys they all paid him a visit;
> A bait in their sacks, too, they fetched;
>   They sweated their duds till they riz it:
> For Larry was ever the lad,
>   When a boy was condemned to the squeezer,
> Would fence all the duds that he had
>   To help a poor friend to a sneezer,
>   And warm his gob 'fore he died.
>
> The boys they came crowding in fast,
>   They drew all their stools round about him,
> Six glims round his trap-case were placed
>   He couldn't be well waked without 'em.
> When one of us asked could he die
>   Without having duly repented,
> Says Larry, "That's all in my eye;
>   And first by the clargy invented,
>   To get a fat bit for themselves."

In the last verse Larry "dies with his face to the city," thus wryly representing the attitude of all real Dubliners who, however much they may curse this city, could not imagine looking for long on anything else.

Stories of the damned and their executioners heard along Kilmainham's spooky corridors may momentarily chill you. Out in the execution yard, where the leaders of the 1916 Rising died and native Dubliners still whisper as if they stood on Calvary, the reminders of men consumed by love

/ 307

of country can exalt you. But as you wander through the museum inspecting the contents of the cases, you come face to face with evidence of a cold contempt for the world that passes itself off as righteous heroism. One of the exhibits is a letter from Patrick Pearse to his mother: "We are ready to die and we shall die cheerfully and proudly. Personally I do not hope or even desire to live. . . . We have preserved Ireland's honour and our own. Our deeds of last week are the most splendid in Ireland's history." Though Behan idealizes his terrorist I.R.A. youth in his autobiography *Borstal Boy*, he elsewhere rejects the heritage preserved in the museum —homemade hand grenades, rifles, land mines, pikes, guns, knives. "What the hell difference does it make, left or right?" says Pat in *The Hostage*. "There were good men lost on both sides."

A ten-minute walk from Kilmainham is the Islandbridge Gate into Phoenix Park, a glorious place on weekends especially. Behan loved all 1,752 acres, but in particular the Zoo, which he often sang about:

> I brought me mot up to the Zoo
> For to show her the lion and the kangaroo;
> There were he-males and she-males of each shade
>   and hue
> Inside the Zoological gardens.
> I went up there on my honeymoon;
> We saw the giraffe and the hairy baboon,
> There were parrots and larks and two doves all a-
>   cooing
> Inside the Zoological Gardens.
>   Trouble and strife, it is no lark,

Dublin city is in the dark;
You want to get out to the Phoenix Park
And view the Zoological Gardens.

The People's Gardens delighted Mary Makebelieve, shy heroine of James Stephen's novel *The Charwoman's Daughter*:

She walked along for some time in the Park. Through the railings flanking the great road many beds of flowers could be seen. These were laid out in a great variety of forms, of stars and squares and crosses and circles, and the flowers were arranged in exquisite patterns. There was a great star which flamed with red flowers at the deep points, and in its heart a heavier mass of yellow blossom glared suddenly. There were circles wherein each ring was a differently-coloured flower, and others where three rings alternated—three rings white, three purple, and three orange, and so on in slendered circles to the tiniest diminishing.

And along came a policeman who sat down beside her and said the park had a fascinating history and geography. Because he didn't believe there was a phoenix in the Zoological Gardens ("He rather inclined to the belief that the phoenix was extinct—that is, died out"), he lost the girl.

Every Dubliner can tell you that you are strolling through one of the largest and most beautiful parks in Europe, that at its far end from the city it opens out on the Liffey and Chapelizod ("The Chapel of Iseult" where the Earwickers of *Finnegans Wake* live), and that a long time ago it was not the place for British civil servants to stroll through after sunset. In 1882 the rebel "Invincibles" assassinated two government officials here—the famous Phoenix

/ *309*

Park Murders. But as Mary Makebelieve knew, you can enjoy the park and be completely innocent of its sinister history, which has nothing to do with the Sunday afternoon children racing around the Wellington Obelisk or squealing over the chimpanzees and flamingoes, the lovers lying in the grass under the willows, or the old women selling apples and violets.

There are more than a thousand pubs in Dublin and, as wags would have it, Behan knew them all. The one he knew best is McDaid's in Harry Street, where he set his typewriter and glass in a corner and worked on his plays. Other southside pubs within walking distance of Grafton Street and still connected in one way or another with Irish writers, living and dead, include: Neary's and Sinnot's in Chatham Street, the latter the scene of weekly poetry readings; the bar at Jury's (now closed) in Dame Street where Donleavy's Ginger Man was wont to be found; the Scotch House in Burgh Quay, the temple of Simon Dedalus as well as the characters of Joyce's story "Counterparts"; the White Horse in George's Quay; the Fleet and the Palace in Fleet Street, haunts of journalists from the *Irish Times*; the Lincoln Inn or the "Poets' Pub" in Lincoln Place where Behan took his bride after their 7 A.M. wedding; O'Donoghue's in Merrion Row, good for music; and Mooney's at Baggot Street Bridge, once a favorite spot of Frank O'Connor. North of O'Connell Bridge you can strike up a conversation with theatre people at the Plough, opposite the Abbey Theatre; with newspaper columnists and broadcasters at Madigan's in Moore Street; with O'Casey characters and Behan's relatives at the Blue Lion in Parnell Street (Adolphus Grigson and Tommy Owens drink here in *The Shadow of a Gunman*); with jazz fans at Slattery's in Capel Street; and, in the morning, with truckers and farmers in the pubs near the Iveagh Market in Mary's Lane. Benedict Kiely, Irish novelist, short-story writer, and journalist, remembers "the mornings I have been aroused at six or seven to find Brendan smiling at the foot of my bed with the bright idea that we could start the day well in the early bars in the fruit markets or on the docks!"

Pub life may unnerve you. By closing time it floods with troubled and exhilarating waters, high with the pull and slap of the Irish character. Behan once said, "In Dublin you have conviviality, but no friendship." He may have had in mind the sting left by pubcrawlers competing for the coveted title of Dublin Wit. Many of them are would-be or one-shot writers, well-known, too, to Patrick Kavanagh, another of McDaid's former writers-in-residence, who tells about a Dubliner he meets in a London pub in "Tale of Two Cities":

> You certainly must have another double whiskey, he
>   cried
> And once again he gripped my hand in his
> And said there was no place like Dublin.
> His friendship wounded, but I dare not complain
> For that would seem boorish. Yet it was this
> Insincere good-nature that hurt me in Dublin.
> The sardonic humour of a man about to be hanged.
> But London would not hang him; it laid him
>   horizontal
> To dream of the books he had written in liquor

/ 311

Once again he would return to Dublin.
Where among the failures he would pass unnoticed,
Happy in pubs talking about yesterday's wits,
And George Moore's use of the semi-colon.

From one point of view, pubs are not healthy for writers and other working men: Behan, Kavanagh, and Flann O'Brien were certainly loyal to the Dublin code that prescribes public drinking as essential to the writer's craft. And several other famous names still walk the streets in stupor. Along with their pints, young writers must swallow big mouthfuls about the glorious past. "How odd it is," boasts Denis Johnston, "that over the past three centuries—from Swift and Sheridan to Shaw and Joyce—this ragbag of misplaced persons, this Seventh City of Christendom, built by fair strangers in one of Europe's backyards—has consistently taught the Englishman how to write in his own tongue." Fledgling writers go home groggy with a sense of the act they have to follow.

But comedy, as well as wounded pride and nostalgia, can carry the night along merrily towards its climactic shout, "Time now, gents!" As in Jewish-America, the Irish comic spirit has flourished amidst defensive conditions and relieves, however briefly, the people's memories of pain and loss. The Irish gift of tongues, which helped the colonized outwit the tyrant, gives this spirit its liberating wings. If you have an ear for Beckett, you'll recognize in these wet, smoky jungles of garrulous comedians the circuitous patterns of Vladimir and Estragon's dialogue in that supremely Irish play, *Waiting For Godot*. In a country whose chief cultural symbol is the Book of Kells, talk does not track towards conclusions. From the snugs you can hear Beckett's Winnie of *Happy Days* chattering on desperately, pronouncing everything "lovely," or "grand," or "wonderful," "laughing wild amidst severest woe." "In Ireland it's bad taste to be serious," says Sean O'Faolain. *"In risu veritas,"* says James Joyce. In laughter, truth. From *Gulliver's Travels* to tonight's crack, this is the Dubliner's triumph over adversity.

CHRONOLOGY

c. 3000 B.C.   Separate waves of Stone Age settlers begin to construct elaborate burial places: court cairns, dolmens, and round-cairn passage-graves.

c. 350   Celtic peoples begin to arrive from the continent. Gaelic-speaking Celts win control. The Iron Age hill-forts and ring-forts are built.

c. A.D. 1   The action of Ireland's epic, the *Tain*. The Gaelic order flourishes: aristocracy of petty kings, warrior-heroes, hereditary poets, and druids, based on land and livestock holdings.

432   Saint Patrick arrives, initiating the age of Christian, monastic Ireland.

795   Vikings begin their raids, establish the first towns and ports.

1170   Strongbow lands: the Anglo-Norman invasion.

1172   The Pope grants Ireland to England's Henry II.

1367   Anti-Irish Statutes of Kilkenny are enacted.

1536   First Protestant Reformation Parliament in Dublin.

1556   The Plantations begin: the English Crown grants confiscated Irish land to English settlers.

1601   Gaelic Ireland is decisively defeated by the English at Kinsale.

1645   Catholic Confederacy, meeting in Kilkenny, fails to agree on a united front against Cromwell.

1649   Cromwell arrives; the massacres begin.

1690	King William wins the Battle of the Boyne.
1692	Catholics excluded from office.
1695	Beginning of penal laws against Catholics.
1724	Swift's *Drapier's Letters*.
1782	Grattan's independent Irish Parliament. Era of Georgian architecture.
1791	Founding of the United Irishmen.
1795	Maynooth Seminary founded; Orange Order founded.
1798	Rebellion against England breaks out, led by Anglo-Irish.
1800	Irish Parliament dissolved by Act of Union with England. Great blow to Irish commerce. Maria Edgeworth's *Castle Rackrent* published.
1803	Robert Emmett's rising.
1829	Daniel O'Connell forces Catholic Emancipation. Gerald Griffin's *The Collegians* published.
1830	William Carleton's *Traits and Stories* published.
1845	Famine. Great emigrations begin.
1848	Rising of the Young Irelanders.
1858	Fenian Movement founded.
1867	Fenian rising; the Manchester martyrs executed.
1869	Disestablishment of the Church of Ireland.
1877	Parnell takes leadership of Irish party in British Parliament.
1879	The Land League, allied with Parnell, organizes tenant farmers to "boycott."
1884	Gaelic Athletic Association founded.
1891	Parnell, deposed for adultery with Kitty O'Shea, dies.
1893	Douglas Hyde founds Gaelic League to revive Irish culture.

1899	Irish Literary Theatre opens.
1904	Ulster Literary Theatre founded. Yeats and Lady Gregory open the Abbey Theatre. The Literary Revival. Joyce leaves Ireland.
1905	Sinn Fein established.
1907	The *Playboy* Riots.
1909	Death of J. M. Synge.
1910	James Connolly returns from America.
1911	George Moore's *Hail and Farewell*.
1912	James Stephens's *The Crock of Gold* published. The Irish Labour Party founded.
1913	The Dublin lockout strike; Irish Citizen Army and Irish Volunteers founded.
1914	Joyce's *Dubliners* published.
1916	Joyce's *A Portrait of the Artist as a Young Man* published. Easter Rising. Irish Republic proclaimed.
1919	Dail Eireann (Irish Parliament) founded.
1919–1921	War of Independence.
1922	Britain and Ireland sign treaty establishing Irish Free State (which excludes the six counties of Northern Ireland still under British rule) and granting Ireland commonwealth status. The I.R.A. (Irish Republican Army), led by de Valera, start Civil War to make Ireland an independent republic and bring an end to partition. *Ulysses* published.
1923	End of Civil War. Partition remains in effect. Irish Free State established. W. B. Yeats receives Nobel Prize.
1925	Liam O'Flaherty's *The Informer* published.
1926	Radio Eireann begins broadcasting. The *Plough* Riots.
1928	The Gate Theatre opens.

1932	...Valera Prime Minister.
1933	...ath of George Moore.
1936	...e Valera's government outlaws I.R.A. I.R.A. goes underground.
1937	New Irish Constitution; Douglas Hyde first President. Liam O'Flaherty's *Famine* published.
1939	Yeats dies. *Finnegans Wake* and *At Swim Two Birds* published.
1941	Death of James Joyce and F. R. Higgins.
1949	Dail Eireann voids Anglo-Irish Treaty, declares Ireland an independent republic.
1951	The Dolmen Press established. Abbey Theatre burnt down.
1953	Samuel Beckett's *Waiting for Godot* published (in French).
1955	Ireland joins the United Nations.
1961	Irish Television Service begins.
1964	Death of Sean O'Casey and Brendan Behan.
1966	Death of Frank O'Connor and Flann O'Brien.
1967	Death of Patrick Kavanagh.
1968	Catholics in Northern Ireland begin drive for enfranchisement and other civil rights. British troops arrive to quell disturbances in Northern Ireland. Beckett receives the Nobel Prize. Northern Ireland Catholics in favor of a united Ireland imprisoned without trial, accused of I.R.A. terrorism.
1972	Stormont, Northern Ireland's parliament, dissolved, and Northern Ireland given status similar to Scotland and Wales. Ireland enters Common Market.

SOME BOOKS
FOR THE ROAD

A Selective Bibliography

BECKETT, SAMUEL

Eh, Joe. New York: Grove Press, 1964; London: Faber & Faber, 1967.

Happy Days. New York: Grove Press, 1961; London: Faber & Faber, 1962.

Krapp's Last Tape. New York: Grove Press, 1958; London: Faber & Faber, 1959.

More Pricks Than Kicks. New York: Grove Press, 1970; London: Chatto and Windus, 1934.

Murphy. New York: Grove Press, 1957; London: Calder and Boyars, 1969.

Waiting For Godot. New York: Grove Press, 1954; London: Faber & Faber, 1965.

BEHAN, BRENDAN

Borstal Boy. New York:Random House, 1971; London: Corgi Books, 1961.

Two Plays. The Quare Fellow; The Hostage. New York: Grove Press, 1965; London: Methuen & Co., 1956, 1958.

BOWEN, ELIZABETH

Bowen's Court. New York: Knopf, 1942; London: Longmans & Co., 1942.

The Last September. New York: Knopf, 1952; London: Jonathan Cape, 1948.

CORKERY, DANIEL. *The Hidden Ireland.* Dublin: Gill & Macmillan, 1970.

CROSS, ERIC. *The Tailor and Ansty.* Cork: The Mercier Press, 1970.

DONLEAVY, J. P. *The Ginger Man.* New York: Berkley Medallion Edition, 1965; London: Penguin, 1968.

EDGEWORTH, MARIA. *Castle Rackrent.* New York and London: Oxford University Press, 1969.

GREGORY, LADY AUGUSTA
Collected Plays. 4 vols. Ed. Ann Saddlemyer. London: Colin Smythe, 1971.
Journals, 1916–1930. Ed. Lennox Robinson. New York: Macmillan, 1947.

GOGARTY, OLIVER ST. JOHN. *As I Was Going Down Sackville Street.* London: Sphere Books, 1968.

JOYCE, JAMES
A Portrait of the Artist as a Young Man. New York: Viking Press, 1965; London: Jonathan Cape, 1956.
Dubliners. New York: Viking Press, 1961; London: Penguin, 1956.
Ulysses. New York: Random House, 1961; London, Penguin, 1969.

KAVANAGH, PATRICK
Collected Poems. Old Greenwich, Conn.: Devin-Adair, 1964; London: Macgibbon & Kee, 1964.
Tarry Flynn. Old Greenwich, Conn.: Devin-Adair, 1949; London: Mayflower Paperbacks, 1970.

KIELY, BENEDICT. *Journey to the Seven Streams.* London: Methuen & Co., 1963.

LAVIN, MARY.
Collected Stories. Boston: Houghton Mifflin, 1971.
Stories. London: Constable & Co., 1964.

MCGAHERN, JOHN
The Barracks. London: Panther Books, 1969.
The Dark. London: Panther Books, 1969.
Nightlines: Stories. Boston: Little Brown, 1971; London: Faber & Faber, 1970.

MOORE, BRIAN. *The Lonely Passion of Judith Hearne.* Boston: Little Brown, 1971; London: Panther Books, 1969.

MOORE, GEORGE. *Hail And Farewell.* 3 vols. New York: D. Appleton & Co., 1911–1914; London: William Heinemann, 1911–1914.

O'BRIEN, EDNA. *A Pagan Place.* New York: Knopf, 1970; London: Weidenfeld & Nicolson, 1970.

O'BRIEN, FLANN. *At Swim-Two-Birds.* New York: Viking Press, 1967; London: Penguin, 1971.

O'CASEY, SEAN
Collected Plays. Vols. 1–3. New York: St. Martin's Press, 1949–1951; London: Macmillan, 1949.
I Knock at the Door. New York: St. Martin's Press, 1964; London: Macmillan, 1963.

O'CONNOR, FRANK
A Set of Variations, Twenty-Seven Stories. New York: Knopf, 1969.
An Only Child. New York: Knopf, 1961; London: Pan Books, 1970.
My Father's Son. New York: Knopf, 1969; London: Pan Books, 1971.

/ 321

My Oedipus Complex and Other Stories. London: Penguin, 1963.
The Mad Lomasneys and Other Stories. London: Pan Books, 1970.

O'FAOLAIN, SEAN. *The Finest Stories of Sean O'Faolain.* New York: Bantam Books, 1965.

O'FLAHERTY, LIAM
Skerret. New York: R. Long & R. R. Smith, 1932; London: V. Gollancz, 1932.
The Informer. New York: Signet Books, 1961; London: Four Square Books, 1958.
The Short Stories of Liam O'Flaherty. London: Digit Books, 1961.
The Stories of Liam O'Flaherty. Old Greenwich, Conn.: Devin-Adair, 1956.

RUKEYSER, MURIEL. *The Orgy.* New York: Pocket Books, 1966; London: New English Library, 1968.

SHAW, GEORGE BERNARD
Back To Methuselah. New York & London: Penguin, 1961.
John Bull's Other Island. New York: Brentano, 1913; London: Constable & Co., 1907.
Sixteen Self Sketches. New York: Dodd Mead, 1949; London: Constable & Co., 1950.
The Matter With Ireland. Ed. D. H. Greene & D. H. Lawrence. New York: Hill & Wang, 1962; London: Hart-Davis, 1962.

SOMERVILLE, EDITH Œ. and ROSS, MARTIN. *Experiences of an Irish R. M.* London: Everyman's Library, 1969.

STEPHENS, JAMES
Collected Poems. New York: Macmillan, 1941; London, Macmillan, 1954.
The Charwoman's Daughter. London & Dublin: Scepter Books, 1966.

SWIFT, JONATHAN

"Cadenus and Vanessa," *Gulliver's Travels*, *The Drapier's Letters*, *The Letters*. In many editions.

SYNGE, JOHN MILLINGTON

Collected Works. Vols. I–IV. Ed. Robin Skelton, Ann Saddlemyer, & Alan Price. London: Oxford University Press, 1962–1968.

Complete Works of John Millington Synge. New York: Random House, 1935. *Note:* This volume actually does not contain the complete works.

YEATS, WILLIAM BUTLER

The Autobiography. New York: Macmillan, 1966; London: Macmillan, 1955.

The Collected Plays. Rev. ed. New York: Macmillan, 1953; London: Macmillan, 1952.

The Collected Poems. New York: Macmillan, 1956; London: Macmillan, 1950.

TRANSLATIONS FROM THE IRISH:

Kings, Lords, & Commons. An Anthology from the Irish translated by Frank O'Connor. Dublin: Gill & Macmillan, 1970.

Love Songs of Connacht. Translated from the Irish by Douglas Hyde. Dublin & London: Irish University Press, 1968.

The Tain. Translated from the Irish by Thomas Kinsella. New York & London: Oxford University Press, 1970.

OTHER SOURCES:

Craig, Maurice. *Dublin 1660–1860.* Dublin: Figgis, 1969.

Ellmann, Richard. *James Joyce.* London: Oxford University Press, 1959.

Harbison, Peter. *Guide to the National Monuments in the Republic of Ireland.* Dublin & London: Gill & Macmillan, 1970.

Kirby, Sheelah. *The Yeats Country*. Dublin: The Dolmen Press, 1969.

Love Poems of the Irish. Ed. Sean Lucy, Cork: The Mercier Press, 1967.

MacCana, Proinsias. *Celtic Mythology*. New York & London: Hamlyn, 1970.

Mercier, Vivian. *The Irish Comic Tradition*. London: Oxford University Press, 1962.

INDEX